Theo Global Vol. I

The Living God
Attributes and Persons

© 2024 Sola Media
13230 Evening Creek Drive
Suite 220–222
San Diego, CA 92128

All rights reserved. No part of this book may be
reproduced or transmitted in any form or by any means,
electronic or mechanical, including photocopying,
recording, or by any information storage and retrieval system,
without permission in writing from the publisher.

Designer: Karly Steenholdt
Copyediting: Isaac Fox

Printed in the United States of America

November 2024

ISBN: 9798344370118

Theo Global

JOURNAL

Vol. I

The Living God
ATTRIBUTES AND PERSONS

Managing Editor
Adam P. Smith

Contents

Preface

ATTRIBUTES

13

The Self-Revealing and Accommodating God
REV. DR. JUSTIN S. HOLCOMB.

33

Divine Impassibility and Self-Limitation
DR. DAVID MUTHUKUMAR SIVASUBRAMANIAN

55

"Something Perfect From Something Perfect"
The Dogmatic and Apologetic Functions of Divine Simplicity

DR. WILSON JEREMIAH

73

The Aseity of God in the Old Testament Creation Discourses
Implications for Christian Spirituality and Society in Africa

DR. MICHAEL PHIRI

89

What's in a Name?
DR. MICHAEL S. HORTON

115

Exploring Divine Providence
Reason, Scripture, Free Will, and the Reality of Suffering

DR. SHERIF A. FAHIM

133

God's Sovereignty Amidst Suffering

DR. KENETH PERVAIZ

143

**Exploring God's Attributes in Dialogue
With the Hymnology of Eastern Women**

DR. GRACE AL-ZOUGHBI

163

**The Fatherhood of God
A Biblical-Theological Reflection and Analysis**

DR. VIJAI SINGH TAGORE

181

**The Attribute of God's Fatherly Love
an African Theological and Leadership Perspective**

DR. WOLE ADEGBILE

197

A Biblical Theology of the Wisdom of God

TSEDEY ALEMAYEHU GEBREHIWOT

TRINITY

221

**Why Historical Theology Matters
The Trinity and the Dangers of Biblicism**

DR. MICHAEL S. HORTON

239

**Trinitarian Heresies
What is Lost?**

REV. DR. JUSTIN S. HOLCOMB

267

Contributors

Preface

In the historic Nicene and Apostles' creeds, Christians throughout the globe and the centuries have held and confessed one holy catholic Church, amongst biblical and central truths to the Christian faith. Fittingly, the Nicene Creed was developed and adopted at the geographical crossroads where East meets West as it addressed challenges to the divinity of Christ and expressed the Church's catholicity. The Jerusalem Council of Acts 15 likewise gathered, discussed, and corresponded in order to bring clarity and unity regarding the matter of Jew and Gentile distinction that threatened to divide the nascent faith. In later centuries, the Reformers also came together in conversation; convening in assemblies, disputations, and even discreet pubs to work through theological identifications, formulations, and commitments.

Since 2015, Theo Global has facilitated annual regional theological forums, publications, and productions among leading Protestant (for lack of a globally better label) theologians around the world, in order to do theology together for the health of the global church. These engagements seek to create a place for new regional, cross-regional, and world-wide theological conversations and relationships for the global church by the global church.

After 10 years of Theo Global, how evident it has become that Christianity is both ancient and expanding in the Majority World – brimming with histories and novel horizons of Christian theological insights, articulations, and applications! The essays in this volume recognize and showcase this. They are a result of the Theo Global symposiums in 2024, which collectively concentrated on the doctrine of God. There, scholars prepared presentations and engaged in discussions on self-selected topics on The Living God: Attributes and Persons. Following these presentations and discussions, they then finalized their papers which are contained in this journal.

At these Theo Global symposiums, half of the presentations are given by representatives from within the region while half are given by scholars from outside the region. This allows local voices to speak prominently while simultaneously hearing and engaging with other parts of the global Church. It also facilitates a degree of continuity and cross-pollination from one regional gathering to another. In 2024 Dr. Michael Horton and Dr. Justin Holcomb (both Senior Fellows for Theo Global), along with Dr. Wilson Jeremiah (from Indonesia) contributed presentations and papers, which this volume contains, at multiple regional symposiums as visitors.

Within the essays contained in this journal, you will find unique and insightful interactions with the biblical doctrine of God and its touchpoints in the Church's life, worship, history, and cultural contexts. Wherever your vantage point may be, may the wisdom and insight from theologians of the global Church enhance your faith, wonder, and confidence in God's majesty. May the goodness, faithfulness, and mercy of God be written ever more upon your mind and your heart by His Spirit's hand as we do theology together. Soli Deo Gloria.

Adam Smith

Adam Smith is the Chief Operating Officer at Sola Media and has led the Theo Global project since 2015. He is a minister in the Presbyterian Church of America.

The Self-Revealing and Accommodating God

REV. DR. JUSTIN S. HOLCOMB
Bishop of the Episcopal Diocese of Central Florida
Senior Fellow with Theo Global
Professor, Reformed Theological Seminary
USA

In what way can the God who is other be revealed? Must not revelation be received? What, then, is the condition of possibility for the reception of such revelation? Must it not be a revelation that is received *secundum modum recipentis recipitur*—according to the mode or condition of the receiver?[1] Is it true that if the God who is wholly other is to reveal, then God must reveal in terms that the recipient of the revelation can understand? How can one suggest the need for God to reveal in terms of the condition of the recipient without it constituting an imposition of those conditions upon God? Does God create in us the condition of possibility for the reception of revelation? How does God reveal himself without exploitation? How does a revelation in terms of the condition of the receiver not deny or nullify the otherness or God?[2]

In revealing himself, God does not give up transcendence. If God did not reveal himself in terms of the conditions of the finite perceiver who is also sinful, there would be only ignorance and no knowledge of God.

I. ESSENCE AND ENERGIES

In considering revelation, it is important to hold to and emphasize the Creator-creation distinction, which is celebrated in the traditions of both Western theology and Eastern Orthodox theology. Both say that God so transcends creation in his incomprehensible majesty that we cannot even know God in his essence or God's being in itself but only in and according to God's works. Yet, God's works are nothing less than God working.

Western theology is usually restricted to the category of essence: either divine or nondivine. Eastern theology introduced the category of God's energies. The Cappadocian fathers and Eastern Orthodox make the helpful distinction between the essence of God (which we cannot know) and God's energies (which we can know).

Where Western theology typically works with the categories of divine essence (source) and human essence (effect), Eastern theology recognizes that God's working is divine without being an emanation or extension of his essence. As

---

1   Thomas Aquinas, *Summa Theologiae*, trans. Fathers of the Dominican Province (New York: Benzinger, 1947), 1a.75.5.
2   These are the questions James K. A. Smith investigates in his "critique of revelation in Levinas and Marion." See James K. A. Smith, *Speech and Theology: Language and the Logic of the Incarnation* (London: Routledge, 2002), pp. 153-160.

Michael Horton explains: "The sun's rays are not the sun itself, but they are also not the ground that is warmed by the sun. Rather, they are the shining forth or effulgence of the sun. Similarly, God's energies (*energia*) are neither God's essence (*ousia*) nor a created effect but are God's knowledge, power, and grace directed toward creatures."[3] We do not know God in himself but are warmed by the effulgence of his being. The "rays" are not an extension of God's being, but of his power and activity.

We come to know God in his works rather than his essence. God's works are neither God's essence nor merely the created effect of his action, but God's effective agency. For example, as Horton writes: "God's act of creating the world by his Word is neither an emanation of God's being nor itself part of creation. Rather, it is God's activity."[4] John Calvin presupposes the essence-energies distinction when he writes: "The Spirit may be regarded as the essential power of God, whose energy is manifested and exerted in the entire government of the world, as well as in miraculous events."[5]

This essence-energies distinction informs how we think about revelation. The patristic rule that the finite cannot comprehend or enclose the infinite is applicable to every form of divine revelation. Eastern Orthodoxy appeals to Exodus 33 for the distinction between the revelation of God in his essence (God's inescapable glory) and in his energies (God's gracious acts). God reveals his attributes or characteristics rather than his hidden essence—what he is like rather than what he is in the inner depths of his hidden mystery.

There is not revelation of God's essence—direct or indirect. Nor is the medium of revelation (the Bible) either God's essence or merely a creaturely witness. Scripture is identified as the locus of God's revelation, even though God infinitely transcends it. As the canonical record of God's acts and speech, it communicates to us here and now God's powerful energies. As God's living speech, the Scriptures are a series of divinely inspired interpretations of God's gracious acts in redemptive history. God's energies, not his essence, are communicated through the human writers of Scripture. They are sent by the Father to proclaim the Son in the power of the Spirit.

---

3   Michael Horton, *The Christian Faith: A Systematic Theology for Pilgrims Along the Way* (Zondervan Academic), 130.
4   Ibid.
5   John Calvin, *A Harmony of the Evangelists*, 1:42.

Concerning these distinctions, Calvin writes, "The essence of God is to be adored rather than inquired into."[6] In fact, "They are mad who seek to discover what God is."[7] Rather, we come to know God through his works in creation but especially through his Word: "Thereupon his powers are mentioned, by which he is shown to us not as he is in himself, but as he is toward us; so that this recognition of him consists more in living experience than in vain and high-flown speculations."[8] This view of revelation and mediation is God's condescending mercy in order to reveal himself without destroying us.

II. THE KNOWLEDGE OF GOD

There would be no knowledge of God without God's condescension to reveal and deal with the difference that finitude posits, as well as the noetic effects of sin. We will explore Aquinas' concept of knowledge "according to the mode of the receiver" and Calvin's concept of accommodation as we consider the Creator-creation distinction as it relates to the knowledge of God given to us by God's self-revealing.

1. *Aquinas and Analogy*

Aquinas denies that we have quidditative knowledge of God (knowledge of what God is in his essential being), whether by reason or revelation, but only analogical knowledge of God.[9] Aquinas' discussion, "How God is Known by Us,"[10] is grounded in his epistemological principle that all knowledge, as a matter of "reception," is possible only according to the mode or condition of the receiver: *quidquid recipitur, secundum modum recipientis recipitur.*[11] Based on this principle, the question is: how will it be possible for us, as finite and conditioned, to know God, who is infinite and unconditioned?

First, Aquinas notes that according to our "natural" powers, this is impossible:

> For knowledge takes place according as the thing known is in
> the knower. But the thing known is in the knower according to

---

6   Calvin, *Institutes*, 1.2.2.
7   Calvin on Roman 1:19 in his *Commentary on Paul's Epistle to the Romans* (1948), 69..
8   Calvin, *Institutes*, 1.10.2
9   See John Wippel, "Quidditative Knowledge of God," in *Metaphysical Themes in Thomas Aquinas* (Washington, D.C.: Catholic University of America Press, 1984).
10   Thomas Aquinas, *Summa Theologiae*, trans. Fathers of the Dominican Province (New York: Benzinger, 1947), 1a.12.
11   Ibid., 1a.75.5, 76.2.ad3.

the mode of the knower. Hence the knowledge of every knower is according to the mode of its own nature. If therefore the mode of being of a given thing exceeds the mode of the knower, it must result that the knowledge of that thing is above the nature of the knower.[12]

However, the impossibility is overcome by grace, which Aquinas applies to the issue of finitude. Calvin's teaching on God's accommodating applies to human finitude, but also human sinfulness.

Second, Aquinas considers the objection that "if God is seen through a medium, he is not seen in his essence. But if seen by any created light, he is seen through a medium."[13] Aquinas' reply to this objection moves toward an account of condescension: "A created light is necessary to see the essence of God, not in order to make the essence of God intelligible, which is of itself intelligible, but in order to enable the intellect to understand."[14] That which is infinite appears in terms that the created intellect can understand, otherwise it would fail to appeal to a finite perceiver. Thus God, in and from himself, concedes to the conditions of human knowing in order to be made known.

Third, Aquinas makes a careful distinction between "knowledge" and "comprehension," which will be crucial to any account of the self-revealing God. While God can be known, God cannot be comprehended by any finite intellect since "what is comprehended is perfectly known."[15] Since all human knowledge is according to the mode of the perceiver, the finite creature cannot perfectly know the infinite God: "[I]n no way is God comprehended either by the intellect or by anything else; for since he is infinite, he cannot be included in any finite being."[16] The belief that God cannot be comprehended does not preclude knowledge of God altogether. Rather, because God reveals in the terms of the conditions of the perceiver, God can be known. Thus the principle of analogy, as well as Calvin's teaching on accommodation, is a matter of God condescending to our finite capacities out of love.

---

12 Ibid., 1a.12.4.
13 Aquinas, *Summa Theologiae*, 1a.12.5.obj2.
14 Ibid., 1a.12.5.ad1.
15 Aquinas, *Summa Theologiae*, 1a.12.7.
16 Ibid.

2. *Calvin and God Accommodating*

Calvin argues that God in the depths of his being is past finding out: "His essence is incomprehensible; so that His divinity wholly escapes all human senses." His theology of God accommodating in revelation, like Thomas Aquinas' use of "analogy," reflects the ontological difference between God and creation as well as takes into account the human condition. According to Calvin, revelation refers to a voluntary, mediated accommodation of what God wills to make known of himself to the capacities and limits of humans.

This seems to be what Calvin thought when we writes that "as nurses commonly do with infants, God is wont in a measure to 'lisp' in speaking to us. Thus such forms of speaking do not so much express clearly what God is like as accommodate the knowledge of him to our slight capacity. To do this he must descend far beneath his loftiness."[17]

In the *Institutes*, Calvin uses either the verb *accommodare* or *attemperare*, when he describes the principle of accommodation. *Accommodare* and *attemperare* refer to the adjustments made by a speaker to the capacities and understanding of the listener they wish to persuade. Just as rhetoricians[18] adjust their use of language and presentation to the level of their hearers, so God "accommodates" his self-revelation to the human condition. In effect, God "lisps" so that finite and sinful humans may hear the divine Word and receive knowledge of God.[19]

Before Calvin went the patristic witnesses who contend that in his self-revealing God was adjusting his revelation to the capacity of the human mind and heart. Unlike Origen, Clement of Alexandria, Augustine, or Chrysostom, Calvin makes this principle a consistent basis for every avenue of relationship between God and humans. Accommodation unlocks for Calvin God's beneficent tutelage

---

17 Calvin, *Institutes*, I.13.i.
18 Ford Lewis Battles traces the use of accommodation in classical rhetoric, in the writings of the early church (Clement of Alexandria, Origen, John Chrysostom, and Augustine), and in Calvin's work. See Ford Lewis Battles, "God Was Accommodating Himself to Human Capacity," in *Readings in Calvin's Theology*, ed. Donald McKim (Grand Rapids: Baker, 1984) pp. 24-29. David F. Wright questions whether the tracing of accommodation to the categories of classical Roman rhetoric is valid. See David F. Wright, "Calvin's Accommodating God," *Papers of the Sixth International Congress on Calvin Research*, Edinburgh, Scotland, 16 September 1995, note 34.
19 For Calvin, the principle of accommodation is understood as God's method of self-disclosure. Scripture portrays God in an accommodated manner in order to communicate the word of God to sinful humans, who have only a limited capacity (*captus*). God uses several avenues of accommodation, including the law, the language of the Lord's Prayer, and the sacraments. We find in the Incarnation God's supreme act of divine accommodation. Regarding the Incarnation, Calvin made substantial use of the principle of accommodation. Also, he particularly depends on accommodation as a context for understanding the nature and function of scripture.

and pedagogy of his children.[20]

For Calvin, accommodation is a major characterization of the knowledge of God: "[God] accommodates to our capacity in addressing us."[21] God "cannot be comprehended by us except as far as he accommodates (*attemperat*) himself to our standard."[22] Calvin also writes: "God in his greatness can by no means be fully comprehended by our minds...there are certain limits within which men ought to confine themselves, in as much as God accommodates to our measure what he testifies of himself."[23] The term *attemperat* includes within its scope all the noetic aspects of the Creator-creation distinction and relationship: "For since he is in himself incomprehensible, he assumes, when he wishes to manifest himself to men, those marks by which he may be known."[24] Accommodation points to the difference between God and humanity that is dealt with only by God "in some way descending" to meet the limitations of human nature, never by humanity overcoming them. Commenting on this, Calvin writes: "It was necessary that he should assume a visible form, that he might be seen by Moses not as he was in his essence but as the infirmity of the human mind could comprehend. For thus we believe that God, as often as he appeared of old to the holy patriarchs, descended in some way from his loftiness, that he might reveal himself as far as was useful and as far as their comprehension would admit."[25]

The essence of God is unknown and inaccessible to us, according to Calvin, and

---

20   Calvin sees human beings—even before the fall—as creatures far removed from their Creator and he sees human language as insufficient to bridge this gap. Therefore, in Calvin's picture of God three biblical themes especially stand out: God is our parent, our divine parent exceeding all human parents; God is also teacher, who well knows God's pupils; and God is physician, who skillfully diagnoses our diseases. Thus at the outset we have the three analogies of parental care, instruction, and healing. The weakness and inexperience of childhood, the ignorance of the student, and the disease of the sick, respectively, correspond to these three divine roles. However, the rhetorician's task is not merely to bridge the gulf of weakness or ignorance. God has to deal not only with inexperience and ignorance but also with willful stubbornness and disobedience. We begin to see that, for Calvin, accommodation has to do not only with scripture and its interpretation, but also with the whole of created reality to which, for Christians, scripture holds the clue. At the heart of God's accommodation to human capacity, however, is God's supreme act of condescension, the giving of Christ to reconcile a fallen world to God. If accommodation is the condescension of the Creator to the creation, the divine to the human, then the Logos who tented among us is the point from which we must view creation, the fall, and all history, before and since the Incarnation. For Calvin, then, in every act of divine accommodation, the whole Trinity is at work.
21   Calvin, *Commentary on First Corinthians*, 337d.
22   John Calvin, *Commentary on Ezekiel*, in *Ioannis Calvini opera quae supersunt omnia*, ed. Wilhelm Baum, Edward Cunitz, and Edward Reuss, vol. XL (Brunsvigae: C. A. Schwetsche, 1863-1900), 196d.
23   John Calvin, *Commentary on Romans*, in *Ioannis Calvini opera quae supersunt omnia*, ed. Wilhelm Baum, Edward Cunitz, and Edward Reuss, vol. XLIX (Brunsvigae: C. A. Schwetsche, 1863-1900), 23c.
24   John Calvin, *Commentary on Genesis*, in *Ioannis Calvini opera quae supersunt omnia*, ed. Wilhelm Baum, Edward Cunitz, and Edward Reuss, vol. XXIII (Brunsvigae: C. A. Schwetsche, 1863-1900), 65d.
25   John Calvin, *Commentary on Exodus*, in *Ioannis Calvini opera quae supersunt omnia*, ed. Wilhelm Baum, Edward Cunitz, and Edward Reuss, vol. XXIV (Brunsvigae: C. A. Schwetsche, 1863-1900), 35c.

all speculations about it are idolatrous and blasphemous. This is the main error of those who discuss the being of God apart from revelation of God's will: "Those, therefore, who in considering this question propose to inquire what the essence of God is (*quid sit Deus*) only trifle with frigid speculations—it being much more important for us to know what kind of being (*qualis sit*) God is, and what things are agreeable to his nature."[26] In his *Commentary on Ezekiel*, he writes: "God appeared under a visible form to his servant: could Ezekiel on that account do as scholastic theologians do—philosophize with subtlety concerning God's essence and know no end or moderation in their dispute? By no means, but he restrained himself within fixed bounds."[27]

The three "epithets" for God's essence, "immensity," "spirituality," and "simplicity," are not positive descriptions that form a base for speculation, but boundaries or limits that deny the access of speculation regarding the essence of God.[28] In other words, these terms mean that God's essence is not finite, not material, and not divisible, and therefore, are not comprehensible. Describing the boundaries of the epithets "immensity" and "spirituality," Calvin writes:

> What is taught in the Scriptures concerning the immensity of spirituality of the essence of God should serve only to overthrow the foolish notions of the vulgar but also to refute the subtleties of profane philosophy...But although God, to keep us within the bounds of sobriety, speaks but rarely of his essence, yet, by those two epithets, which I have mentioned, he supersedes all gross imaginations, and represses the presumption of the human mind. For surely, his immensity ought to deter us that we may not attempt to measure him with our sense; and his spiritual nature prohibits us from entertaining any earthly or carnal speculations concerning him.[29]

Calvin continues that God's simplicity, when viewed alone as a positive attribute, gives us a "bare and empty name of God, which flits about in our brains," and not the true God.[30] In connection with the doctrine of the Trinity, Calvin further writes: "For how can the infinite essence of God be defined by the capacity of the

---

26 Calvin, *Institutes*, I.2.ii.
27 Calvin, *Commentary on Ezekiel*, 57c.
28 Calvin, *Institutes*, I.13.i-ii.
29 Calvin, *Institutes*, I.13.i.
30 Ibid., I.13.ii.

human mind, which could never yet certainly determine the nature of the body of the sun, which the eye behold daily? Indeed, how can it, by its own efforts, penetrate into an examination of the substance (*substantiam*) of God, when it is totally ignorant of its own? Wherefore let us willingly leave to God the knowledge of himself."[31]

It is the work, power, or activity of God that we know, not God's essence or being.[32] And even then, we know God's work, power, or activity only in so far as they are directed toward us:

> Whence we conclude this to be the right way and the best method of seeking God: not with presumptuous curiosity to attempt an examination of his essence, which is rather to be adored than too minutely investigated; but to contemplate him in his works, in which he approaches and familiarizes himself to us...Although he is himself invisible, in a manner he becomes visible to us in his works."[33]

Thus, according to Calvin, theology does not handle what God is, only what God is in relation to the world: "His essence is indeed incomprehensible, so that his divinity is not to be perceived by the human senses, but on each of his works he has inscribed his glory in characters so clear, unequivocal, and striking that the most illiterate and stupid cannot exculpate themselves by the pleas of ignorance."[34] By this Calvin reminds us that humans must keep their thoughts within the limits imposed by the temporal and spatial creation. Speculations about infinite time and space are forbidden, and even within our temporal and spatial limitations, humans know God's will only in a very limited way.

From the first edition of the *Institutes* to the latest, Calvin opens with the category of

---

31 Calvin, *Institutes*, I.13.xxi.
32 This is similar to what Aquinas writes in *Summa Theologiae*, 1a.3- "Now we cannot know what God is, but only what he is not; we must therefore consider the ways in which God does not exist rather than the ways in which he does." Also see *Summa Theologiae*, 2a2ae.8.7- "The better we know God the more we understand that he surpasses whatever the mind grasps." Elsewhere Aquinas writes: "Wherefore man reaches the highest point of his knowledge about God when he knows that he knows him not, inasmuch as he knows that that which God is transcends whatsoever he conceives of him" (Thomas Aquinas, *On the Power of God*, trans. Laurence Shapcote (Westminster: Newman, 1952), 7.5.14. Again, he writes: "We cannot know of the existence of something without also knowing its essence in some way" (Thomas Aquinas, *Commentary on Boethius' "De Trinitate"*, trans. Armand Brennan (Toronto: Pontifical Institute of Mediaeval Studies, 1987), 6.3.
33 Calvin, *Institutes*, I.5.ix; and I.14.1.
34 John Calvin, *Commentary on Hebrews*, in *Ioannis Calvini opera quae supersunt omnia*, ed. Wilhelm Baum, Edward Cunitz, and Edward Reuss, vol. LV (Brunsvigae: C. A. Schwetsche, 1863-1900), 146a.

"the knowledge of God and ourselves" and not with speculations about being and existence.[35] For Calvin, creation's reason for being—the goal of accommodation—is God's revelation to humanity and the resulting glory to and worship of God.[36] Calvin writes: "No sooner was the world created than the Word of God came forth into external operation; having been formerly incomprehensible in his essence, he then became publicly known by the effect of his power."[37] Calvin warns against human speculation about God. Early in the *Institutes*, he describes the human mind's powerful tendency to move away from God and how we always wander in error and never reach our goal if we leave the accommodated paths of revelation, which alone give us knowledge of God: "Suppose we ponder how slippery is the fall of the human mind into forgetfulness of God, how great the tendency to every kind of error, how great the lust to fashion constantly new and artificial religions."[38] Faithful listening to Scripture prevents us from turning to either side.

When we turn to God's work of redemption, we find the accommodation of God to humanity capacities extended. The redeeming Word, like the creative Word, is accommodated to the aggravated condition of sinful creatures:

> For there are two distinct powers which belong to the Son of God: the first, which is manifest in the architecture of the world and the order of nature; and the second, by which he renews and restores fallen nature. As he is the eternal Word of God, by him the world was made, by his power all things continue to posses life which they once received; man was endued with a unique gift of understanding, and though by revolt he lost the light of understanding, yet still sees and understands, so that what he naturally possess from the grace of the Son of God is not entirely destroyed. But since by his stupidity and perverseness he darkens the light which still dwells in him, it remains that a new office be undertaken by the Son of God, the office of Mediator, to renew by the spirit of regeneration man, who has been ruined.[39]

---

35   Richard Muller, "Establishing the Ordo docendi: The Organization of Calvin's Institutes, 1536-1559," in *The Unaccommodated Calvin* (New York: Oxford University Press, 2000), pp. 118-139.
36   . John Calvin, *Commentary on Isaiah*, in *Ioannis Calvini opera quae supersunt omnia,* ed.Wilhelm Baum, Edward Cunitz, and Edward Reuss, vol. XXXVI (Brunsvigae: C. A. Schwetsche, 1863-1900), 589b; Calvin, Commentary on Genesis, 27d; and John Calvin, Commentary on Psalm, in Ioannis Calvini opera quae supersunt omnia, ed. Wilhelm Baum, Edward Cunitz, and Edward Reuss, vol. XXXI (Brunsvigae: C. A. Schwetsche, 1863-1900), 92b.
37   Calvin, *Commentary on John*, 2a.
38   Calvin, *Institutes*, I.6.iii.
39   Calvin, *Commentary on John*, 3b.

God's special accommodation to human sinfulness occurs exclusively though the self-revealing that God undertook in the Incarnation: "[G]od himself would remain absolutely hidden (*procul absconditus*) if we were not illuminated by the brightness of Christ."[40] No redemptive knowledge is available apart from the mediatorial work of Christ: "For he assumed the character of Mediator in order to approach to us by descending from the bosom and incomprehensible glory of his Father."[41]

Calvin argues that the principle of accommodation intervenes where the temptation of idolatry is strong—to say that God is known immediately. Examples of Calvin's response to the idol of immediacy is found in his commentaries concerning the giving of God's name—Yahweh. This name of God "is to be understood of the knowledge of him in so far as he makes himself known to us, for I do not approve of the subtle speculations of those who think the name of God means nothing else but God himself. It ought rather to be referred to the works and properties (*virtutes*) by which he is known, than to his essence."[42] To guard against idolatry regarding the name of God, Calvin notes "that we may not suppose that his eternal essence only is here exhibited, but also his power and goodness, which he constantly exercises toward us and by which he abundantly reveals himself...The world falls into the mistake of giving a naked and empty name to God, meanwhile transferring his authority to another."[43] He continues to argue against idolatrous names: "The name 'strong' is attributed to God...because it is not enough to acknowledge God's eternal essence unless we also ascribe strength to him. But for this we shall leave him nothing but a bare and empty name, as the wicked do, who with the mouth confess God and then transfer his power to this and that."[44]

God's essence is a mystery even to those who know God's name. Calvin writes that the Psalmist does not "speak of the hidden essence of God (*absconditus Dei essentia*), which fills heaven and earth, but of the manifestations of his power, wisdom, goodness, and righteousness, which appear publicly, although they may exceed the measure of our understanding."[45] The appearances of God are moments

---

40 Calvin, *Institutes,* III.2.i.

41 Ibid., II.15.v.

42 Calvin, *Commentary on Psalm,* 88c. Also, in the name Yahweh the "eternity and primary essence of God is expressed." See Calvin, *Commentary on Ezekiel,* 53d. In *Commentary on Exodus,* 44a, Calvin asks: "How would it have profited Moses to gaze upon the secret essence of God as if it were shut up in heaven, unless, being assured of his omnipotence, he had obtained from thence the buckler of his confidence?"

43 Calvin, *Commentary on Isaiah,* 89d.

44 Ibid., 111c.

45 Calvin, *Commentary on Psalm,* 71b. Also see Calvin, *Commentary on Psalm,* 794a.

of concealing and revealing. The presence of God is not as exhibition of God's essence but an illustration that God's essence is unknowable—moments of God's gracious veiled appearance that is accommodated to human capabilities. There is a double aspect to God's communication, to reveal character and to conceal essence: "For when the Lord gives tokens (*signa*) of his presence, he employs at the same time some coverings to restrain the arrogance of the human mind...this admonition also pertains to us, that we may not seek to pry into secrets which lie beyond our perception, but rather that every man may keep within the limits of sobriety, according to the measure of his faith."[46] Calvin also writes: "As therefore our capacity cannot endure the fullness of the infinite glory which belongs to the essence of God, it is necessary whenever he appears to us that he put on a form adapted to our capacity."[47]

The giving of God's name and celebration of Yahweh's redeeming activity are all within the economy of accommodation to the human condition and are subordinate to the final accommodation to human sinfulness, the Incarnation. Here, just like elsewhere, God's accommodating character guards the borders. The Incarnation follows the same pattern as before: essence unknown, power exerted for the sake of revelation, with the main emphasis placed upon the revelation itself. Commenting on John 14:10, "I am in the Father and the Father is in me," Calvin writes:

> I do not consider these words to refer to Christ's divine essence, but to the manner of revelation; for Christ, so far as regards his hidden divinity, is not better known to us than the Father. But he is said to be the express image of God because in him God has fully revealed himself, so far as God's infinite goodness, wisdom, and power are clearly manifested in him. Yet the ancients are not wrong when they quote this passage as a proof for defending Christ's divinity; but as Christ does not inquiry simply what he is in himself, but what we ought to acknowledge him to be, this description applies to his power rather than his essence. The Father, therefore, is said to be in Christ, because full divinity dwells in him and displays its power; and Christ, on the other hand, is said to be in the

---

46 Calvin, *Commentary on Matthew*, 487c.
47 Calvin, *Commentary on Daniel*, in *Ioannis Calvini opera quae supersunt omnia*, ed. Wilhelm Baum, Edward Cunitz, and Edward Reuss, vol. XLI (Brunsvigae: C. A. Schwetsche, 1863-1900), 55b-c.

Father because by his divine power he shows that he is one with the Father.[48]

While Calvin believes that Christ participates in an identity of essence with the Father, he insists that the "main thing is, in what manner the Father makes himself known to us in Christ." Commenting on Colossians 1:15, Christ is "the image of the invisible God," Calvin writes:

> [T]he term image is not related to essence, but has a relation to us. For Christ is called the image of God on this ground, that he makes God in a manner visible to us...[but] we must not insist on essence alone. The sum is this—that God in himself, that is, in his naked majesty, is invisible, and that not to the eyes of the body only, but also to the minds of men, and that he is revealed to us in Christ alone, that we may behold him as in a mirror.[49]

Calvin continues on this theme in regard to Second Corinthians 4:4:

> When, however, Christ is called the image of the invisible God, this is not meant merely of his essence, as being the 'co-essential of the Father,' as they say, but rather has reference to us, because he represents the Father to us. The Father himself is represented as invisible, because he is in himself not apprehended by the human understanding. He exhibits himself, however, to us by his Son, and makes himself in a manner visible.[50]

---

48   Calvin, *Commentary on John*, 326a. Also in *Commentary of John*, 387c, Calvin writes: "Again, it ought to be understood, that in every instance in which Christ declares, in this chapter [John 17] that he is one with the Father, he does not speak simply of his divine essence, but he is called one as regards his character as Mediator, and in so far as he is our Head. Many of the fathers, no doubt, interpreted these words as meaning absolutely that Christ is one with the Father, because he is the eternal God. But their dispute with the Arians led them to seize on detached passages, and to twist them into alien meanings. Now, Christ's design was widely different from that of raising our minds to a mere speculation about hidden divinity. Thus, he reasons from the end, by showing that we ought to be one, otherwise, the unity which he has with the Father would be fruitless and unavailing. To comprehend aright what was intended by saying that Christ and the Father are one, we must take care not to deprive Christ of his character as Mediator, but must rather view him as Head of the Church, and unite with his members. Thus it agrees best with the context, that in order to prevent that unity of the Son with the Father from being fruitless and unavailing, the power of that unity must be diffused into the whole body of the pious. Hence, too, we infer that we are one with Christ, not because he transfuses his substance into us, but because by the power of his Spirit, he imparts to us his life and all the blessings which he has received from the Father."
49   John Calvin, *Commentary on Colossians*, in *Ioannis Calvini opera quae supersunt omnia*, ed. Wilhelm Baum, Edward Cunitz, and Edward Reuss, vol. LII (Brunsvigae: C. A. Schwetsche, 1863-1900), 84d-85a.
50   Calvin, *Institutes*, II.6.iv.

In the Incarnation, Christ's hidden divinity or essence remains unchanged[51] and was veiled under the form of flesh, but in such a way as yet to be revealed.[52] In the concealing-revealing character of the Incarnation, the "divine incognito," the double aspect of accommodation is at its sharpest and most paradoxical. God's deepest condescension or descent from God's essence is both the high-point of humanity's knowledge and the limit of it: "God is not to be sought out in his unsearchable height, but is to be known by us in so far as he manifests himself in Christ."[53] And again: "If God, then, has spoken now for the last time, it is right to advance thus far; so also when you come to [Christ], you ought not to go further."[54]

Calvin describes our *captus* in many and varied ways. Sometimes it is our vision that is single out—we suffer from *lippitudo* (bleary eyes). Sometimes it is our *hebetudo*, our sluggishness, which stands in the way. However, it is our *captus* that God knows so well. As Calvin puts it, commenting on Psalm 78:60: "God, it is true, fills both heaven and earth; but we cannot attain to that infinite height to which God is exalted, in descending among us by the exercise of God's power and grace, God approaches as near to us as is needful, and as our limited capacity will bear."[55]

Calvin's theology of accommodation offers an understanding of how God reveals according to the mode of the receiver but avoids the pitfalls of pantheistic immediacy on one hand and ignorance or agnosticism on the other hand. He argues that we come to know God through the revelatory Word of God. Beyond this, any supposed knowledge of God is speculative and must be avoided lest one, in deluded arrogance, pretends to grasp the hidden mind of God. One cannot get behind the act of God's revelation and know the essence of God.

Calvin mentions the importance of accommodation (*accommodare*) several times. When he describes God's revelatory activity, Calvin depicts God as a grand

---

51   "Although the infinite essence of the Word is united in one person with the nature of man, yet we have no idea of its incarceration or confinement. For the Son of God miraculously descended from heaven, yet in such a manner that he never left heaven; he chose to be miraculously conceived in the womb of Virgin, to live on the earth, and to be suspended on the cross; and yet he never ceased to fill the universe, in the same manner as from the beginning" (Calvin, *Institutes*, II.13.iv).

52   See John Calvin, *Commentary on Philippians*, in *Ioannis Calvini opera quae supersunt omnia*, ed. Wilhelm Baum, Edward Cunitz, and Edward Reuss, vol. LII (Brunsvigae: C. A. Schwetsche, 1863-1900), 26c-d: "[T]he abasement of the flesh was, notwithstanding, like a veil, by which his divine majesty was concealed... Finally, the image of God shone forth in Christ in such a manner that he was the same time abased in his outward appearance and brought down to nothing in the estimation of men." See Calvin, *Commentary on John*, 15b: "The majesty of God was not annihilated, although it was surrounded by flesh; it was indeed concealed under the low condition of the flesh, but so as to cause its splendor to be seen."

53   John Calvin, *Commentary on Second Corinthians*, in *Ioannis Calvini opera quae supersunt omnia*, ed. Wilhelm Baum, Edward Cunitz, and Edward Reuss, vol. L (Brunsvigae: C. A. Schwetsche, 1863-1900), 53c.

54   Calvin, *Commentary on Hebrews*, 10b.

55   Calvin, *Commentary on Psalm*, 74c.

orator who speaks to an audience and thus uses a language that is clear and comprehensible. The most general form of this accommodation comes in the beauty of creation. In the splendor of creation, God "renders himself near and familiar to us, and in some manner communicates himself."[56]

Similarly, scripture is accommodated to our limited capacities and understanding. In his description of the process by which Moses wrote the creation account, Calvin writes: "Moses, accommodating himself to the rudeness of common folk, mentions in the history of Creation no other works of God than those which show themselves to our own eyes."[57] This is illuminating in that it portrays the accommodating Spirit of God working through the accommodating rhetoric of a human.

Calvin refers to accommodation in terms of a human teacher and not just in terms of divine accommodation. This can give insight on his understanding of God's accommodation. In his *Commentary on First Corinthians*, Calvin reflects: "A wise teacher accommodates himself to the understanding of those who must be taught. He begins with the first principles in teaching the weak and ignorant and should not rise any higher than they can follow. In short, he instills his teaching drop by drop, lest it overflow."[58]

III. CONCLUSION

We should not speak about God in ungodly terms but to speak of God in God's terms given to us. We are always already immersed in the human condition of sinfulness and finitude. Humans can have knowledge of God only because God first condescends and accommodates to human capacity to reveal to us truth about himself. We have seen that humans cannot arrive, by themselves, at the truth about God. Left on our own, we are only good idolaters. Revelation is self-authenticating and God's accommodation is the means by which God's revelation is mediated. The acceptance of what is given in revelation is an acceptance made by humans in and by faith—a faith that is from God.

---

56 John Calvin, *Institutes of the Christian Religion*, ed. J. T. McNeill and trans. Ford Lewis Battles (Westminster Press, 1960), I.5.ix.
57 Ibid., I.14.iii.
58 John Calvin, *Commentary on First Corinthians*, in *Ioannis Calvini opera quae supersunt omnia*, ed. Wilhelm Baum, Edward Cunitz, and Edward Reuss, vol. XLIX (Brunsvigae: C. A. Schwetsche, 1863-1900), 347a.

3. *Archetypal and Ectypal theology*

Christian theology rests on the self-revelation of God in human history to human ears. It is a claim that God is speaking God—a God who has spoken and still speaks. He discloses himself to us such that we can know him – and but not fully understand him.

In the opening pages of his *Elenctic Theology*, Francis Turretin writes:

> When God is set forth as the object of theology, he is not to be regarded simply as God in himself (for thus he is incomprehensible to us) but as revealed and as he has been pleased to manifest himself to us in his word, so that divine revelation is the formal relation which comes to be considered in this object. Nor is he to be considered exclusively under the relation of the deity (according to the opinion of Thomas Aquinas and many Scholastics after him, for in this manner the knowledge of him could not be saving but deadly to sinners), but as he is our God (i.e., covenanted in Christ as he has revealed himself to us in his word not only as the object of knowledge, but also of worship).[59]

Turretin argues that theology deals with the revealed knowledge of God—but that in doing so, it does not claim that that is all there is to know about him. Theology should be divided into archetypal theology and ectypal theology.

Archetypal theology is the infinite knowledge of God that only God possesses and which is known only to God himself. It is the original whereas all else is the copy (ectypal knowledge). Archetypal knowledge is the pattern for all true theology. Ectypal theology is knowledge of God to which finite minds have access. It is creaturely knowledge that is revealed by God and accommodated to our finite capacities. Creaturely knowledge is always imperfect, incomplete, and dependent on God's perfect and complete knowledge. Archetypal theology is simply not what creatures have ever had, can have, or will ever have. Our knowledge of God—ectypal—will never be comprehensive, even while it is true.

Turretin calls for *theologia viatorum*—a "theology on the way." The theology of the journeying Christian as he or she heads towards the heavenly rest, but knows all along that what he or she knows now is not complete, and may even at points be faulty.

---

59   Francis Turrentin, *Elenctic Theology*, 1.5.4.

Ectypal theology helps us to be both confident and humble. We can be confident that what knowledge we have of God is true knowledge – a knowledge that is saving, personal, and real. We can make meaningful statements about God, because he has made meaningful statements about himself to us.

But we also ought to be humble. We should be aware of our own capacity for error. We should be aware that whatever we say about God is not a mastery or a limitation of who he is. We speak of God with confidence, but also with reverence and humility because cannot comprehend God, but we can apprehend God.

4. *Language about God*

It is important to hold to the distinction between the Creator and creation and we must never confuse the two. This leads us to the question of language about God. To maintain this Creator/creature distinction, theologians have used the terms univocal, analogical, and equivocal when speaking about how we know God. Those who argue for some type of univocal understanding (e.g. John Duns Scotus in the 13th century) seem to believe "some predicates applied to God and humans must be univocal (i.e., mean exactly the same thing)."[60] The opposite makes God unknowable. And then others, like Thomas Aquinas (12th century), argued for an analogical view.

Michael Horton offers a careful explanation about the differences:

> Neither being nor knowledge is ever shared univocally (i.e., identically) between God and creatures. As God's being is qualitatively and not just quantitatively distinct from ours, so too is God's knowledge. God's knowledge is archetypal (the original), while ours is ectypal (a copy), revealed by God and therefore accommodated to our finite capacities. Our imperfect and incomplete knowledge is always dependent on God's perfect and complete knowledge.
>
> A covenantal ontology requires a covenantal epistemology. We were created as God's analogy (image bearers) rather than as self-existent sparks of divinity; therefore, our knowledge is also dependent rather than autonomous. So there is indeed such a

---

60   Michael Horton, *Justification*, vol. 1, 139.

The Self-Revealing and Accommodating God

thing as absolute, perfect, exhaustive, and eternal truth, but this knowledge is possessed by God, not by us. Rather, we have revealed truth, which God has accommodated to our capacity.

Following Thomas Aquinas (1225–74), our older theologians therefore argued that human knowledge is analogical rather than either univocal or equivocal (two terms are related analogically when they are similar, univocally when they are identical, and equivocally when they have nothing in common).

When we say that God is good, we assume we know what good means from our ordinary experience with fellow human beings. However, God is not only quantitatively better than we are; his goodness is qualitatively different from creaturely goodness. Nevertheless, because we are created in God's image, we share this predicate with God analogically. Goodness, attributed to God and Sally, is similar but always with greater dissimilarity. At no point is goodness exactly the same for God as it is for Sally. The difference is qualitative, not just quantitative; yet there is enough similarity to communicate the point.

God reveals himself as a person, a king, a shepherd, a substitutionary lamb, and so forth. These analogies are not arbitrary (i.e., equivocal), but they are also not exact correspondence (i.e., univocal). Even when we attribute love to God and Mary, love cannot mean exactly the same thing for a self-existent Trinity and a finite person. In every analogy, there is always greater dissimilarity than similarity between God and creatures. Nevertheless, God judges that the analogy is appropriate for his self-revelation. We do not know exactly what divine goodness is like, but since God selects this analogy, there must be a sufficient similarity to our concept of goodness to justify the comparison.

This doctrine of analogy is the hinge on which a Christian affirmation of God's transcendence and immanence turns. A univocal view threatens God's transcendence, while an equivocal view threatens God's immanence.[61]

---

61 Horton, *The Christian Faith,* 53–55.

Adopting a view of God's revelation accommodated to our human capacities and an analogical view of our knowledge of God guards against collapsing the Creator/creature distinction. We are, indeed, created in the image of God. Yet, we are not *exactly* like God.

Remembering God's transcendence humbles us. God is far above humanity. He is high and lifted up. Remembering the utter uniqueness of God moves us to adoration, reverence, and worship. We must remember that our knowledge of God is dependent upon God's accommodating self-revelation. Because God is beyond us, if we are to know him rightly, then he must stoop to our level. Graciously, he has done just that. God has "accommodated" to our capacities and we can know him truly—though never exhaustively. Our imperfect and incomplete knowledge is always dependent on God's perfect and complete knowledge.

Divine Impassibility and Self-Limitation

DR. DAVID MUTHUKUMAR SIVASUBRAMANIAN
Associate Professor,
South Asia Institute of Advanced Christian Studies
India

Anselm of Canterbury writes in *Cur Deus Homo* ("Why God Became Man"), "For we affirm that the divine nature is undoubtedly incapable of suffering and cannot in any sense be brought low from its exalted standing..."[1] For Anselm, and most of the early Christian theologians, it is paramount to protect the divine nature from any attribution of change or modification. Nevertheless, Christian salvation is deeply reliant on the understanding that God in Christ suffered and died on the cross and was resurrected on the third day. So, in order to balance the unchangeable nature of God with the suffering aspect of Christ, Anselm quickly adds the following words,

> But we say that the Lord Jesus Christ is the true God and true man, one person in two natures and two natures in one person. In view of this, when we say that God is suffering some humiliation or weakness, we do not understand this in terms of the exaltedness of his nonsuffering nature, but in terms of the weakness of the human substance which he was taking upon himself.[2]

Anselm acknowledges the necessity of articulating that "God suffered," but he insists that this suffering should be ascribed to the "human substance" rather than the "divine essence," which is essentially incapable of suffering. Not only did Anselm confront this theological conundrum, but the traditional formulations of the doctrine of God also wrestled with the paradox of reconciling God's suffering with the attributes of "impassibility and immutability" as fundamental characteristics of the divine essence.

As suffering signifies deep psycho-physiological change within the human being, transposing the same notion to the divine person would challenge these notions of impassibility and immutability. However, perceiving God as a co-suffer with humanity, as the Gospels portray, is essential to our faith understanding (which Anselm also recognized).

However, can this paradox be answered adequately by just attributing the suffering to the "human Christ" and preserving the "divine Christ" from all affects? Contemporary theologians such as Jürgen Moltmann would contend that the suffering of God in Christ must be understood as the suffering of the Trinitarian Godself as the salvation of humanity depends on the efficacy of

---

1 Anselm of Canterbury, *The Collected Works,* (Oxford, 2008), 274. Italics mine.
2 Ibid.

God's identification with human misery. Moltmann revisits the doctrine of divine self-limitation (through a panentheistic framework) to articulate God's full identification with human miseries in the Person and Work of Jesus Christ. Thus, there is a challenge to the traditional articulation of God's impassibility and immutability in contemporary theological reflections.

This paper will seek to explore this paradox by exploring the concepts of divine impassibility and self-limitation as articulated by select theologians in the history of the Church. This study will argue that a re-examination of divine impassibility in light of the doctrine of divine self-limitation does provide a better framework to comprehend the paradox of God's suffering, albeit certain cautions are warranted in this process.

I. METAPHYSICAL AND ONTOLOGICAL DISCUSSION

The divine attributes of impassibility and immutability are deeply rooted in classical theism and evoke a rich tradition of metaphysical and ontological discourses. However, I suppose a brief overview of it for this paper will suffice. Impassibility, derived from the Latin *impassibilis*, traditionally denotes God's immunity to suffering or emotional changes. This attribute is grounded in the belief that God transcends the vicissitudes and vulnerabilities inherent in the created order and underscores divine transcendence and perfection. And Immutability refers to God's unchangeableness in essence, attributes, and will. This concept is also linked to the philosophical notion of perfection. A perfect being, it is argued, would not undergo change, for change implies imperfection. In their usage, both impassibility and immutability are used in a complementary sense—God cannot suffer because God cannot change.

The influence of Greek philosophy, especially that of Plato and Aristotle, is significant in shaping the early Christian understanding of God, especially the development of the understanding of God's immutability and impassibility. Plato's conception of the "Forms" as unchanging and eternal ideals and Aristotle's concept of the "Unmoved Mover" as pure actuality are foundational in developing the metaphysical background for understanding these divine attributes. The Neoplatonist emphasis on the absolute transcendence and immutability of the One God is an undeniable influence in Christian articulations. Also, Aristotle's Unmoved Mover, being perfect and complete in itself, necessitated the understanding that no essential change or modification is possible within God's Being.

However, if the "Perfect Being" cannot undergo change as the change would imply an imperfection, how do we understand the nature of the immutable God interacting with a dynamic, ever-changing world? And can a God who is impassible truly empathize with human suffering? Moreover, this challenge is particularly acute in the context of the Incarnation Christology—of God entering into the temporal, ever-changing realm of human existence, where the unchangeable God is affirmed to have taken on human nature and has ostensibly undergone suffering and change. Therefore, both divine impassibility and divine suffering present a paradoxical interface between the transcendence and a personal, relational understanding of God, and theology has to grapple with this mystery in its articulation.

I. SCRIPTURAL BASIS

The notion of God's impassibility is often inferred from Biblical texts emphasizing God's perfection and completeness. For instance, in Psalm 102:26-27, the psalmist contrasts the temporal nature of creation with the eternal, unchanging nature of God as he affirms that the "[heavens and earth] will perish, but you [YHWH] endure; they will all wear out like a garment... but you [YHWH] are the same, and your years have no end." Similarly, James 1:17 speaks of God as the "Father of lights, with whom there is no variation or shadow due to change," underscoring God's constancy and perfection. The immutability of God is also pivotal in understanding God's character. Malachi 3:6 declares, "For I the Lord do not change; therefore you, O children of Jacob, have not perished." This verse not only speaks to God's unchanging nature but also signifies the reliability of God's faithful commitment to his promises and covenants. Hebrews 13:8 explicates this steadfast reliability of God in Christological terms by stating, "Jesus Christ is the same yesterday and today and forever."

Theologians have often interpreted these texts to affirm God's unchanging and unaffected nature. They are meant to affirm that God's essence, will, knowledge, and divine decrees remain constant despite the changing nature of the world and human history. This immutability was not seen as a limitation but as an aspect of God's divine perfection. Also, God's unchanging nature is a source of comfort and assurance for believers, as it guarantees the steadfastness of God's love, grace, and justice.

However, the Old Testament is full of anthropopathic representations of God's dealings with his people. The OT talks about the sorrow or the affliction that God experiences in his relationship with the Israelites and the creation. Genesis 6:6 states that "the Lord was sorry that he had made humans on the earth, and it grieved him to his heart," which expresses God's deep disappointment over his creation and the consequent affliction he experiences. Also, Judges 10:16 talks about how the Lord "could no longer bear to see Israel suffer" as they were oppressed by their enemies. Isaiah 63:9 talks about God's anguish toward the condition of the exiled Israelites: "In all their affliction he was afflicted." Though the OT tests are often explained in an anthropomorphic sense, the import of these passages in expressing God's loving, vulnerable relationship toward his people cannot be merely explained away. Moreover, the Gospel accounts candidly portray the human limitations and passions that Jesus endured in his life on earth.

II. THE UNCHANGEABLE GOD AND DIVINE IMPASSIBILITY

While the Hebrew representations of God are unabashedly full of God's passions, the Early Church Fathers and Medieval theologians had to grapple with the Greek philosophical concept of the unchangeableness of God. They strived to strike a balance between the conception of an impassible, immutable God with the OT and the Gospel accounts portrayal of God as deeply involved in human history through suffering and change. In their attempt to articulate this paradox, we can see at least two strands of emphases: some of them stressed (or overstressed) the unchangeableness of God over God's passions and attempted to confine God's passion to Christ's human nature, while some others relied on the conceptual possibility of attributing human experiences onto the divine nature. We will look at some of the theological conceptions of select theologians who broadly fall under the aforementioned criterion of prioritizing the unchangeableness of God while finding ways to understand the suffering of Christ.

III. HUMAN CHRIST AND DIVINE CHRIST

1. *Athanasius*

Athanasius' understanding of divine impassibility is intricately linked to his defense of the full divinity of Christ against Arianism. His Christology cannot be understood apart from his soteriology, as for him, the central question is not only who Christ is but also what Christ's incarnation achieves for humanity. In his writings Against the Arians and On the Incarnation, Athanasius posits that salvation involves the restoration of human beings to the divine likeness, which was marred by sin, and the Word (Logos) becoming flesh is essential for this restorative work. Athanasius argues that only someone who is fully divine can restore humanity to the divine image, and only someone who is truly human can represent humanity and die in its place. Thus, by affirming the full divinity and humanity in Christ, Athanasius has to account for the suffering of God in Christ.

However, for Athanasius, the impassibility of God is a given; God cannot suffer because God is perfect and unchangeable. And suffering implies change, limitation, and a response to external forces, all of which are incompatible with the divine nature. The incarnation, for Athanasius, is the act by which the impassible Word assumes a passible human nature. He, therefore, concludes that the Logos does not suffer in his divine nature; rather, he suffers in and through the human nature he assumed. For Athanasius, the Word experiences human suffering without the divine nature itself being altered, and he avers that this is possible because the Word's assumption of human nature is a voluntary act of condescension and love. Athanasius, thus, limits God's passions to Christ's human nature.

2. *Augustine of Hippo*

Augustine of Hippo also upheld the classical understanding of God as impassible. For him, impassibility meant that God does not experience emotional changes or physical suffering, as these are characteristics of temporal, created beings. In Confessions, he contends that any emotion ascribed to God is not to be understood as implying changeableness in God or any disturbance (*perturbatio*) within divine life. He interpreted God's emotions, as described in Scripture, not as literal affective changes in God but as metaphorical expressions that describe God's actions and attitudes in terms humans can understand.

Augustine explained that it was through Christ's human nature that Christ experienced suffering and death. Augustine did not see the suffering of Christ as implicating the divine nature in change or suffering.[3] Instead, he viewed the incarnation as the means through which the impassible God entered into the human condition to bring about redemption.[4]

---

3 Augustine, *Letters* 100-155, (United Kingdom: New City Press, 2002), 137:12.
4 Ibid, 219:3.

3. *Thomas Aquinas*

In Summa Theologica, Aquinas articulates the immutability of God, arguing that God is altogether immutable. For him, divine impassibility means that God cannot suffer or be acted upon in any way. Using the Aristotelian metaphysics, Aquinas understands God as Actus Purus, or "Pure Act."[5] This term Pure Act denotes that God is the perfect realization of Being, without any potentiality. Since change implies moving from potentiality to actuality, a being that is pure actuality cannot change, and therefore, God cannot suffer (impassibility) or change (immutability) because suffering implies a kind of defect or lack, and God, being perfect, cannot lack anything.

However, in the later part of his Summa, Aquinas, while discussing the suffering of Christ, does acknowledge that Scripture speaks of God in terms that imply passions (like anger, sorrow, etc.).[6] While denying that God experiences emotions as humans do, Aquinas agrees that God has love toward his creation. However, he conceives this love as of an intellectual nature and not as a psychological response. Also, he interprets the descriptions of God as expressing anger or sorrow in a metaphorical or anthropopathic sense, as they are the means to understand God's actions from a human perspective. Thus, Aquinas tries to safeguard the integrity of God's internal nature against all external stimuli.

IV. COMMUNICATION OF PROPERTIES

1. *Gregory of Nazianzus*

Gregory of Nazianzus also maintained the classical understanding of God as perfect and unchangeable. In his Five Theological Orations, especially Oration 29 and 31, Gregory articulated the nature of God, emphasizing God's transcendence and unchangeableness. Gregory spoke of the impassibility of God as essential to divine perfection. He insisted that any talk of change in God can only be in terms of God's actions, not his essence. By maintaining this distinction between actions (energeia) and essence, Gregory spoke of the dynamic nature of God's interactions with the world while preserving the immutability of God's divine nature. He famously stated in his Letter to Cledonius (Epistle 101), "That which He has not assumed He has

---

5   Thomas Aquinas, *Summa Theologica,* (United States: Coyote Canyon Press, 2018), Part I, Q. 9, Art. 1.
6   Ibid., Part III, Q. 46.

not healed; but that which is united to His Godhead is also saved." Thus, He also acknowledged the fullness of human and divine nature being present in Christ, which will necessitate the understanding of the Second Person in the Trinity suffering.

Gregory employed the concept of the hypostatic union—the unique union of divine and human natures in the person of Christ—to understand the impassible God's suffering in the Person of Christ. He asserts that by assuming human nature, the Logos made possible the healing of that nature, including its capacity for suffering. Gregory maintained that while the divine and human natures in Christ remain distinct, they are united in one person, so the experiences of the human nature, including suffering and death, can be spoken of as experiences of the Person of the Son. Gregory's understanding laid the groundwork for what would later be known as the *communicatio idiomatum*, the communication of properties, where the attributes of both natures are ascribed to the one person of Christ. Gregory thus attributed God's suffering to the unified Person in Christ, albeit through the human nature.

2. *Martin Luther*

Luther's education in nominalism, study of Augustine, and familiarity with medieval catechetics heavily influenced his inheritance of classical theism. He asserted that it is "fundamentally necessary and salutary for a Christian, to know that God foreknows nothing contingently, but that he foresees and purposes and does all things by his immutable, eternal, and infallible will."[7] For Luther, the Word of God was "immutable and insuperable."[8] In his Lectures on the book of Genesis, he described the Law of God as "the eternal and immutable decree of God concerning the worship of God and the love of one's neighbor,"[9] For Luther, the immutable nature of God's Word was essential as it is through this unchanging Word that one's faith is engendered and affirmed.[10]

---

7 Martin Luther, *The Bondage of the Will* (Createspace Independent Pub, 2012), 37.
8 Martin Luther, *Luther's Works*, American Edition, eds. Jaroslav Pelikan and Hilton C. Oswald, Vol. 25, *Lectures on Romans* (St. Louis: Concordia Publishing House, 1972), 371.
9 Martin Luther, *Luther's Works*, American Edition, ed. Jaroslav Pelikan, Vol. 3, Lectures on Genesis Chapters 15-20 (St. Louis: Concordia Publishing House, 1961), 84.
10 Luther defends God's immutability through the paradoxical tension between *deus absconditus* and *deus revelatus*. God's self-disclosure and workings are made manifest in his Word, which is most fully expressed in the incarnation of Jesus Christ, the Deus Revelatus, or God revealed. While Christ stands at the core of Luther's theological framework, Luther acknowledged the existence of aspects of God that remain unrevealed to us. These dimensions, either exceeding our grasp or deliberately concealed by God, constitute the *Deus Absconditus*, or the hidden God. (Gerhard O. Forde, Theology Is for Proclamation (Minneapolis: Fortress Press, 1990), 22.) Luther contends that the workings of God should not be misconstrued as indicative of divergent wills within God but rather as manifestations of a consistent and unchanging God. (Timothy

In his "Heidelberg Disputation," Luther introduces the theology of the cross (*theologia crucis*). Luther's interpretation of the cross transcends mere theological symbolism. It touches upon the profound existential anxieties experienced by humans in the midst of suffering, fears of death, and eternal judgment.[11] The cross serves to dismantle our flawed preconceptions about our own self and clears the path for the emergence of an authentic theology that confronts and interprets these deep-seated human concerns.[12] His theology of the cross asserted that God reveals Himself most profoundly in the weakness and suffering of the cross. While God in his divine essence is impassible, God willingly enters into the human condition, including suffering, in the person of Jesus Christ.[13]

Luther further developed his understanding of the passions of Christ in the economy of salvation through the doctrine of communicatio idiomatum (the communication of properties) in his two great Christological disputations "The Word became Flesh" (1539) and "On the divinity and humanity of Christ" (1540). Luther elucidates the doctrine by stating that the properties of Christ's human nature can be attributed to his divine nature and vice versa. Luther endeavors to portray God as One who is transcendent and unchangeable in essence, yet intimately involved in the human condition through the person of Jesus Christ. He remarks that Christ participated in the full extent of human experience, even to the point of suffering and death on the cross, which is the ultimate expression of God's love and the primary locus of divine self-disclosure. Luther claims that because of the union of divine and human natures in Christ, it is appropriate to attribute characteristics of one nature to the entire person, even if those characteristics originate from the other nature. This means that, for Luther, we can speak of the Son of God as suffering and dying on the cross (attributes of His human nature) and the man Jesus as omnipotent and eternal (attributes of His divine nature).

3. *John Calvin*

For Calvin, God's immutability is a cornerstone of divine perfection. In his

---

Roser, Can God Be Persuaded: A Discussion of the Immutability of God in Luther's Catechesis on Prayer, [Unpublished doctoral dissertation], Concordia Seminary, St. Louis.) Any seeming variability in God's nature or perceived discrepancies in God's actions are attributed through faith to the mysteriousness of God.

11   Alister E. McGrath, *Luther's Theology of the Cross: Martin Luther's Theological Breakthrough*, (Oxford, UK: Wiley-Blackwell, 2011), 204.

12   Ibid.

13   *Luther's Works*, vol. 31, 39–40.

Institutes of the Christian Religion (Book 1, Chapter 10), Calvin emphasizes that God is unchangeable in essence, will, and purpose. This immutability is contrasted with the variability and mutability of creation. He views God's promises and covenants as expressions of this unchangeable nature. For Calvin, the reliability of God's promises, such as the covenant of grace, hinges on the fact that God does not change. The attribute of immutability also plays a significant role in Calvin's understanding of predestination and providence. God's eternal decrees are unchanging, and his providential care for the world is consistent and reliable, reflecting God's immutable nature.

Calvin's conception of divine impassibility is tied to the idea that God is not subject to human passions or emotions. He asserts that God is beyond the vicissitudes and weaknesses that characterize human emotional life. However, Calvin does not deny that the Bible frequently attributes human emotions to God. He interprets these descriptions metaphorically, understanding them as accommodations to human understanding. When Scripture speaks of God as angry, grieved, or loving, it is speaking in human terms to make God's actions and moral will comprehensible to us.

In his theology of incarnation, Calvin posits that Jesus Christ, within his human essence, underwent the entirety of human emotions and afflictions (Book 2, Chapters 12 and 16). Yet, Calvin strives to carefully navigate the relationship between Christ's divine and human natures. While affirming that Christ, in his human nature, could suffer and die, he preserves the integrity of the divine nature as impassible by maintaining a clear distinction between the two natures in the person of Christ.[14] Calvin articulates the relationship between Christ's divine and human natures as "distinction and union," maintaining that while these two natures are intimately united within the single Person of Christ, they remain distinct without any corruption of their individual integrity.[15]

This inseparable yet distinct union forms the basis for the hypostatic union, where Christ is fully recognized as both God and man.[16] Consequently, Calvin concedes that the attribution of the properties of one nature to the other, the *communicatio idiomatum*, is "not without reason."[17] Nevertheless, he denies any direct transfer

---

14   John Calvin, *Institutes of the Christian Religion,* J.T. McNeill (ed.), transl. F.L. Battles, 2 vols, (Philadelphia: Westminster Press, 1960), 486.
15   Ibid., 486–487.
16   Ibid., 482.
17   Ibid., 1402.

of attributes between the natures, upholding the complete integrity of both Christ's divinity and humanity.[18] Calvin's nuanced approach to the communion of attributes through the doctrine of hypostatic union ensures that the properties of the two natures are justifiably and fittingly ascribed to the entire Person of Christ while the unique qualities of each nature are affirmed in their distinction.[19]

While the Lutheran's exposition of the doctrine of communicatio idiomatum, especially in the context of the Eucharist, asserts a fuller exchange of attributes, endorsing the idea that Christ's human nature can partake in divine attributes, such as omnipresence, Calvinists maintain a more distinct separation between the two natures, allowing no transfer of divine properties to the human nature except in the unity of the Person of Christ. This is in alignment with Calvin's qualified acceptance of the *communicatio idiomatum* in terms of the profound union of the divine and human natures in the One Person of Christ.[20]

V. THE SUFFERING GOD AND DIVINE SELF-LIMITATION

The theological deliberations, as outlined in the previous section, in a general sense, prioritize the unchangeable nature of God while trying to understand the mystery of the Incarnation, where God has entered human existence through the very life, suffering, and death of Jesus Christ. As the event of the Incarnation is not merely a symbolic or metaphorical occurrence but a real and substantial union of divine and human natures in the One Person, theologians have strived to articulate this through the doctrine of two natures (divine nature being the predominant partner), the doctrine of the hypostatic union (distinction in unity), and the communion of properties (across the two natures on in the Person.) The challenge is to uphold the genuine humanity of Christ without compromising either the divine or human attributes.

1. *Jürgen Moltmann*

However, some contemporary theologians, such as Jürgen Moltmann, have found these early theological articulations inadequate in balancing this mystery of the transcendent God becoming fully enfleshed and embodied in the Incarnation. He

---

18   Sung W. Park, "The question of deification in the theology of John Calvin," *Verbum et Ecclesia*, 38(1), 3. https://doi.org/10.4102/ve.v38i1.1701.
19   Calvin, *Institutes,* 1403.
20   Ibid., 1402. Also see, Sung W. Park, "The question of deification."

questions the relevance of the classical doctrine of impassibility and immutability in depicting the Christian God and argues that a God who suffers is more consistent with the biblical testimony of a God who is deeply involved in the world and responsive to human suffering.[21] In his book The Crucified God, Moltmann critiques the notion of the "impassibility of God" that was "cherished by the Greek Fathers... and by the medieval theologians.[22] Moltmann alleges that the early Christian theologians' emphasis on divine immutability and impassibility is an indication that "a mild docetism runs through the Christology of the ancient church."[23] He contends that the idea of the "passion of the passionate God" is antithetical to Aristotelian metaphysics, as it specializes in God's "essential apathy" rather than in his crucial identification with the suffering humanity.[24]

Moltmann's critique of the theologies that prioritize impassibility and immutability is rooted in his theology of the cross (theologia crucis). He argues that the traditional doctrine of two natures that seeks to "make a neat separation between the natures of Godhead and Manhood" should rather be understood in their "reciprocal relationship" constituting the personal union in the "God-man" Christ.[25] In contrast to the notions of God's impassibility and immutability, Moltmann argues that God's suffering is most profoundly revealed in the crucifixion of Jesus Christ. The cross, for Moltmann, is the central event in the life of God. It is the ultimate expression of God's love, revealing God's true nature.[26] He sees God's suffering as an expression of divine love and solidarity with humanity.[27] A God who cannot suffer, according to Moltmann, is a God who cannot love.[28] For Moltmann, God's nature understood through the event of the cross manifests God's vulnerability and suffering, as in "crucified Christ," God binds himself in solidarity with human suffering and abandonment.[29]

Moltmann interprets the suffering and death of Jesus as not merely human experiences but as events that involve the very being of God.[30] According to him, the crucifixion is an event within the life of the Trinity, which means that

---

21   Jürgen Moltmann, *The Crucified God: The Cross of Christ as the Foundation and Criticism of Christian Theology* (New York: Harper & Row, 1974), x.
22   Ibid.
23   Ibid., 89.
24   Ibid., x.
25   Ibid, 81.
26   Ibid., 89.
27   Ibid., 223.
28   Ibid.
29   Ibid., 25.
30   Ibid.

the Father also experiences the Son's suffering.[31] On the Cross, Moltmann sees a correspondence between God's *ad intra* and *ad extra* Trinitarian relations as he avers that God's "outward acts correspond to inward suffering, and outward suffering corresponds to inward acts."[32] The cross is not just an act of God in the world but an event in which all the Persons of the Trinity participate.

In the garden of Gethsemane, Jesus prayed to the Father to remove the cup of suffering but received no answer, and on the cross, Jesus cried through the words of Psalm 22:2, "My God, my God, why have you forsaken me?" Moltmann concludes that these instances signify Christ's experience of abandonment as God the Father had forsaken God the Son to the "experience of hell and judgment."[33] Jesus' agony was more than "suffering in his human nature."[34] Moltmann observes that Jesus was "not merely assailed by fear and suffering in his human nature, as scholastic tradition" portrays; rather, "He was assailed in his person, his very essence, in his relationship to the Father - in his divine sonship."[35] The Son suffers a godforsaken death, and the Father suffers the Son's death. On the cross, "the pain of the Father corresponds to the death of the Son... Here, the innermost life of the Trinity is at stake."[36] The Father forsakes the Son "in order to become the Father of those who have been delivered up."[37] Moltmann's understanding of the Incarnation as having implications for the Trinitarian Being of God is based on his understanding of divine self-limitation.

Moltmann uses the Kabbalistic doctrine of *zimsum* ("contraction" or "self-limitation") to understand the relationship between God and Creation.[38] He argues that while God is omnipresent, he is capable of self-limitation in order to create a domain for creatures to dwell. He argues that in Scripture, as recounted in Exodus 25:22, God demonstrates his ability to differentiate from his omnipresence by localizing his presence as the Shekinah glory within the Tabernacle.[39] He further states that the act of creation, which is analogous to God's self-differentiation

---

31 Jürgen Moltmann, *The Trinity and the Kingdom: The Doctrine of God* (San Francisco: Harper & Row, 1981), 98. The influence of Process theology can be inferred here.
32 Ibid., 77. See also Moltmann, *The Crucified God,* 149-153.
33 Ibid.
34 Ibid.
35 Ibid.
36 Ibid., 81.
37 Ibid.
38 Jürgen Moltmann, *God in Creation: A New Theology of Creation and the Spirit of God* (San Francisco: Harper & Row, 1985), 86. Also see, Gershom G. Scholem, Major Trends in Jewish Mysticism (New York: Schocken Books, 1946).
39 Ron Highfield, "Divine self-limitation in the theology of Jurgen Moltmann: A critical appraisal," *Christian Scholar's Review,* Holland, Vol. 32, Iss. 1, (Fall 2002): 53.

in the Shekinah, is effected through a divine contraction (*zimsum*) where God voluntarily recedes in his Being to create a space by a form of self-denial.[40] Moltmann observes that in this process of *zimzum*, God brings out Creation through a conscious "inward act" of "self-humiliation" and "self-limitation."[41]

Moltmann applies the doctrine of *zimzum* to discuss the inner trinitarian reflection of the creation as "out of God and in God."[42] According to Moltmann, Creation is "a process of reflection to the inner relationship of the Trinity."[43]

> ... [I]t means that the Father, through an alteration of his love for the Son (that is to say through a contraction of the Spirit), and the Son, through an alteration in his response to the Father's love (that is, through an inversion of the Spirit) have opened up the space, the time and the freedom for that "outwards" into which the Father utters himself creatively through the Son. For God himself this utterance means an emptying of himself - a self-determination for the purpose of a self-limitation.[44]

For Moltmann, the event of creation itself is thus a self-limitation of God within the internal Trinitarian Being. Moltmann also claims that both the Father's love for the Son and the Son's response of obedience and surrender to the Father arise "out of the necessity" in God's nature.[45] And thus, creation is not a Sovereign act of God; rather, it is a necessary act, integral to the very Being of God.[46]

Moltmann extends the divine self-limitation in Creation to the event of the Cross. He conceives the Cross as the instance in the life of the Trinity where the Father, Son, and Spirit experience human alienation and suffering. He says, "The communicating love of the Father turns into infinite pain over the sacrifice of the Son," and "the responding love of the Son becomes infinite suffering over his repulsion and rejection by the Father."[47] On the cross, the Spirit of God represents the Father and the Son in a "single surrendering movement."[48]

---

40 Moltmann, *God in Creation, 15.*
41 Moltmann, *The Trinity and the Kingdom,* 59.
42 Ibid., 111.
43 Ibid., 112.
44 Ibid.
45 Ibid., 58.
46 Ibid., 112
47 Ibid.
48 Ibid., 82. The Spirit is "the link joining the bond between the Father and the Son, with their separation."

Moltmann thus conceives the Cross as the ad extra event in creation through which we understand the internal self-limitation of God ad intra in which all the three Persons of the Trinity partake. Moltmann, thus, by attributing the suffering in the Person of Jesus Christ to the Trinitarian Being of God, emphatically argues that the Triune God whom we worship is not a disconnected and apathetic God who is unable to share in the existential realities of humanity but the God who is fully present and participates as a co-suffer with us.

Moltmann's theological quest to comprehend God as a co-sufferer in human affliction stems from his personal history as a German soldier during the Nazi era, where he had first hand experienced unparalleled human catastrophes. This unique *sitz im leben* informs his compelling portrayal of the Triune God's immanence and participation in human realities. The Liberation theologians have greatly appropriated Moltmann's conception of the Crucified God, making it relevant to the theological expressions of issues of social justice and emancipation of the poor and the marginalized.

However, Moltmann's use of *zimzum* within his panentheistic worldview does raise some significant theological problems. If creation is a necessary act of God's Being, how do we understand the *ex nihilo* creation that the Scripture affirms? Wolfhart Pannenberg criticizes Moltmann's attempt to combine the Kabbalistic concept of *zimsum* with traditional theological explanations of creation. Pannenberg states that Moltmann's use of *zimsum* is a "materially unfounded mystification."[49] He finds Moltmann as confounding the *creatio ex nihilo* doctrine by making creation essential to God's Being.

Also, the Kabbalistic myth of *zimsum* is a metaphorical extension of the notion of physical space, and it conceives "God as his own space—the container and its contents, so to speak."[50] Moltmann envisions God as shrinking into himself in order to create a space within his Being for creatures.[51] If "God is in everything and everything is in God" then how do we maintain the mystery of God's transcendence and immanence in the world through this space myth? Also, Moltmann rejects "the distinction made by the early church between theology as the doctrine of God and economy as the doctrine of salvation."[52] He states, "Statements about the

---

49 Wolfhart Pannenberg, *Systematic Theology: Volume 2*, trans. G.W. Bromiley (Edinburgh: T&T Clark, 1994), 14.
50 Highfield, "Divine self-limitation," 53.
51 Ibid.
52 Moltmann, *The Crucified God*, 67

immanent Trinity must not contradict statements about the economic Trinity."[53] Moltmann sees a direct correspondence between the immanent Trinity and the economic Trinity, and his assertions that the Triune God's Being is involved in the experience of Christ's suffering on the Cross would dissolve the distinction between God's Being and his action in the word.

We can perceive that Moltmann's theology is apparently influenced by his panentheistic worldview, which he derived from Process theology. Through this panentheistic framework, he conceives God as being affected by the events within creation. Though his "theology of hope" expounds on the eschatological redemption through Christ's death and resurrection, his unconventional use and exposition of *zimsum* do create theological issues. While we uphold the merit of Moltmann's presentation of God as a co-sufferer with humanity, we do recognize that his use of the Kabbalistic myth does confound the distinction between the Creator and the creation and the Immanent and Transcendent Reality of God's Being. Therefore, while striving to understand the divine self-limitation in suffering, if we can identify an approach that steers us away from the Kabbalistic doctrine, it will be helpful. In this regard, we will turn to Torrance's exposition on kenosis.

2. *Thomas Torrance*

Torrance's kenotic theology also touches on the idea that God, in Christ, suffers with humanity. God's self-limitation makes it possible for him to experience human suffering and death, thereby providing a profound solidarity with the human condition. Torrance writes, "Kenosis has to be understood as the utterly astonishing and incomprehensible act of God's self-humiliation and self-abnegating love in which he freely made himself one within our actual existence in order to share the shame of our sin and guilt and through atoning sacrifice to effect our salvation."[54] Torrance articulates that the Incarnation—the event of God becoming human— signifies God operating and existing within the limitations and conditions that are inalienably and fittingly human.[55] God, in Christ's embodied existence, has willingly entered into the human existential realities.

However, Torrance cautions that the divine entry into the realm of space and

---

53 Moltmann, *The Trinity and the Kingdom*, 153.
54 T.F Torrance, "Hugh Ross Mackintosh: Theologian of the cross," *Scottish Bulletin of Evangelical Theology*, 1987:163.
55 T.F. Torrance, *Theology in Reconciliation: Essays Towards Evangelical and Catholic Unity in East and West* (MI, Grand Rapids: Eerdmans, 1975), 163.

time should not be viewed as a dissolution or complete fusion of divine Being into a human form.[56] Instead, it should be understood as a deliberate act of self-emptying (kenosis), in which the Son of God, while remaining unaltered in his divinity, voluntarily takes on human nature, embodying humanity in its fragility, impoverishment, and marginality.[57] The Son, while remaining fully God, chose to live a fully human life within the conditions of space and time, which entailed limitations on the exercise of his divine attributes.[58]

Torrance challenges the traditional Greek philosophical understanding of space as a container (the notion also seen in Moltmann's understanding of zimzum) in which objects are placed. Instead, he draws from the relational and dynamic view of space that emerges from modern physics, where space is not a neutral container but is determined by the relations and interactions of objects within it.[59] Torrance applies this relational and dynamic understanding of space to the incarnation, suggesting that in Christ, God enters into our space and time without being contained by it. Torrance extends the self-limitation of God in Christ within the spatiotemporal existence to the Trinitarian relations. He states, "[when] the Word [is] made flesh, he really is in himself; that he is in the internal relations of his transcendent being the very same Father, Son and Holy Spirit that he is in his revealing and saving activity in time and space toward mankind."[60]

Kenosis involves God's deliberate choice to undergo humiliation and death as a means to pardon our sins.[61] In this act of kenosis, God willingly enters into our existence, fully embracing the disgrace of our transgressions and culpability. Torrance avers that this self-emptying in Christ is an expression of Triune God's love and desire for genuine fellowship with humanity.

For Torrance, the kenotic act is not only a revelation of God's character but also an act of reconciliation.[62] In the self-limitation of the Son, God enters into the brokenness of human life to heal, redeem, and reconcile humanity to Himself. He writes,

> [R]esurrection tells us that the life and person of Jesus are not
> held under the tyrant forces of this world, that though he was

---

56 T. F. Torrance, *Space, Time and Incarnation* (London: Oxford University Press,1969), 52.
57 Ibid., 52.
58 Ibid.
59 Ibid., 15.
60 Thomas F. Torrance, *Trinitarian Faith: Evangelical Theology of the Ancient Catholic Church: The Evangelical Theology of the Ancient Catholic Faith* (London: T.& T.Clark Ltd, 2000), 130.
61 Ibid.
62 T. F. Torrance, *Incarnation: The Person and Life of Christ* (Downers Grove, IL, Inter Varsity Press, 2008).

born of woman and made under the law, Jesus Christ was not dominated and mastered by our fallen flesh and its judgment, but is triumphant over it all, in achieving his redeeming purpose of reconciling our humanity to fellowship with God."[63]

Torrance avers that despite God willingly taking on humanity's shame, sin, and guilt, this act of incarnation does not diminish his transcendence and holiness, nor does it restrict his freedom.[64] And through the Sovereign act of divine self-limitation, God accomplishes the reconciliation of humanity to himself.

Torrance also infers a direct correspondence and coherence between God's being and God's actions. He states that since God is Triune, all his acts toward us cannot but be acts of the Trinity in Unity and of the Unity in Trinity.[65] For Torrance, the way God reveals himself in history (economically) is a true reflection of the internal relations of the Trinity (immanently). He remarks that the Economic Trinity reveals the Immanent Trinity (God-in Self), and God's actions in the world are rooted in and are consistent with who God is in essence, as it constitutes God's Self-Revelation.[66] However, by maintaining the priority of the immanent Trinity over the economic Trinity, Torrance avoids the tendency to subsume the former with the latter, a tendency identified within Moltmann's conception.[67]

Thus, while emphatically arguing for the aspects of self-negation and self-limitation in Christ's enfleshment, Torrance also maintains the distinction between God's transcendence and immanence. By maintaining the integrity of both natures while emphasizing the depth of God's love and the profound implications for the Trinitarian Godhead in the incarnation within the bounds of space and time, Torrance provides a corrective to Moltmann's confusion of categories (Creator–creation) and Being (Immanent and Economic Trinity) in the doctrine of *zimsum*.

VI. CONCLUSION

The theological exploration of divine impassibility and divine self-limitation reveals a dynamic exchange of ideas within Christian thought. The traditional

---

63 Torrance, *Incarnation,* 97.
64 T. F. Torrance, *The Christian doctrine of God, One Being Three Persons* (Edinburgh: T. & T. Clark, 1996), 108.
65 Ibid., 141.
66 Ibid., 145.
67 Ibid., 200.

emphasis on impassibility by early church fathers like Athanasius, Augustine, and Aquinas has been instrumental in shaping the classical understanding of God as unchangeable and unaffected by external events or emotions. This perspective, while safeguarding the divine transcendence and perfection, has confined the possibility of God's sharing in human experiences to either anthropopathic representations or as privy only to Christ's humanity. The communion of properties, as propounded by Gregory of Nazianzus and developed within the Reformation insights of Martin Luther, attempts a relational and participatory view of God's interaction with creation. However, by construing the communion of properties across the two natures, a criticism arises whether this is in alignment with the Chalcedonian Christological distinctions of "without confusion, change, division, or separation." Calvin's qualified approach to the *communicatio idiomatum* refines the conversation by acknowledging the possibility of the communion of properties in relation to the unified Person of Jesus Christ and not across the two natures. This range of theological articulations thus represents a rich exchange of ideas in balancing divine impassibility and suffering.

However, in contemporary settings, Jürgen Moltmann and others challenge these traditional articulations of impassibility and immutability. By engaging with the Kabbalistic doctrine of *zimzum*, Moltmann offers a radical account of a self-limiting God within the Trinity. Moltmann understands the creation itself as an extension (or rather contraction) of God's Being. He understands the Cross as the event where Christ demonstrates his kenotic love as he unreservedly experiences human misery and suffering, in which the very Being of the Triune God participates in this kenotic experience. However, Motlmann's elucidations also result in the identification of Creation with the Creator and the blurring of the distinction between transcendence and the immanence of God.

Torrance, while avoiding the problem of confounding the immanence and the transcendence of God's presence in Christ, explicates the self-emptying of the Son as a means through which God accomplishes the reconciliation and redemption of humanity in a Sovereign act of self-negation and self-humiliation. It is in the hypostatic union of the eternal Son with the human Jesus that this divine relationship is specifically actualized, and the suffering and death on the cross are personal experiences of God the Son encountered in the unified experiencing Subject, the Person of Jesus Christ. Torrance presents this act of kenosis as embodying God's essential self-giving and self-emptying love, which inherently involves Triune God's relationship with the "Other," humanity, and creation. In this self-limiting experience of the Second Person of the Trinity, the Father, and the Spirit also participate in the experiences of humanity. And it is in this communion that humanity experiences God's redemptive power in and through Christ and the Spirit.

"Something Perfect From Something Perfect"

The Dogmatic and Apologetic Functions of Divine Simplicity

DR. WILSON JEREMIAH
Lecturer in Systematic Theology,
Southeast Asia Bible Seminary
Indonesia

I. PROLOGUE: THE LOSS OF SIMPLICITY?

Christian theology has long regarded the attribute of simplicity as part and parcel with the classical understanding of God. However, divine simplicity has fallen out of favor since modernity, and the reasons for its rejection are still being rehearsed even until this very moment. In my Eastern-Asian-Indonesian context within the last few decades, there has been almost no new engagement or retrieval, perhaps to the point of neglect of the doctrine, as witnessed in some recent publications.[1] A more charitable analysis of such a lacuna could be because the concept of simplicity is too abstract and not directly relevant to the present contexts in the Eastern world, so many do not feel the need to mention or even defend the idea of a simple God. The well-known Christian philosopher-theologian Nicholas Wolterstorff once recounted his bewilderment of finding no mention of simplicity in John Calvin (most likely his Institutes) and thought probably Calvin "did not regard divine simplicity as a topic of burning importance for the life of the church in that boisterous refugee city which was Geneva."[2] To be sure, this does not necessarily amount to a rejection of the doctrine, even when theologians of Calvin's stature do not explicitly mention simplicity in their works.[3] Perhaps, then, Christians today implicitly affirm simplicity without feeling the urgency to keep restating and defending it more intentionally. After all, as Ronald Nash once said, simplicity has "a public relations problem"— i.e., that it is difficult to explain the meaning to those without proper and deep theological training.[4]

Nevertheless, I suspect that these comments made in a recent theology textbook about simplicity are also representative of why many (evangelical) theologians

---

1 For example, the massive tome edited by Gene L. Green, Stephen T. Pardue, and K. K. Yeo, *Majority World Theology: Christian Doctrine in Global Context* (Downers Grove: IVP Academic, 2020) does not include a separate section on the attributes of God, and there is no meaningful discussion on simplicity in the section on the Trinity written by various authors from different locations. The most recent and perhaps the only "systematic" theological text in Indonesian by Joas Adiprasetya, *Berteologi dalam Iman: Dasar-Dasar Teologi Sistematika Konstruktif* (Jakarta: BPK Gunung Mulia, 2023) have no mention of the attribute of simplicity.
2 Nicholas Wolterstorff, "To Theologians: From One Who Cares about Theology but is Not One of You," *Theological Education* 40, no. 2 (2005): 89.
3 See e.g., Richard A. Muller, "Calvin on Divine Attributes: A Question of Terminology and Method," *Westminster Theological Journal* 80 (2018): 199–218.
4 Ronald H. Nash, *The Concept of God: An Exploration of Contemporary Difficulties with the Attributes of God* (Grand Rapids: Zondervan, 1983), 85. In Indonesian language (Bahasa), translating "simplicity" proves to be an uneasy task. Directly translating it into "kesederhanaan" is understood more as "modesty" or "humility" in English, which is not appropriate. Other options are to translate it as "ketunggalan" (oneness) or better still "kesempurnaan" (perfection).

in the East and West neglect the doctrine: "Most Christians have not even heard of the doctrine of divine simplicity." And why is that so? It is most likely because simplicity "has no real biblical basis and has in fact worked to defeat the resources of a full-fledged trinitarianism."[5] In my estimation, such comments betray to us how many have failed to observe our catholic tradition since, as Richard Muller rightly states, "The doctrine of divine simplicity is among the normative assumptions of theology from the time of the church fathers, to the age of the great medieval scholastic systems, to the era of Reformation and post-Reformation theology, and indeed, on into the succeeding era of late orthodoxy and rationalism."[6] We somehow have not paid enough attention to able thinkers like Athenagoras, Irenaeus, Augustine, Gregory of Nyssa, and Thomas Aquinas, or even confessional documents like the Belgic Confession, the Augsburg Confession, the Westminster Confession of Faith, the Thirty-Nine Articles of Religion, among others. In other words, we somehow have forgotten the true meaning of the doctrine of divine simplicity and what it was for.[7]

This paper thus has a twofold aim, namely, to demonstrate why the doctrine of divine simplicity is indispensable to the Christian faith. First, I summarize how theologians across the centuries have used simplicity to ground and support these biblical doctrines, without which the Christian faith cannot be meaningfully defended: the Trinity, incarnation, and atonement. Second, I argue that we will lose so many opportunities to dialogue with our Muslim brothers and sisters if we reject simplicity, and I establish this by retrieving some of the ways in which the early Arab Christian theologians or apologists attempted to convince their Muslim interlocutors that the Christians do not worship three gods. In short, I attempt to show why we cannot afford to discard divine simplicity by explicating the dogmatic and apologetic functions of the doctrine. Lastly, I conclude with some reflections on the practicality and catholicity of the doctrine.

---

5   Richard J. Plantinga, Thomas R. Thompson, and Matthew D. Lundberg, *An Introduction to Christian Theology,* 2nd ed. (Cambridge: Cambridge University Press, 2023), 116.

6   Richard A. Muller, *Post-Reformation Reformed Dogmatics: The Rise and Development of Reformed Orthodoxy, ca. 1520 to 1725; vol. 3: The Divine Essence and Attributes* (Grand Rapids: Baker Academic, 2003), 39.

7   Cf. Stephen Holmes, "'Something Much Too Plain to Say': Towards a Defence of the Doctrine of Divine Simplicity," *Neue Zeitschrift für Systematische Theologie und Religionsphilosophie* 43, no. 1 (2001): 137, who said more than two decades ago that simplicity seems "either already forgotten or regarded as best-forgotten." There are probably other reasons as mentioned in Thomas Joseph White, O.P., "Divine Simplicity," *St. Andrews Encyclopaedia of Theology,* ed. Brendan N. Wolfe et al., 2022, https://www.saet.ac.uk/Christianity/DivineSimplicity, that could have influenced the neglect of simplicity such as the theory that theology has drunk too much from the well of Hellenistic Philosophy, the trinitarian renewal in the twentieth century, or other hosts of objections raised by analytic theists. I perceive the second of these as another significant reason why Indonesian theologians feel that the idea of a simple God runs counter with the triune God. More on this below.

II. THE DOGMATIC FUNCTION: HOW SIMPLICITY CHANGES EVERYTHING

There are many ways divine simplicity can be defined, but we can at least agree with Stephen Holmes that "to describe God as 'simple' means that God is ontologically basic. Any attribution of ontological complexity, any postulation of distinction or division into ontological parts, is excluded by this doctrine."[8] Many of the confessional documents that I mentioned above agree that it is essential to add to the clear biblical affirmation that "there is but one only, living, and true God" (Deut. 6:4; Isa. 44:6; 45:5) these descriptions about God: "infinite in being and perfection, a most pure spirit, invisible, without body, parts, or passions" (The Westminster Confession of Faith, 2.1; cf. Thirty-Nine Articles of Religion, 1). James Dolezal accurately explains the purpose of the doctrine:

> This curious verbiage signifies the Westminster divines' commitment to the simplicity that enables the Christian to meaningfully confess that God is most absolute in his existence and attributes. Adherents to this doctrine reason that if God were composed of parts in any sense, he would be dependent upon those parts for his very being, and thus the parts would be ontologically prior to him. If this were the case, he would not be most absolute, that is, wholly self-sufficient and the first principle of all other things. Thus, only if God is "without parts" can he be "most absolute."[9]

Francis Turretin likewise explains why it is necessary to say that God is "perfectly simple" and "free from all composition" for the following reasons. If God is independent (a se), then he cannot be composite for whatever is composed is composed by another. If God is singular and absolute, then he can neither be divided nor composed for something would have to precede God and put his being in all its parts together. If God is truly perfect, then he cannot be composite again because it implies passive potency, dependency and mutability.[10] Therefore,

---

8 Holmes, "'Something Much Too Plain to Say,'" 139. For good discussions on the various definitions of simplicity, see Thomas H. McCall, "Trinity Doctrine, Plain and Simple," *Advancing Trinitarian Theology: Explorations in Constructive Dogmatics,* ed. Oliver D. Crisp and Fred Sanders (Grand Rapids, MI: Zondervan Academic, 2014), 42–59; Gavin Ortlund, "Divine Simplicity in Historical Perspective: Resourcing a Contemporary Discussion," *International Journal of Systematic Theology* 14, no. 4 (2014): 436–53; Oliver Crisp, "A Parsimonious Model of Divine Simplicity," *Modern Theology* 35, no. 3 (2019): 558–73.

9 James E. Dolezal, *God Without Parts: Divine Simplicity and the Metaphysics of God's Absoluteness* (Eugene, OR: Pickwick, 2011), 1–2.

10 Francis Turretin, *Institutes of Elenctic Theology,* 3 vols., ed. James T. Dennison, Jr., trans. George Musgrave Giger (Phillipsburg, NJ: P&R Publishing, 1992), III.7.4.

God "receives no perfection from another."[11]

This is why even critics like Alvin Plantinga say that the "sovereignty-aseity intuition" behind the doctrine "must be taken with real seriousness."[12] This is because even when simplicity may not have a direct "proof text," the doctrine is a consequence of the biblical affirmations that God is sovereign over all things and independent of all things (e.g., Exod. 3:14; 33:19; Acts 17:24-28; Rom. 9:15-23). In other words, rejecting simplicity means that the absolute sovereignty-aseity of God is questionable.[13]

Holmes suggests another reason why simplicity is important: "If we accept the linked scholastic account of God's nature as dynamic, as pure act, then this doctrine means that God does one thing, and that is to be God – perfectly, eternally, and incomprehensibly."[14] Turretin agrees that simplicity can be deduced "from his activity, because God is a most pure act having no passive admixture and therefore rejecting all composition."[15] In the Bible, God is often described not just by abstract names—truth, righteousness, life, light, love, and wisdom, but also concretely regarding his actions—truthful, righteous, living, illuminating, loving, and wise (e.g., Jer. 10:10; 23:6; John 1:4–5, 9; 14:6; 1 Cor. 1:30; 1 John 1:5; 4:8, 16). All these references about God signify his simplicity which, as Adonis Vidu puts it, "qualify divine agency in a distinct way and differentiate it from any human agency."[16]

In short, divine simplicity is affirmed throughout history to maintain a strict Creator-creature distinction in terms of their natures and actions or agencies. Although the concept itself seems to defy logic and irrational, it continues to have some tractions since the doctrine "allows" God to define logic for "he is the ground of all rules and Rule itself, and as such utterly unique."[17] Hence, in doing all kinds of theological tasks, all human epistemologies and ontologies must be disciplined by the confession that God is absolutely and perfectly simple.

---

11 Steven J. Duby, "Receiving No Perfection from Another: Francis Turretin on Divine Simplicity," *Modern Theology* 35, no. 3 (2019): 526.

12 Alvin Plantinga, *Does God Have a Nature?* (Milwaukee: Marquette University Press, 1980), p. 34.

13 For more discussions on how simplicity has bearings on various doctrines that are well-attested in the Scriptures, see Steven J. Duby, *Divine Simplicity: A Dogmatic Account* (London: T&T Clark, 2016), 91–176.

14 Holmes, "Something Much Too Plain to Say," 139.

15 Turretin, *Institutes,* 1:III.7.4.

16 Adonis Vidu, *Atonement, Law, and Justice: The Cross in Historical and Cultural Contexts* (Grand Rapids: Baker Academic, 2014), 240.

17 Ortlund, "Divine Simplicity in Historical Perspective," 447.

III. THE ONENESS AND THREENESS OF GOD

When the Westminster divines then continue to affirm the doctrine of the Trinity, we cannot but see that simplicity is presupposed: "In the unity of the Godhead there be three persons, of one substance, power, and eternity: God the Father, God the Son, and God the Holy Ghost" (WCF, 2.3). So Turretin, as he lists all the doctrines that almost all the Reformed orthodox agree to be counted among the so-called "fundamental articles of faith" that are essential to maintain Christian orthodoxy, it is not enough just to emphasize the Trinity but also the "unity of God."[18] As Herman Bavinck rightly stresses that "the oneness of God does not only consist in a unity of singularity . . . but also in a unity of simplicity."[19] It is no wonder, then, that Muller can claim that "from the time of the fathers onward, divine simplicity was understood as a support of the doctrine of the Trinity."[20]

It is interesting that in his Grassroots Asian Theology, the Singaporean Pentecostal theologian Simon Chan singles out the negative influence of Jürgen Moltmann's well-known tritheistic model of the Trinity in modern theology as he discusses the convergences between the God of Islam and Christianity.[21] It is likewise the case that, in the Indonesian context, the most well known academic theologian, Joas Adiprasetya, is heavily influenced by Moltmann.[22] Like Moltmann, Adiprasetya makes much use of the concept perichoresis, including Moltmann's panentheism in his most recent systematic theological work, Berteologi dalam Iman, as well as in his previously published dissertation, An Imaginative Glimpse.[23] Although I find that Adiprasetya is much more sympathetic to confess monotheism and the unity of God in his latest work, I believe that more work needs to be done by supplying the concept of perichoresis with simplicity in order to safeguard trinitarian monotheism from tritheism.

Dolezal has rightly called into question, in my opinion, many recent attempts by

---

18 Turretin, *Institutes*, 1:I.14.24.

19 Herman Bavinck, *Reformed Dogmatics*, 4 vols., ed. John Bolt, trans. John Vriend (Grand Rapids: Baker Academic, 2003-2008), 2:173.

20 Muller, *Post-Reformation Reformed Dogmatics*, 3:276, emphasis added. White also notes the two medieval figures whose teachings on the Trinity which led to the ecclesiastical formulations of simplicity, namely Gilbert of Poitiers (d. 1154)—rejected by the Council of Reims in 114, and Joachim of Fiore (d. 1202)—rejected by the Fourth Lateran Council in 1215 ("Divine Simplicity").

21 Simon Chan, *Grassroots Asian Theology: Thinking the Faith from the Ground Up* (Downers Grove: IVP Academic, 2014), 49.

22 An associate of mine recently pointed out that references to Moltmann's work is among the most frequent as witnessed by the bibliographical list in Adiprasetya's Berteologi dalam Iman.

23 For the latter, see Joas Adiprasetya, *An Imaginative Glimpse: The Trinity and Multiple Religious Participations* (Eugene, OR: Pickwick, 2013).

evangelical theologians and (analytic) philosophers alike to construct the doctrine of the Trinity without simplicity, precisely because they think that the two are mutually exclusive.[24] Many then opt for what Dolezal calls "the compositional models of divine unity" or "social trinitarianism" which very much depends on the idea of perichoresis. Thus Moltmann: "The unity of the triunity lies in the eternal perichoresis of the Trinitarian persons. Interpreted perichoretically, the Trinitarian persons form their own unity by themselves in the circulation of the divine life."[25] Nevertheless, Dolezal insists that "Without a sufficiently strong doctrine of simplicity, it becomes unclear why the three persons are not three gods (or three parts of the essence that are themselves less than wholly divine) and why the divine unity is not merely a moral and communal unity."[26] Gavin Ortlund similarly finds that perichoresis alone is not enough:

> The reason is that divine simplicity is able to bind the three persons, not merely into each other, but into the one divine essence. Strictly on the grounds of interpenetration, we are left further to explain why the interpenetration of the Father, the Son and the Spirit does not entail three interpenetrating gods. Why should the interpenetration of three persons yield one undivided unity, and not some complex aggregate? What is needed is not simply a mechanism by which to bring the divine persons into proximity with each other in the "circulation of the divine life," but a mechanism by which to unite the divine persons as one. Where perichoresis may make oneness among the three persons possible, divine simplicity makes it necessary.[27]

In other words, Ortlund does not argue that we should discard perichoresis from our understanding of the Trinity, but that even the prominent defender of perichoresis, John of Damascus, did not merely appeal to perichoresis but also

---

24   See especially James E. Dolezal, *All That Is in God: Evangelical Theology and the Challenge of Classical Christian Theism* (Grand Rapids: Reformation Heritage Books, 2017), 105–34. For example, Cornelius Plantinga, Jr., "Social Trinity and Tritheism," in *Trinity, Incarnation, and Atonement: Philosophical and Theological Essays* (Notre Dame: University of Notre Dame Press, 1990), 39, explicitly rejects simplicity as antithetical to the biblical doctrine of the Trinity: "Simplicity theory of the Augustinian, Lateran, and Thomistic sort cannot claim much by way of biblical support...Simplicity doctrine finds its way into Christian theology via Neoplatonism, and ought therefore to be viewed with the same cool and dispassionate eye as any other potentially helpful or harmful philosophical contribution to theological elaborations of biblical truth."
25   Jürgen Moltmann, *The Trinity and the Kingdom*, trans. Margaret Kohl (Minneapolis: Fortress, 1981), 175.
26   Dolezal, *All That Is in God*, 106.
27   Ortlund, "Divine Simplicity in Historical Perspective," 452.

divine simplicity to uphold trinitarian monotheism.[28] Augustine's explanation is helpful here: "It is for this reason, then, that the nature of the Trinity is called simple, because it has not anything which it can lose, and because it is not one thing and its contents another, as a cup and the liquor, or a body and its color, or the air and the light or heat of it, or a mind and its wisdom."[29] His point is again on the non-composite nature or essence of God, where the persons of God are not three separate parts yet somehow are united in perichoretic relations. Therefore, I agree with Scott Swain who says it rather bluntly, "There was and is no need for the doctrine of the Trinity if God is not simple, for there were and are plenty of sophisticated and unsophisticated ways of conceiving how three persons may compose one complex divine being or community."[30]

IV. THE COMMUNICATIO IDIOMATUM AND THE TELOS OF THE INCARNATION

Theologians has also used divine simplicity to construe a fuller picture of the incarnation as part of the redemptive history. In the writings of the late fifth century theologian Pseudo-Dionysius, the unity-in-diversity of the simple God is used as the ground to show how the incarnation communicates something to us about the telos of creaturely redemption from fallenness. Pseudo Dionysius calls God "the principle of simplicity for those turning toward simplicity, point of unity for those made one."[31] Further, the one God in his "supernatural simplicity and indivisible unity" possess the "unifying power [by which] we are led to unity. We, in the diversity of what we are, are drawn together by it and led into a godlike oneness, into a unity reflecting God."[32] It is here that the incarnation of the Son is aimed toward redemption and to bridge the gap, so to speak, of creaturely complexity into divine simplicity (theosis): "the simplicity of Jesus became something complex, the timeless took on the duration of the temporal."[33] We are

---

28   See further John's view on simplicity in Ortlund, "Divine Simplicity in Historical Perspective," 440–41, 449–50.
29   Augustine, *City of God,* 11.10.
30   Scott R. Swain, "Divine Trinity," in *Christian Dogmatics: Reformed Theology for the Church Catholic,* ed. Michael Allen and Scott R. Swain (Grand Rapids: Baker Academic, 2016), 102–3. I think the best analogy for the perfectly simple Triune God is the musical analogy of a three-note chord by Jeremy Begbie, "Through Music: Sound Mix," in *Beholding the Glory: Incarnation through the Arts,* ed. Jeremy Begbie (Grand Rapids: Baker, 2001), Kindle, ch. 8.
31   Pseudo-Dionysius, *The Complete Works,* trans. Colin Luibheid (New York: Paulist Press, 1987), 51, cited in Ortlund, "Divine Simplicity in Historical Perspective," 442–3.
32   Pseudo-Dionysius, *The Complete Works,* 51, in Ortlund, "Divine Simplicity in Historical Perspective," 443.
33   Pseudo-Dionysius, *The Complete Works*, 52, in Ortlund, "Divine Simplicity in Historical Perspective," 443. John of Damascus agrees: "The divine effulgence and energy, being one and simple and indivisible,

reminded here of the famous quote by Athanasius: "He indeed assumed humanity that we might become God."[34]

But here the question regarding the final state of such a union can be asked: will we be truly become part of God or even become (one with) God? Again, Moltmann imagines such a state in these intriguing terms:

> Once God finds his dwelling place in creation, creation loses its space outside God and attains to its place in God. Just as at the beginning the Creator made himself the living space for its creation, so at the end his new creation will be his living space. A mutual indwelling of the world in God and God in the world will come into being. The mutual indwellings then issue in a cosmic *communicatio idiomatum*, a communication of idioms, to use a scholastic phrase—that is to say, mutual participation in the attributes of the other.[35]

Here we can see how the language of perichoresis coupled with the technical term "communication of idioms or attributes" are invoked to paint a picture of the eschatological state of God-world union. Moltmann is clearly on to something here, especially by invoking scriptural and scholastic languages. But is it the correct use of the communicatio, including what Scripture taught about our final states? If we are not careful like Moltmann (including other Lutheran theologians who teach that there can be a *genus maiestaticum* resulting from the communicatio), it is difficult not to fall into panentheism which construes the world in God and that there is indeed sharing of attributes between the two parties. But how does this not imply pantheism, where the distinction between God and creation is lost?

It is instructive, then, to see how Turretin explicates the doctrine of Christ's two natures in relation to simplicity:

> The Son of God is God-man (theanthrōpos) not by composition properly so-called, but by hypostatical union (by which the Word [logos] indeed assumed human nature in one hypostasis,

---

assuming many varied forms in its own goodness among what is divisible and allotting to each the component parts of its own nature, still remains simple and is multiplied without division among the divided, and gathers and converts the divided into its own simplicity" (On the Orthodox Faith, 1.14.17, in Ortlund, "Divine Simplicity in Historical Perspective," 443).

34   Athanasius, "On the Incarnation," in *Nicene and Post-Nicene Fathers*, ed. Philip Schaff et al., 2nd series (Grand Rapids: Eerdmans, 1982), 4:65.

35   Jürgen Moltmann, *The Coming of God*, trans. Margaret Kohl (Minneapolis: Fortress, 2004), 307.

but was not compounded with it as part with part; but stood to it in the relation of perfecter and sustainer to make perfect and sustain an essential adjunct, so that the human nature indeed did thence receive perfection, but nothing was added by it to the divine nature).[36]

Similarly, Turretin incorporates the simplicity of the divine nature in the polemic against the Lutherans whether certain divine attributes (e.g., ubiquity, omniscience, omnipotence, etc.) are communicated to Christ's humanity. His answer is no, since "either all the properties of the divine nature were communicated or none because they are inseparable and really one. Now of things which are really one, one being communicated, the other is necessarily communicated."[37] In other words, "[God's] simplicity hinders him also from being compounded with any created things so as to hold the relation of some part either of matter or form.... This is so both because he is altogether diverse from creatures, and because he is immutable and incorruptible."[38] Such an understanding of the communicatio should lead one to construe the God-world relation not panentheistically but in a different plane altogether. As Turretin explains Acts 17:28, a verse commonly understood as a support for panentheism, that "we are called the race and offspring of God...not by a participation of the same essence, but by similarity of likeness; efficiently not essentially."[39] As I emphasized earlier, therefore, simplicity is important to maintain a strict Creator-creature distinction, while at the same time showing us how it can enrich our idea of the incarnation and redemption in Christ. Ortlund thus stresses that we cannot remove simplicity from our doctrine of God without some loss or damage to our understanding of redemption in Christ that has inspired the church's worship and liturgy.[40]

V. THE ATONEMENT AND THE PERFECTIONS OF DIVINE ACTION

As noted previously, simplicity not only speaks to us about the divine nature, but it also makes a difference in how we talk about the divine action. As Vidu puts it, the doctrine "yields the following rule: in any divine action all divine attributes are

---

36   Turretin, *Institutes*, 1:III.7.7, emphasis added.
37   Turretin, *Institutes*, 2:XIII.8.11.
38   Turretin, *Institutes*, 1:III.7.6.
39   Turretin, *Institutes*, 1:III.7.7.
40   Ortlund, "Divine Simplicity in Historical Perspective," 445.

present as its ground."[41] I think that is especially true as we come to understand the fuller picture of the atoning work of Christ.

Vidu has helpfully summarized some implications of the doctrine of simplicity to the atonement.[42] First, divine simplicity means that we should not emphasize one divine attribute against another, as if there is a conflict between them. One popular understanding of the atonement is how there is a strife within God's being, particularly in terms of his justice and mercy (cf. Hos. 11:8-9). Another is a way of understanding the concept of propitiation in Scripture (e.g., in Rom. 3:24-26) as the pagans do—that God somehow needs to be appeased from his boiling wrath. Another related view is the idea that the Father is wrathful toward the Son and that He must punish Jesus on the cross. These common views related to the atonement are misguided when we take divine simplicity into consideration. It is in fact impossible for God to have a conflict within himself, as if our problem then becomes his! It is also an overly anthropomorphic reading of texts that seem to indicate change from wrath to love in God, when there are other texts that indicate otherwise. And the language of the Father punishing the Son is inappropriate for the idea that God is simple stands behind the dictum "opera Trinitatis ad extra sunt indivisa" (the outer works of the Trinity are undivided). I. Howard Marshall's comments are spot on: "There is an indissoluble unity between Father, Son, and Spirit in the work of redemption. The recognition that it is God the Son, that is to say quite simply God, who suffers and dies on the cross, settles the question finally. This is God himself bearing the consequences of sin, not the abuse of some cosmic child."[43] This last part is also instructive, as it is a modern caricature to paint penal substitution as cosmic child abuse, precisely because they do not understand the language of divine accommodation or condescension in the Scriptures.[44] The point is, again, the doctrine of divine simplicity protects us from making those mistakes by giving us a better lens not to read the Bible literalistically.

Second, divine simplicity also implies that we cannot prioritize one model or theory of the atonement and pit it against the other. On the one hand, there is a tendency to accept all theories like recapitulation, satisfaction, penal substitution, moral influence, ransom, among others as equally valid and argue that no single theory

---

41   Vidu, *Atonement, Law, and Justice,* 256.

42   Vidu, *Atonement, Law, and Justice,* 256–64.

43   I. Howard Marshall, *Aspects of the Atonement: Cross and Resurrection in the Reconciling of God and Humanity* (London: Paternoster, 2007), 56.

44   As Marshall puts it, for instance, that the Gethsemane scene where the Son is pleading with the Father is really "a condescension to human beings who might think of God as other than the Jesus they know as the friend of sinners and assures them that the Father is in agreement with him" (*Aspects of the Atonement,* 56).

can claim monopoly over the others.[45] On the other hand, there is a tendency to isolate one theory from another as if they are not connected at all. There is a case study in Indonesia where Joas Adiprasetya wrote a response to his colleague, Ioanes Rakhmat, who was outspoken about his liberal theology and had written a book just to overturn the penal substitutionary model of the atonement.[46] Part of Adiprasetya's response was to say that if it is the case that Rakhmat is rejecting penal substitution, then it is no matter since there are other theories like Christus victor, moral influence, etc., that are available for Christians to uphold.[47] I think both tendencies can and need to be chastised by a firm understanding of God's simplicity. As Adam Johnson writes, "The divine attribute(s) stand at the center of any theory of the atonement, shaping its constituent parts and determining its insights and limitations."[48] So, regarding the first tendency, there are some good works that attempt to combine all theories together, but nonetheless without an adequate grounding with simplicity doctrine.[49] Regarding the second, I also do not think it is correct to accept that penal substitution, or other theories for that matter, to be overturned and move on as if nothing has happened, because even if it is just one theory, it has its place among the larger scheme of God's redemptive work and it certainly has a role to display certain among the many attributes of God. But again, without simplicity doctrine, we have no reasonable ground to construe the atonement in such a way that perceives the various models as integrated to one another.[50]

---

45   Such an approach is dubbed as the "egalitarian approach to atonement doctrine" by Oliver D. Crisp and Fred Sanders, "Introduction," in *Locating Atonement: Explorations in Constructive Dogmatics,* ed. Oliver D. Crisp and Fred Sanders (Grand Rapids: Zondervan Academic, 2015), 13.

46   Ioanes Rakhmat, *Membedah Soteriologi Salib: Sebuah Pergulatan Orang Dalam* (n.p.: Borobudur Indonesia, 2010); Joas Adiprasetya, *Berdamai dengan Salib: Membedah Ioanes Rakhmat dan Menyapa Umat* (Jakarta: Grafika Kreasindo, 2010).

47   One Indonesian New Testament scholar agrees with Adiprasetya's assessment and explains that Rakhmat is "just throwing a stone" to the Christian faith if what he is doing is rejecting penal substitution instead of "a bomb." Chandra Gunawan, "Signifikansi Kematian Yesus: Evaluasi Perdebatan Ioanes Rakhmat dan Joas Adiprasetya," *Jurnal Amanat Agung* 7, no. 2 (2011): 222–23.

48   Adam J. Johnson, *Atonement: A Guide for the Perplexed* (London: Bloomsbury, 2015), 96.

49   E.g., Joshua M. McNall, *The Mosaic of the Atonement: An Integrated Approach to Christ's Work* (Grand Rapids: Zondervan Academic, 2019).

50   Vidu adds that we cannot also prioritize the cross as more important than the other "discrete" actions of the so-called Christ event, where in "his temptation, teaching, obedience, miracles, crucifixion, descent into hell, resurrection, glorification, ascension, return cannot be read as stand-alone actions that achieve certain ends independently of the other 'segments' and of the overarching divine intention (*Atonement, Law, and Justice,* 263).

VI. THE APOLOGETIC FUNCTION: OUR COMMON YET CONFLICTING GROUND WITH THE MUSLIMS

We now come to the second part of my argument that divine simplicity has been and can further be utilized for apologetic purposes.[51] In his discussion about God in Asian contexts, Chan suggests that "a better case could be presented to the Muslim via a Thomistic conception of the Trinity." He goes on to say how "Thomas's concepts of God as 'pure act' (simple, perfect, without potentiality and change) and of divine 'operations' (such as 'generation' and 'procession') might serve as a better point of contact between the Muslim and the Christian." According to Chan, it is because such an understanding of God "makes distinction in God conceivable without compromising the divine perfection and oneness."[52] I agree with his judgment and further demonstrates that his suggestions are indeed viable as we look back into how the medieval Arab Christian thinkers, namely Theodore Abū Qurra (c. 750–c. 830), Abū Rā'iṭa Al-Takrītī (c. 755–c. 835), and ʿAmmār al-Baṣrī (d.c. 840) have engaged their Muslim counterparts as they responded to the objection that Christian understanding of the Trinity is absurd.[53]

To begin with, it is important to summarize some of the apologetic steps that the three thinkers did have in common (though not necessarily explicit or in that precise order). The first step is to set up some common ground with the Muslims by arguing that Christians also believe in the one God—monotheism. They also seem to understand the Islamic understanding of God very well and can recognize some of the attributes they can agree with, even when they are quick to add that the two faiths understand "oneness" differently. The second step, which is the one in focus, is to make the move to argue for the Trinity through the simple essence or substance of God, especially by showing how the Muslims have tended to misunderstand what the doctrine of simplicity entails.[54] And the third step is they make frequent use of the tools from (Aristotelian) philosophy and categories to define terms and make distinctions. In this regard, they deploy everyday analogies

---

51   For instance, Ortlund notes that Athenagoras used divine simplicity to reject polytheism in his apology to the Emperors Aurelius and Commodus in the late second century ("Divine Simplicity in Historical Perspective," 441).

52   *Grassroots Asian Theology,* 49.

53   For the following, I rely heavily on Sara Leila Husseini, *Early Christian-Muslim Debate on the Unity of God: Three Christian Scholars and Their Engagement with Islamic Thought* (9th Century C.E.) (Leiden: Brill, 2014)

54   The three theologians mentioned here seems to have engaged primarily with the Muʿtazilites, so we need to be careful with which idea of God they are dialoguing with. But it seems that generally the different types of Islamic theism do hold to some kind of simplicity doctrine. See further, Enis Doko and Jamie B. Turner, "A Metaphysical Inquiry into Islamic Theism," in *Classical Theism: New Essays on the Metaphysics of God,* ed. Jonathan Fuqua and Robert C. Koons (London: Routledge, 2023), 149–66.

in a careful and qualified way and with some anticipation that the Muslims will not easily accept them. In what follows, I focus more on Abū Rā'ita's structure of argumentation and supply it with the other two where appropriate.

For starters, Abū Rā'ita establishes the monotheistic common ground by listing the Muslim conception of God's attributes that are mentioned in the Qur'an and that Christians can likewise affirm:

> ...God is one, [who] has never and will never cease to be living (ḥayy), knowing ('ālim), seeing (bashīr), hearing (samī'), without companion (lā sharīk lahu) in his substantial nature (jawhariyyatihi) or his dominion. He is the first and the last (al-awwal wa-l-akhir), the creator of the seen and the unseen, free from want, perfect [in] His essence, he cannot be described by those who [try to] describe him, elevated above imperfection and incapacity, not described by division (tab'īḍ) nor partition (tajazz'u), reigning, powerful, acting according to what He wishes, not seen, not felt, not comprehended and not limited, encompassing everything in His knowledge.[55]

'Ammār similarly appeals to simplicity in warding off polytheism when speaking about the Triune God: "We have informed you earlier that He who created creatures with His Word and Spirit is without a doubt one in his substance and unique (munfarid) in His nature, division does not reach him, partition does not apply to Him."[56] However, Abū Rā'ita is quick to point out the crux of the Christian and Islamic difference in understanding the oneness of God. In response to the Muslims charges the Christians with worshipping three gods or that they confuse the one with the three, Abū Rā'ita shows how the Muslims is misattributing the type of oneness that the Christians hold, namely "one in number" (al-'adad) instead of "one in substance" (jawhar): "We described Him as one perfect in substance not in number, because in number, that is to say hypostases, He is three; so indeed this description of Him is perfect in both aspects."[57] We can see here that Abū Rā'ita is using simplicity to say that it is wrong to construe the simple nature of God in terms of numbers. He elaborates:

---

55 Husseini, *Early Christian-Muslim Debate on the Unity of God,* 82.
56 Husseini, *Early Christian-Muslim Debate on the Unity of God,* 112.
57 Husseini, *Early Christian-Muslim Debate on the Unity of God,* 87. Abū Rā'ita also identifies the irony with which Muslims is committing an anthropomorphism (tashbīh) by thinking of God in terms of number, which clearly contradicts their own principle of shirk.

> With your description of Him by number, you describe him with divisions and imperfections. Do you not know that the individual 'one' in number is a part of the number? Since the perfection of the number is that which comprises all types of number. So the number 'one' is part of number and this is a contradiction of the words that He is "perfect" [and] "undivided."[58]

What Abū Rā'iṭa is doing is forcing the Muslims to define what they mean when they charge that the Christian God is "three" instead of "one," and using the doctrine of simplicity to the Christian's advantage to establish the oneness of God in ousia even when God has three hypostases. In explaining that the oneness and threeness are not a numerical issue, both 'Ammār and Abū Qurra make use of analogies to make this point. So asks 'Ammār: "'Does fire need its heat and dryness, and does water need its coldness and moistness?'...you know that the natural constitution (sūs) of the substance of fire is heat and dryness, and the natural constitution of the substance of the water is its coldness and moistness."[59] 'Ammār's point is that although one can distinguish between the fire, its heat and dryness, or the water, its coldness and moistness, one would not refer to it as three fires or three waters. Similarly, Abū Qurra:

> We are not of the opinion that the heat is more related to the fire than the Son is related to the Father nor that the heat is more connected to the fire than the Son is to the Father, and each one of them [Father and Son] is a hypostasis, because the divine nature does not accept composition as bodies do. Nor is there matter and form in them [the hypostases] and one does not find difference (ghayriyya) in a certain hypostasis from among them. But the position of the Son [in relation to] the Father is

---

58 Husseini, *Early Christian-Muslim Debate on the Unity of God,* 85.

59 Husseini, *Early Christian-Muslim Debate on the Unity of God,* 119. With incredible clarity and sharpness, 'Ammār continues to employ the analogies and show how the divine ousia and hypostases can be seen as superior and thus perfect compared to those creaturely elements: "For you know that things must fall into four categories. Either substance, as one might say 'human'; hypostasis such as one might say Moses and David and Solomon; capacities like heat of fire and rays of the sun; or an accident like blackness of something black and whiteness of something white. The most perfect of these four things are substances (jawāhir) and hypostases (aqānīm). For all substances have this capacity like heat to the fire, rays to the sun, and they also have the ability to support accidents. Every substance also has two capacities, such as the earth having coldness and dryness; water having coldness and moisture; fire having heat and dryness; and air having heat and moisture. They are therefore single in their substances and tripled in their entities. And the hypostases too, as one could say of Moses, David and Solomon, that each one is subsistent in himself, not needing the others, whereas accidents and capacities are single in their entities, they cannot stand by themselves like the substance and the hypostasis, they have need of the substance which supports them and in which they exist," p. 121.

> the same as the position of the heat of the fire [in relation to] the fire and the ray to the sun and the word to the mind, though the Son is a complete hypostasis, because the divine nature is too refined to have difference in terms of its hypostases.[60]

Again, the takeaway is not that the simple nature of God is like that of fire, water, the sun, or the mind; rather it is the indivisibility or inseparability of the various aspects within those entities that help us to establish the necessity of the one simple God with three eternally subsisting persons.

Abū Rā'iṭa goes further to elucidate how the aforementioned divine attributes are related within God's substance or essence by delineating these possibilities: "[1] either as entities other than Himself, 'as one partner is related to another'; [2] 'from Him,' as an action He has made; or [3] 'from His substance.'"[61] The first two are obviously unacceptable for the Muslims (and the Christians), leaving the third with two further possibilities: "[3.1] either they are 'parts of something perfect,' which neither party can accept as this allows division in the Godhead, leaving the only other option...that these attributes are [3.2] 'something perfect from something perfect.'"[62] Through this process of analysis and elimination, Abū Rā'iṭa then sets up the stage to argue for the Trinity, particularly the Christian understanding of eternal generation and the deity of the "two hands" of God (Word and Spirit), by establishing what the Muslims and the Christians would want to affirm regarding divine simplicity.[63]

We could go further in analyzing how the three Arab Christian thinkers establish the doctrine of the Trinity and respond to the Muslim objections, but my point here is clear: they all appeal to divine simplicity as the doctrine that serves as the common yet conflicting ground with Muslims. Without some understanding of the doctrine, it would be difficult for Christians to help Muslims grasp why the triunity of God does not amount to positing three gods. Even when the two faiths

---

60   Husseini, *Early Christian-Muslim Debate on the Unity of God*, 70, emphasis added.
61   Husseini, *Early Christian-Muslim Debate on the Unity of God*, 89.
62   Husseini, *Early Christian-Muslim Debate on the Unity of God*, 89.
63   See further Husseini, *Early Christian-Muslim Debate on the Unity of God*, 90–97. Such a move can also be seen in Abū Qurra's clever maneuver in shifting the burden of proof to his Muslim interlocutors to explain how God can communicate with his "Word" that is neither considered as separated nor as part of God. As Husseini explains: "'Does God have a Word?' [Abū Qurra] concludes immediately that if his interlocutor says no, then he would be making God mute and a lesser being than humans; therefore he must say yes. [Abū Qurra] then moves onto a follow up question: 'Is the Word of God a part of God?' If his opponent replies that God's Word is a part of God then he allows composition in God's nature, which Abū Qurra knows the Muslims will not allow. Therefore his opponent is forced to make God's Word a full hypostasis, with the same being said about His Spirit," p. 72.

clearly have different conceptions of God and his simple nature, there are great similarities and the two are much closer to one another compared to other non- or pantheistic religions.[64]

VII. CONCLUDING REFLECTIONS

I have attempted to show why the doctrine of divine simplicity is essentially valuable not just to secure biblical and rigorous accounts of the Christian doctrines of the Trinity, incarnation, and atonement, but how it can provide opportunities to dialogue with, including perhaps to evangelize the Muslims who likewise affirm simplicity yet reject the Trinity. By demonstrating the dogmatic and apologetic functions of the doctrine as I have done here, I hope to stimulate further thinking at least in two areas. First, it is important for pastor-theologians in any context to be able to provide explanations as to why any doctrine is indispensable by precisely showing the implications of one's rejection of it. A common and well-spread posture of Christians in the East is that doctrine has no practical relevance whatsoever for daily living.[65] Such a posture will remain, I am afraid, if we continue to talk about theology or doctrine in an abstract and theoretical way (not that I think it has no place to do so or that its mysterious elements must always be explained away). Second, it is instructive for pastor-theologians in any context to master historical theology and continue to retrieve it for the sake of the contemporary church. As I intimated earlier, the loss of divine simplicity in the contemporary scene is most likely due to unfamiliarity with the catholic teaching on the Trinity. By familiarizing ourselves with how theologians across the centuries have taught simplicity, we can minimize errors while continuing to profess our reasonable faith as we witness the beauty of the perfectly simple Triune God of the Gospel.

---

64   A good example can be gleaned to how a Muslim philosopher Khalil Andani defends divine simplicity against one supposedly formidable objection, namely the modal collapse argument, not only by appealing to Islamic Neoplatonic thinkers such as Avicenna and the Shi'i Ismaili tradition but also Jonathan Edwards. See Khalil Andani, "Divine Simplicity and the Myth of Modal Collapse: An Islamic Neoplatonic Response," *European Journal of Analytic Philosophy* 18, no. 2 (2022): 5–33.

65   In relation to this fact, philosophy and logical-critical thinking are generally not encouraged in Indonesia as reflected in its educational systems from the primary school to university levels. Only those Indonesians who take an undergraduate or graduate studies in philosophy (and possibly some degrees with a minimal requirement to take philosophy courses) are ever exposed to philosophy and logic—and I dare say 80-90% of them still do not really get why they study it and how to use them in their lives apart from successfully making other people think that they are geeks or nerds who know not how to make money!

The Aseity of God in the Old Testament Creation Discourses

Implications for Christian Spirituality and Society in Africa

DR. MICHAEL PHIRI

Lecturer, Quality Assurance Officer and Head of Research

Evangelical Bible College of Malawi

Malawi

seity is a term that derives from the Latin *a se*, which means "from oneself": thus, aseity denotes God's incommunicable attribute of self-existence.[1] God exists apart from and independently of any other being. God is clearly distinguished from creatureliness. John Webster argues that the difference between the Creator and creatureliness is not a "distinction within created being but one between different orders of being."[2] he states that the relations within the triune God "constitute God's immanent perfection anterior to creation."[3] God is the self-motivated as well as the ultimate motivating being of the entire creation. Gerald Bray argues that God has no external origin—one could also add internal—and that in modern theology, the three attributes of "without beginning, uncreatedness and unbegottenness are often lumped together under the heading of aseity,"[4] We draw that God exists beyond time and space. According to John S. Feinberg, the idea of the aseity of God could be understood in one or two ways or both: that "the ground of God's being is within himself" and that "there are not properties independent of God upon which he depends in order to have the constitutional attributes he possesses."[5] Nevertheless, caution should be exercised when saying that the ground of God's being is within himself. The idea is not to identify any internal origins of Godself but to stress his self-existent and self-explaining character.

I. THE ASEITY OF GOD IN THE OLD TESTAMENT

1. *Genesis*

In the Genesis creation account, 'In the beginning' refers to the beginning of the universe. The expression bespeaks of the pre-existence of God. God created *ex nihilo*.[6] he did not create out of his being – hence, creation is not an extension of God's being. The fact presented there is cosmogony. In the Ancient Near East,

---

1 Stanley Grenz, David Guretzki, and Cherith Fee Nordling, *Pocket Dictionary of Theological Terms: Over 300 Terms Cleary and Concisely Defined* (Downers Grove: InterVarsity Press, 2002), 16.

2 John Webster, "Trinity and creation." *International Journal of Systematic theology* (2010), vol. 12, issue 1, 12.

3 Webster, "Trinity and creation." 4.

4 Gerald Bray, *The attributes of God: An introduction* (Wheaton: Crossway, 2021), 50. Bray (125) presents the thinking that "aseity was represented in the early Christian teaching by the term *autotheos* (God by himself), first used by Origen to designate the Father." Later, the term *autotheos* was used to designate the Son and the Holy Spirit.

5 John S. Feinberg, *No one like him: The doctrine of God* (Wheaton: Crossway, 2006), 239-40.

6 For Feinberg (p. 552), the Greek maxim *ex nihilo nihil fit* (One cannot get something out of nothing) contrasts the doctrine of creation out of nothing. However, the biblical creation discourses indicate creation out of the absolute absence of anything.

there were both cosmogonies and theogonies. Their gods had beginnings and were identified with the basic elements of the cosmos. For instance, in Akkadian literature, "the first twenty lines of the first tablet of *Enuma Elish* contain a theogony that brings the gods connected to the primal elements into existence."[7] The attribute of aseity could not be ascribed to such Ancient Near Eastern gods because their existence was conditioned by some antecedent elements. Walther Eichrodt argues that "By their unqualified rejection of theogony the Old Testament affirmations establish the unconditional dependence of the world on God."[8] We can comfortably ascribe aseity to the God of Israel because he has no beginning and he pre-existed created reality. The Israelites' God is a being who did not come into being – he is an eternally and sufficiently existing being. In John Webster's articulation at the 2009 Hayward lecture at Acadia University in Canada, creation does not bring any perfection and enhancement to God nor does God create due to any external compulsion.[9] God is absolute and the reason behind creation was not to meet any insufficiency. Webster adds that creation is not a modification of any pre-existing entity. Further explanation comes from Aleke who adopts Kasper's description that "God is the ultimate, ungrounded Ground of all reality that sustains and moves everything."[10] Aleke's conceptualization is in line with the doctrine of creation *ex nihilo*.

The Genesis creation account in chapter 1 and 2 indicates God's independence and freedom. God positioned each creature on its proper place. he freely created Adam and Eve in his own image and likeness. he gave dominion to humanity not because of any insufficiency on his part but because he graciously chose to partner with humanity in caring for the earth. The beginning of Genesis 1:1 also marked the beginning of time and space. In other words, God pre-exists time and space and exists independently of history.

2. *Job*

In the book of Job, one notes that Job and his three friends believed the retributive justice scheme of interpretation whereby the righteous prosper and the wicked

---

7   J.H. Walton, "Creation." *Dictionary of the Old Testament Pentateuch*, ed. T. Desmond Alexander and David W. Baker (Downers Grove: IVP Academic, 2003), 162.
8   Walther Eichrodt, *Theology of the Old Testament*, vol. 2, trans. J.A. Baker (Philadelphia: The Westminster Press, 1967), 99.
9   John Webster, *Creator, creation and creature: God and his world* (Acadia University: Hayward 2009 Lecture 2: 20 October 2009). https://www.youtube.com/watch?v=4R9JpVyx3cA, accessed on 31 July 2024.
10   Patrick O. Aleke, "God, Philosophers and Theologians in Africa." *Religions* 15: 739 (2024), 1. https://doi.org/10.3390/rel15060739

suffer. Job was perplexed because he suffered while being righteous. He held that God had perverted justice, was throwing arrows of poison against him and had become his (Job's) enemy. The three friends, believing that Job was suffering because of wrongdoing, appealed to revelation, tradition and observation to try to convince Job to repent in order to experience renewal from God.

Noting the shortcomings of the arguments of the four men, Elihu was compelled from inside to declare his wealth of wisdom. Elihu referred to God's wisdom, justice, righteousness, mystery and sovereignty in his response to the four men. Elihu asks in 34:13 whether anyone appointed God over the earth and put him in charge of the whole world. God has power to give and withdraw life because he is independent and self-sufficient. The mighty creatures are under his control. One could deduce from passages such as Job 35:5-8, 36:24-33 and 37:1-20 that Elihu premises his stance on the aseity of God. he shows that God alone created and has power over nature and that humanity adds nothing to the essence of God. Commenting on Job 33:13, Andersen interprets Elihu's stance that "Job has dared to ignore the dividing line between Creator and creature; he has made a cognitive image of God in order to become a judicial counterpart to him."[11] Andersen could be construed as stressing the ontological distinction between the Creator and creature.

God makes two discourses from chapter 38 to 41 with an interlude on 40:3-5 in which he affirms Elihu's strand of thought. God poses a barrage of questions to Job which could be interpreted to underline his attribute of aseity. God created Job and the rest of the created order including the leviathan and behemoth that Job cannot control. God's cosmic design and governance identified in the discourses point towards creation *ex nihilo*. God's existence is independent of any being whereas that of created entities is contingent upon him. God laid the foundations of the earth and marked off its dimensions without any helper. The Creator sustains the earth. Even the inanimate creation testifies to God's sovereignty and surpassing wisdom. The responses of Job signify that God does not share anything with creation in terms of being.

For some scholars, "The theophany has seemed so obtuse to some that it stands as a classic example of obfuscation — changing the subject to avoid the issue, distracting the questioner and inspiring terror all at once."[12] Some go further to claim that Job's

---

11   Ragnar Andersen, "The Elihu speeches: Their place and sense in the book of Job." *Tyndale Bulletin*, 66.1 (2015), 84.
12   J.H. Walton, "Job 1: Book of." *Dictionary of the Old Testament Wisdom, Poetry and Writings*, ed. Tremper Longman III and Peter Enns (Downers Grove: IVP Academic, 2008), 339.

responses in 40:3-5 and 42:1-6 may have resulted from terror from God's discourses. To the contrary, the character of Job in the book reveals his understanding of God as the wholly Other. Job's response actually shows his submission to the will of God. God maintains order in the universe. Job willingly acknowledges his creaturely limitedness and humbly submits that he is not part of God.

3. *Psalms*

The book of Psalms displays God's majesty in creation. Selected Psalms like Psalm 136 (especially verses 1-9) teach that God created and he was not created. The Creator is designated the God of gods and Lord of lords. Some sections of scholarship suggest monolatry saying that the Israelites acknowledged the existence of many gods but chose to worship only one, the God of their fathers Abraham, Isaac, and Jacob. A closer look at the Psalm indicates monotheism in such passages. God made the heavens and spread out the earth upon the waters. The pre-existence of God is taught in this Psalm. Psalm 139 (especially verses 13-19) portrays God as the maker of humanity and the earth. Psalm 104, which some have described as the second creation account, celebrates the providence, majesty, and sole creatorship of God. God created the heavens and the earth majestically. The Psalm denotes creation *ex nihilo*. It also shows that the created reality is not an extension of the being of God and that God sustains creation by his majesty. Verse 24 teaches that God created in wisdom. The verse is reminiscent of Proverbs 3:19-20 which states that God created by wisdom where wisdom is construed by some scholars as the attribute of God, not a pre-existing entity which God used to create the world. The earth is endowed with wisdom. In a nutshell, creation theology in the Psalms affirm the aseity of God whereby God pre-existed and that he exists in a supremely distinctive category as contrasted with existence of creation. The Psalter presents God as the wholly Other who created and reigns over all creation. Creation declares the aseity of God.

II. SELECTED SCHOLARS ON THE ASEITY OF GOD

Scholars have argued for an acknowledgement of the aseity of God from various perspectives. Their arguments could be used to augment the case advanced in this article where the aseity of God is identified from the Old Testament creation discourses. For instance, Brent Rempel argues that "The aseity and particularity of God converge in 'God's self-correspondence', that is, in the notion that God's antecedent existence corresponds with God for us."[13] Rempel continues that "In Webster's hands, the principles of particularity and aseity lead to a form of 'holism', in which God's being-in-act is viewed as a coherent whole." Tyler Wittman argues that John Webster discusses "relations of origin as materially transparent to the perfect movement of God's life in and from himself."[14] Reference here is to God's self-sufficiency, self-communication, self-reference and self-preservation. Wittman contends:

> The distinction between uncreated and created is basic to the doctrine of creation. As the creator of all things *ex nihilo*, God is uncreated and therefore qualitatively distinct from all things. Whereas creatures move towards their perfection as they enact their natures, God is simply perfect and has no distinction between his being and his act, or his essence and existence.[15]

To paraphrase Wittman, God is perfect in uncreatedness. Wittman further states that "When set forth in this manner, God's perfection is not an 'inclusive,' but 'exclusive' one in that it does not have creatures as an integral aspect of the fullness it describes."[16]

Rempel continues that "The doctrine of divine aseity denotes God's self-existent triune life, which anchors God's bestowal of life. Construed negatively, aseity establishes the incommensurability of God and creatures by distinguishing, without sundering, scripture and God's self-communicative presence."[17] Shannon adds by arguing that "And with tri-unity as primary, God's simple unity entails affirmation of the Son's (and the Spirit's) aseity."[18] Shannon further argues for the aseity of all persons of the Godhead and the mystery of the triune God.

The creation stories lead us to recognize that God is self-existent, immutable, mysterious and particular. His perfection is inherent and infinite rather than adventitious. However, LaCugna and Eiesland both regarded divine relationality

---

13   Brent Rempel, "'God Corresponds to Godself': John Webster's Doctrine of God 'After' Karl Barth." *Scottish Journal of Theology* (2023), 76, 165. doi:10.1017/S0036930622000941

14   Tyler Wittman, "John Webster on the Task of a Properly Theological Theologia." *Scottish Journal of Theology* (2020), 23, 103. doi:10.1017/S003693062000023X

15   Wittman, "John Webster on the Task of a Properly Theological Theologia." 104-5.

16   Wittman, "John Webster on the Task of a Properly Theological Theologia." 109.

17   Brent Rempel, "'A Field of Divine Activity': Divine Aseity and Holy Scripture in Dialogue Between John Webster and Karl Barth." *Scottish Journal of Theology* (2020), vol. 73, issue 3, 203. doi:10.1017/S0036930620000320

18   Nathan Shannon, "Aseity of Persons and the Otherness of God: A Review Essay of Brannon Ellis on Calvin's Trinitarian theology." *Philosophia Christi*, vol. 16, no. 1 (2014), 213.

and aseity as mutually exclusive.[19] In fact, modern theologians "misconstrue divine aseity as imputing solitariness, narcissism, self-indulgence, and non-relationality to the nature of God, and, therefore, reject such a divine perfection."[20] This modern theological rejection of aseity is indeed premised on an assumption that "otherness" is at odds with communion. To address the concerns, the present argument holds that relationality is intrinsic to the essence of the triune God apart from creation. There is no deficiency in God's being and relational quality that require human complement. In this case, God does not require creation in order to be relational.

Karl Barth mentions scholars who have spoken forcefully of God but whose accounts fall short of the biblical understanding of the aseity of God. For instance, Barth refers to Kant who defined God as "the necessary postulate of the limit and goal of pure reason and the equally necessary presupposition of the law-giver and guarantor of practical reason," Hegel who defined God as "the process of absolute spirit which exists eternally in itself" and Schleiermacher who described God as "the source of the absolute dependence of our consciousness."[21] Such ideas portray God as only the projection of humanity. The creation narratives further affirm the primacy of God's attribute of aseity. It could be realized that pre-existence denotes self-existence.

Barth continues that "God's revelation draws its authority and evidence from the fact that it is founded on itself apart from all human foundations."[22] This means God's existence is absolute whereas that of creation is contingent upon the absolutely existing God. The Old Testament accounts mentioned above show the transcendence and freedom of God above creation. Though distinct from creation, God conditions and associates with creation. he remains self-conditioning and unconditioned by anything else. In his freedom and sovereignty, God creates and exercises power over creation. The selected Old Testament creation narratives display God as the sole ultimately existing being. Logically, God exists ultimately whereas created reality exists penultimately. So, ultimating any dimension and system of creation becomes idolatry.

---

19 Jacqueline Service, "Trinity, Aseity and the Commensurability of the Incommensurate One." *St. Mark's Review* (December 2019), no. 250, 67.
20 Service, "Trinity, Aseity and the Commensurability of the Incommensurate One." 67.
21 Karl Barth, *Church Dogmatics* vol. 2, part 1, The Doctrine of God, ed. G.W. Bromiley and T.F. Torrance (London: T & T Clark International, 2004), 270.
22 Barth, *Church Dogmatics*, 271.

III. THE ASEITY OF GOD AND PANENTHEISM

This section seeks to highlight the aseity of God through a critique of panentheism. Philip Clayton defines panentheism as "the view that all things are contained within the divine, although God is also more than the world."[23] Clayton employs the 'cosmic Christ' New Testament passages like Col. 1-2 and Paul's address to the Areopagus in Acts 17 to advance his panentheistic teaching. The *Oxford Dictionary of the Christian Church* defines panentheism as "the belief that the Being of God includes and penetrates the whole universe, so that every part of it exists in Him... that His Being is more than, and is not exhausted by, the universe." Panentheists hold that God creates not *ex nihilo* but out of his own being. They boast that their stance affirms immanence and shows closer relationship between God and created order. Clayton further claims that panentheism is preferable in that it offers a "more effective response to various theological, philosophical, ethical, social-political difficulties."[24] he claims that classical theism fails to mediate biblical theology to the contemporary challenges facing the world. Some scholars today, regarding classical theism as inadequate, are using panentheism to engage the scientific age and to foster dialogue between Christianity and other religions. Nevertheless, panentheists' ontological identification of God and creation, to some extent, renders all their promises impotent. From the theistic vantage point, any being that is ontologically part of creation could not sufficiently engage the scientific age nor direct inter-religious dialogue.

Benedikt Paul Göcke justifies and clarifies Karl Krause's panentheistic philosophy of science. he construes Krause as arguing that "the existence and nature of the world is an essentiality of God as such...an intrinsic determination of God...a finite realization of the essentialities of God and thereby yet already in God."[25] In this understanding, the world is a constitutive element of the whole that is God. The world is an inner structure of God and God is both foundational to and beyond the world. Panentheists believe that the being of God is both indistinguishable and distinguishable from that of the world. For them, world history is the history of the self-transformation of God. Göcke's and Krause's stance stands against the theistic teaching of the immutability of God.

---

23   Philip Clayton, "Panentheism." *The Routledge Companion to Modern Christian Thought*, ed. Chad Meister and James Beilby (New York: Routledge, 2013), 692.
24   Clayton, "Panentheism", 694.
25   Benedict Paul Göcke, *The Panentheism of Karl Christian Friedrich Krause (1781---1832): From Transcendental Philosophy to Metaphysics* (New York: Peter Lang, 2018), 44.

Göcke holds that "Monotheism in general has a problem in making plausible *creatio ex nihilo* before the Court of Reason."[26] he agrees with Griffin who argues that *creation ex nihilo* was an innovation of second-century theologians as Tertullian and Irenaeus in response to Marcion's gnostic theology. Panentheism then will be inconsistent with the doctrine of creation out of absolute nothingness.

Barth argues that "God does not form a whole with any other being either in identity with it or as compounding or merging with it to constitute a synthesis."[27] Created reality does not form part of God. Barth designated panentheism as "The mythology of a merely partial and to some extent selected identity of God with the world."[28] he categorizes panentheism among the outlooks which "seek to represent the relation between God and the reality distinct from Himself as the relation of mutual limitation and necessity."[29] As argued above, creation did not proceed from the essence of God. Paraphrasing Barth, the existence of created reality does not in any way belong to the essence and existence of God himself. Further inspiration is drawn from Webster's notion of "a radical distinction between uncreated and created being...that the doctrine of creation concerns an external work of God."[30] Such logic excludes any possibility of an internal becoming on the part of the Creator. Webster further comments that God's invisible nature, though manifest in the visible world, exceeds the limits of creaturely intelligence.

In the final analysis, the aseity of God renders panentheism redundant. The foregoing discussion suggests that the ethical and epistemological implications of panentheism would be unfulfilling. Feinberg contends that "Aseity is best understood as God's self-existence...and independence in will, purposes and desires."[31] While acknowledging Feinberg's statement, God's independence should include ontology.[32] God is ontologically independent. For an ontologically dependent being can be independent in terms of will, purposes and desires. So, aseity should be ascribed primarily in the realm of ontological independence—which could be basic for other dimensions of independence. God is unbecoming—he is not a being of potentialities.

---

26 Göcke, *The Panentheism of Karl Christian Friedrich Krause (1781---1832)*, 124.
27 Barth, *Church Dogmatics*, 512.
28 Barth, *Church Dogmatics*, 512.
29 Barth, Church Dogmatics, 562.
30 John Webster, "Creator, Creation and Creature: God and His World" (Acadia University: Hayward 2009 Lecture 1: 19. October 2009). https://www.youtube.com/watch?v=urNEROEk2AK&t=786s, accessed 31 July 2024.
31 Feinberg, *No One Like Him*, 242.
32 Elsewhere, Feinberg (p. 573), Feinberg writes that ontologically, God transcends all that is. However, ontology should actually be mentioned in connection with independence in this discussion.

IV. IMPLICATIONS FOR CHRISTIAN SPIRITUALITY IN AFRICA

After establishing the aseity of God, we explore its implications for Christian spirituality in Africa. Olabamiji argues that "Theological assessment of the notion of divine aseity from a Christian perspective in the African context is traceable to the Africans' knowledge of God and the existence of God."[33] Africans knew the self-existence of the Supreme Being even before the proclamation of the gospel on the continent. For the sake of illustrating the significance of the doctrine of the aseity of God to Christian spirituality in Africa, two challenges have been singled out in this paper: syncretism and the related ideologies of naturalism and scientism.

Syncretism comes from the Greek word '*synkretismos*,' and it originates from the tradition of the Island of Crete, where various quarreling groups, who under normal circumstances would not agree, joined forces together against a common enemy.[34] It is the amalgamation of Christian and African traditional values which are incompatible to such an extent that the identity of the Christian faith becomes blurred. In such scenarios, there is fusion of the fundamental tenets of the gospel and the elements of African traditional cultures and religions. The doctrine of the aseity of God becomes important. The pre-existent and self-existent God, the Creator of the universe, is sovereign and all-powerful. All forces standing against him will not prevail. Some church members consult spirit mediums in times of sickness, death, and other hard experiences of life. The attribute of the aseity of God bespeaks of sovereignty, among others. With good understanding, Christians would not seek divination and protective charms in touch times. The Creator God has powers over the opposing forces. He pre-existed and exists sufficiently apart from all the powers and principalities of the world. And so, believers should seek refuge in him at all times both in the presence and absence of life-threatening experiences like witchcraft. And ancestral worship, be it explicit or implicit, is critiqued on the basis of the aseity of God. Worship should be directed solely to the self-existent God. In some instances, syncretism arises from the over-affirmation of African traditional religions and cultures. For instance, Brand argues that "the ancestors could conceivably act in ways that are beneficial to their kin, and to that extent deserve to be called agents of salvation."[35]

---

33 Elisha Olabamiji, "A Theological Appraisal of the Notion of Divine Aseity." *Pharos Journal of Theology*, Vol. 104, Issue 1 (2023), 1. doi: https://doi.org/10.46222/pharosjot.10428
34 Mangaliso Matshobane, "New prophetic Churches and Syncretism: A Critical View." *Religions* 14: 1383 (2023), 3. https://doi.org/10.3390/ rel14111383
35 Gerrit Brand, *Speaking of a Fabulous Ghost: In Search of Theological Criteria, With Special Reference to the Debate on Salvation in African Christian Theology* (Frankfurt am Main: Peter Lang, 2002), 138

In Brand's theological project, the ancestors are accorded secondary or penultimate agency of salvation in relation to Christ. Brand argues for the continuation of the ancestral cult within Christianity whereby "such a cult need not only consist in the remembrance of, and prayers for the dead, but can also include requests for help addressed to them."[36] Clearly, our ancestors did not pre-exist creation and so could not be self-sufficient. And the agency of salvation, whether ultimate or penultimate, could not be ascribed to non-self-existent entities.[37] This viewpoint could find support in Kato who listed syncretism as one of the threats to biblical Christianity in Africa. Kato critiqued Idowu's radical continuity between African traditional religions and Christianity. For Kato, "The final challenge for the African Christian is to make Christianity culturally relevant while holding fast to its ever-abiding message."[38] One should agree with Kato that the gospel message is inspired and the modes of transmission should be rightly contextualized. The aseity of God would enable us to do legitimate contextualization with the recognition that no elements of any traditional cultures and religions in the world share in the self-sufficiency of God. hence, the freedom of the gospel to examine and shape world cultures. The approach would guide us to avoid tampering with the gospel message lest we produce our own gospel which cannot be the gospel at all.

The second challenge is posed by the related ideologies of naturalism and scientism. The teachings under these ideologies question the supernatural and over-affirm nature and scientific reasoning. Subtly, there develops a religion of science. For instance, secular humanism in Malawi is founded upon the basic assumptions of naturalism and scientism. Phiri recounts that in scientism (as well as naturalism), "science becomes Godless and turns into a god."[39] Furthermore, the questioning of creationism in favor of Darwinian evolution and the denial of the eschatological teaching of the end of this age are informed by the ideologies of naturalism and scientism. However, the Old Testament creation narratives inculcate God's pre-existence and self-existence over and above both the natural

---

36 Brand, *Speaking of a Fabulous Ghost*, 138. Brand finds theological support for his stance from some theology including the Sierra Leonean Anglican theologian Edward Fasholé-Luke, the British missionary John Taylor and the Zambian Roman Catholic theologian Emmanuel Milingo.

37 Some African theologians base the inclusion of the ancestral cult within Christianity on Hebrews 11. However, their position is characterized by exegetical inaccuracies. The author of Hebrews did not intend to introduce or augment any levels of ancestral cult within the Hebrews' spirituality. The author's goal when mentioning the ancient paragons of faith was to encourage the Hebrew Christians to persevere in the faith.

38 Byang Kato, *Biblical Christianity in Africa*, edited by Tite Tiénou (Accra: African Christian Press, 1985), 31.

39 Michael Phiri, Bonhoefffer on Salvation: "Towards an Adequate Soteriology for Engaging Secular Humanism in Malawi" Unpublished doctoral dissertation submitted to the Faculty of Theology at Stellenbosch University in 2021, 199.

phenomena and intellectual domains. In this case, science and other domains of knowledge should be construed from the doctrine of the aseity of God. The premise of this assertion is that these noble domains find their true foundation, identity, meaning and utility in the God who fully grounds their essence. At this juncture, one would get inspiration from Eichrodt who states that "creation is understood as the free institution of the conditioned by the Unconditioned, it is not possible for the life of the creature to be an independent unfolding of its own nature under its own authority."[40] In our context, we argue that science is not self-governing nor self-sufficient but conditioned by the self-existing Creator. Ideally, intellectual domains draw their authority from the Creator.

Additionally, the aseity of God could lead us to take our cue from Elihu when responding to the puzzles and mysteries of life. Based on Elihu's (as well as God's) speeches, the answer to Job's concerns lay in accepting the aseity of God and its import for existential reality. The self-existent and self-sufficient God is mysterious. We would not seek to have all the answers to life's dilemmas but rather submit to the sovereign will and purposes of God. Christians would not insist on self-made schema and frameworks of interpretation but rather acknowledge our limitedness and humbly submit to the unlimited authority of God. The aseity of God gives room for acceptance of the supernatural things and explanations. It leads people to humbly acknowledge insufficiency and contingent character of scientific reasoning and human capacities. Attempts at human autonomy would constitute a denial of God's aseity and an ascription of self-existence and self-sufficiency to human beings.

Despite the critique from the panentheists against classical theism, the doctrine of the aseity of God affirms the immanence of God. In his freedom and self-existence, and without deifying creation, the transcendent God becomes immanent in the world for the sake of communion with his creatures. Theistic transcendence is distinct from panentheistic transcendence. The non-historical Creator freely enters the historical realm without compromising his aseity. The aseity calls upon humanity to praise God for his grace to reveal himself to us. For without his self-revelation, nothing of him could be known to humanity—no anthropocentric system could comprehend God. The notion of the aseity of God leads humans to awe and humility before God. For how could a contingent being fully comprehend a self-existent one?

---

40   Eichrodt, *Theology of the Old Testament*, vol. 2, 100.

The notion of the aseity of God is found in traditional African thought. For instance, E. Bolaji Idowu remarks that "The absolute control of the universe and of all things is due, in African thought, basically to the fact that all other beings exist in consequence of him; and that whatever power or authority there may be exists in consequence of him; because it derives from him."[41] The Supreme Being exists independently of all other beings. The Creator exists absolutely and exercises absolute control over his creation. The traditional understanding advances that the Creator is the reason for the existence of all other beings. The aspect of immanence makes the Christian understanding of the aseity of God unique as contrasted with that of some sectors of African traditional religions where the wholly Other is over-transcendent.[42]

V. IMPLICATIONS FOR THE SOCIETY IN AFRICA

The society in Africa is experiencing manifold challenges including poverty, corruption, poor political governance, wars and the attendant refugee crisis, ecological imbalance and diseases. Many initiatives done by governments and other stakeholders to address these challenges only bear minimal fruits. Mostly, the cause of these societal challenges is the human condition. So, anthropocentric strategies could not succeed to address the challenges. For instance, the corruption by government officials subject the masses to poor health services. And we read in book of Romans that the reality created by the self-sufficient, self-existing God is groaning because of the transgressions of humanity. The aseity of God means that nature and the world order are neither self-existing nor self-motivating but dependent on God. Attempts to manage them apart from God constitute a departure from God's intent. In the Old Testament creation narratives one could discern God's original intent for humanity and the rest of the created reality. Accordingly, the notion of the aseity of God could offer promise to Christians in their engagement with the public square. Truly, God as the ultimate ungrounded Ground of all reality becomes in control of the social and natural life. he then is our hope in the wake of social and natural ills facing the African society. If the social and natural are part of the being of God, as panentheists claim, then there

---

41   E. Bolaji Idowu, *African Traditional Religion: A Definition* (London: SCM Press Ltd, 1973), 156.
42   Nieder-heitmann presents an alternative view of Mbiti and Idowu that God is important in the African cosmology, ritual and ethics. In that perspective, God is both transcendent and immanent for many Africans. Henri Mbaya and Ntozakhe Cezula, "Contribution of John S. Mbiti to the Study of African Religions and African Theology and Philosophy." *Stellenbosch Theological Journal* 2019, Vol. 5, No. 3, 424. DOI: http://dx.doi.org/10.17570/stj.2019.v5n3.a20

is no hope. How could one ascertain that the part of God that is not creation is capable of addressing the challenges disturbing creation? If there are problems in the created part of God's being, can one have confidence that the uncreated part of God's being bears no responsibility for such problems since both the uncreated and created portions constitute the ontology of God?

Following panentheistic reasoning, neither the uncreated nor created part of God would be self-sufficient. Self-sufficiency would dwell in the whole being – the two combined. The challenge would be that the social and natural problems exist in the created part which itself is part of the self-sufficient being. In other words, the problems exist within the God. Logically, if creation would be part and parcel of God, then God cannot give promise to address the problems that exist within his ontology. The cosmic dislocation would suggest ontological dislocation within the reality that is God. Humanity cannot turn to the panentheistic God to worship and seek guidance from him.

Even if the uncreated part of God would address the problems in the created order, the development would signify the presence of contradictory elements within the whole being of God. The problems may suggest the imperfection of the uncreated part of God. The uncreated part of God could not claim sovereignty and independence.

According to Arno Meiring, "Africans believe that God is the creator of everything including society. Society ... is a moral entity since the Creator provided a moral code which directs individual behaviour patterns."[43] This demonstrates that in the African traditional understanding, the Creator is distinct from society and that ethics is grounded in the Creator. A contention could be made here that traditionally, Africans subscribe to what could be called the 'from above approach' regarding the origins and content of ethics. Christian theology builds on that understanding in teaching the aseity of God and engaging with the social ills.

VI. CONCLUSION

The paper discussed the notion of the aseity of God as drawn from the Old Testament creation narratives in three books of Genesis, Job and Psalms. It further critiqued panentheism to underscore the theistic notion of the aseity of

---

43   Arno Meiring, "As Below, So Above: A Perspective On African Theology." *HTS* 63(2) 2007, 739.

God and proceeded to proffer implications of the notion to Christian spirituality and society in Africa. In view of the foregoing discussion, one could advance that the notion of aseity could constitute the prolegomena to the doctrine of God. The hope is that the doctrine of the aseity of God, drawn from the Old Testament creation discourses, could inspire a vibrant Christian spirituality and flourishing society in Africa. Further exploration should be done on how the notion of the aseity of God could inform the projects of cultural renaissance and theological decolonization which, if taken to the extreme and absolutized, could devitalize Christian spirituality in Africa.

What's in a Name?

DR. MICHAEL S. HORTON
Founder and Editor-in-Chief, Sola Media
Professor of Systematic Theology and Apologetics,
Westminster Seminary California
USA

There are "names" and "*the* Name." Scripture introduces us to the divine names rather than the divine essence, and this is sufficient since the purpose of such revelation in the first place, as we have seen in the opening chapter, is to call upon or invoke the Lord of the covenant. Hence, the prohibition against taking God's name in vain (Ex 20:7). "It is a designation of him, not as He exists in the depths of His divine Being, but as He reveals Himself especially in His relations" to us, as Louis Berkhof concludes.[1] Or, as Pannenberg expresses the same point, "In the Bible the divine name is not a formula for the essence of deity but a pointer to experience of his working (Exod. 3:14)."[2] God gives his name not as a window into his being or as a means of harnessing cosmic forces, but as a pledge. Thus, the name is *invoked*, not decoded or used. "Whoever calls upon the name of the Lord shall be saved" (Joel 2:32, with Acts 2:21 and Ro. 10:13; cf. Gen 4.26; Ps. 18:3; 145:18; Is 55:6; Mal 3:12).

Therefore, the title "Lord," however analogical, and the name YHWH, are at the heart of the biblical conception of God. To adopt any conception that circumvents "lordship" is to describe a religion other than the faith that knows "no other name in heaven and earth by which we may be saved" (Ac 4:12). It is by this name that we are rescued and in this name that every kingdom activity is effectual (Mk 9:38). In the context of bringing the Lord's "indictment against Judah," the prophet announces, "The LORD the God of hosts, the LORD is his name!" (Hos 12:4). There is no way around this name (YHWH) and this title (*Adonai*), for those who belong to God: the suzerain-vassal structure of divine-human relationships is not accidental but essential. That more can be said—must be said, and in fact is said, is of course granted. But biblical faith is surely not less than this affirmation.

Of course, there is plenty of debate over God's *communicable* attributes. But over the last half-century, it has become common to criticize the so-called *incommunicable* attributes as more appropriate to a Stoic or Buddhist sage than to the living God of the Bible. It's not a new thesis, of course. At the turn of the twentieth century Adolf von Harnack classified the bulk of the Apostles' Creed as the product of "Hellenization." Even further back, the Socinians in the sixteenth century tread this path, rejecting classical theism along with the Trinity, deity of Christ, the substitutionary atonement, and so forth. Francis Turretin observed, "They say the whole doctrine is metaphysical rather than biblical." My goal in this paper is

---

1   Louis Berkhof, op.cit., 47.
2   Wolfhart Pannenberg, *Systematic Theology*, vol. 1 (hereafter ST I), tr. G. W. Bromiley (Eerdmans, 1991 ET), 360.

to show that these great attributes of God's lordship are grounded in Scripture either explicitly or by good and necessary consequence of many biblical passages.

I. COVENANT LORD OR STOIC SAGE?

It is the *Sh'ma* and not pantheistic Stoicism that emphasizes the sole lordship of YHWH as king. And it is precisely Israel's narrative identity, constantly reasserted, of having been slaves liberated from bondage and taken into God's care as a community founded on a covenant rather than racial and social hierarchies that makes this God's sole kingship the basis for freedom in contrast to the nations.

In fact, it is important to remember that the point of having no other king than YHWH was to guard Israel itself from the oppressive hierarchies of the nations. The laws given to Israel defy the traditional social, economic and racial stratifications of their neighbors. The judges applied this law. But before long, Israel wanted a king "like the nations" (Dt 17:14). "Yet that the step was taken almost tentatively and, on the part of some, with great reluctance is likewise not surprising," writes John Bright, "for monarchy was an institution totally foreign to Israel's tradition."[3] Even in God's concession to a monarchy, strict limitations were to be placed on royal power: the ruler "must not acquire many horses for himself" or wives or "silver and gold...in great quantities for himself" and above all must school himself in the law, "neither exalting himself above other members of the community nor turning aside from the commandment..." (Dt 17:14-20). It had after all been the covenant Israel made with YHWH at Sinai that had made an earthly king of the confederacy unnecessary and perhaps even disloyal. As early as the first king (Saul), the saga of corrupt power taints Israel's history. YHWH's status as Israel's sole king was not the validation to the rise of oppressive hierarchies, but their rival.

Suzerainty treaties assumed that the suzerain or lord of the covenant was independent of obligation, except to the suzerain's own aims and objectives. However, once the suzerain accepts self-imposed obligations on the vassal's behalf, the suzerain's character is on trial. The suzerain must be reliable. This is also an assumption of the biblical narrative with respect to YHWH.

---

3   John Bright, *A History of Israel*, 3rd ed. (Philadelphia: Westminster Press, 1972, 1981), 187.

The so-called incommunicable attributes specify characteristics unique to God, attributions that cannot even analogically be said to describe creatures. Since most of the biblical evidence falls on the side of God's *analogical* self-disclosure in the narrative of a covenant, the incommunicable attributes are understandably the most susceptible to philosophical abstraction and speculation.[4] Historically, they are also the most dependent on the *viae negationis* and *eminentiae*, since they are expressions of divine transcendence—hence, the recurring alpha-privative as a prefix (aseity, apatheia, impassibility, immutability, independence, infinity) and the superlative ("omni") prefix (omnipotence, omniscience, omnipresence). It is no doubt true that the so-called metaphysics of perfection / infinitude can easily end up justifying Feuerbach's theory of religion as projection. That which constitutes an ideal or perfect being varies, of course, and we do not achieve much in the way of identifying the God of biblical revelation by substituting a priori definitions. One important difference between the Thomist and Reformed approaches to analogy is that the latter is suspicious of the claim that we can know what God is *not* any more than we can know what God *is*, apart from God's own self-disclosure in revelation. We cannot start with our idea of perfect being, in either a way of eminence or negation.

However, the challenge for us today is to patiently attend to what the Christian tradition has meant to claim by appealing to these predicates without immediately dismissing them as a metaphysics of presence/infinitude in the light of modern philosophy (especially Descartes, Spinoza and German idealism). The criticism of the classical Christian doctrine of God as "metaphysical" (specifically, Stoic) was launched by the Socinians in the sixteenth century and reached its zenith in the post-Kantian theologies of Ritschl and Harnack.[5] This charge has underwritten a century of modern theology, not only in neo-Protestantism but in neo-orthodoxy and in the version of the "biblical theology" movement identified especially with G. E. Wright. According to Wright, the God of systematic theology was the deity of static order, while the God of biblical theology is dynamic, a claim that seems to ignore the different objectives of theological sub-disciplines (systematics being

---

4   Cf. Turretin, op. cit., 190.
5   On the Arian criticism of the orthodox doctrine as philosophical, while Arianism itself was entangled in philosophical assumptions, see Jaroslov Pelikan, *The Emergence of the Catholic Tradition* (100-600) (Chicago: University of Chicago Press, 1971), 194. The Socinians, according to Genevan theologian Francis Turretin, reproached classical theism on the same basis; viz., that "the whole doctrine is metaphysical" rather than biblical (Francis Turretin, *Institutes of Elenctic Theology*, vol. 1, tr. George M. Giger; ed. James T. Dennison, Jr. [Phillipsburg, NJ: Presbyterian and Reformed, 1992], 191). On Harnack, see his *History of Dogma*, vol. 1, translated from the third German edition (Boston: Little, Brown and Company, 1902), 48ff..

concerned with logical connections and biblical theology interested in organic and historical development).[6] But the twentieth century, especially through the work of Barth and Brunner, also witnessed the rehabilitation of the sixteenth-century reformers in this respect, shifting the blame for "Hellenistic" theology to their systematizing successors instead.[7] In a chapter of *Most Moved Mover* titled, "Overcoming a Pagan Influence," evangelical theologian Clark Pinnock takes this well-traveled road, but with the entire classical tradition from the church fathers to current orthodoxy dismissed in one stroke as hopelessly trapped in ancient paganism.[8] This does not keep Pinnock, any more than Harnack, from reading scripture through the lens of modern thought, especially Hegel, in addition to Teilhard de Chardin and Alfred North Whitehead, a debt that Pinnock readily acknowledges.[9] But in this case the philosophical debt is evidently justified, since "modern culture...is closer to the biblical view than classical theism."[10]

More recently, however, this thesis has been unraveling. On the biblical-theological side, James Barr led the way to its demise[11] and subsequent research has raised serious questions about its viability: in relation to Jesus (Hebrew) vs. Paul (Greek)[12] and the Reformers vs. the Protestant scholastics.[13] In fact, although he himself rejects divine simplicity, immutability and impassibility, William P. Alston demonstrates that for Aquinas and others, the whole point

---

6   G. E. Wright, *God Who Acts: Biblical Theology as Recital* (London: SCM Press, 1952), esp. 35, 81, 111.
7   This was the working assumption of neo-orthodoxy (particularly evident in Brunner and Barth), in its attempt to rescue the Reformers while eschewing the systems of their successors. On the Reformed side, it is the controlling presupposition of T. F. Torrance, James B. Torrance, Michael Jinkins, Jack Rogers, B. A. Armstrong, R. T. Kendall and others.
8   Clark Pinnock, *Most Moved Mover* (Grand Rapids: Baker, 2001). First, Pinnock does not seem to grant that in the Hellenistic world are many mansions: not only Parmenidean stasis, but Heraclietean flux. To reduce Hellenism to the Stoics and Plato is to ignore the fact that even Hegel et.al. appealed to important streams of Greek thought (especially Aristotle, oddly enough). Cf. Clark Pinnock, "Theological Method," in *New Dimensions in Evangelical Thought: Essays in Honor of Millard J. Erickson*, ed. David S. Dockery (Downers Grove: IVP, 1998), 197-208.
9   Clark Pinnock, *Most Moved Mover*, op.cit.,142ffClark Pinnock, "From Augustine to Arminius: A Pilgrimage in Theology, in Clark Pinnock, ed., *The Grace of God and the Will of Man* (Grand Rapids: Zondervan, 1989), 24..
10   Clark Pinnock, "From Augustine to Arminius: A Pilgrimage in Theology, in Clark Pinnock, ed., *The Grace of God and the Will of Man* (Grand Rapids: Zondervan, 1989), 24.
11   James Barr, "The Old Testament and the New Crisis of Biblical Authority," *Interpretation*, vol. XXV (January 1971), number 1: 24-40; cf. Barr, *The Semantics of Biblical Language* (Oxford: Oxford University Press, 1961); *Biblical Words for Time* (London: SCM Press, 1962).
12   Against the application of the Harnack thesis to the so-called "Jesus vs. Paul" antithesis, see the recent collection, Troels Engberg-Pedersen, ed., *Paul Beyond the Judaism/Hellenism Divide* (Louisville: Westminster John Knox Press, 2001).
13   For the criticism of the Luther/Calvin vs. Lutheranism/Calvinism version, see particularly Richard Muller, "Calvin and the 'Calvinists': Assessing Continuities and Discontinuities between the Reformation and Orthodoxy," *Calvin Theological Journal* 30 (1995), 345-75 and 31 (1996), 125-60; cf. Robert Preus, *The Theology of Post Reformation Lutheranism*, 2 vols. (St. Louis: Concordia, 1970-72). Articles and monographs by Willem van Assalt, David Steinmetz, Susan Schreiner, Irena Backus, Robert Kolb, among others, have contributed significantly to this field.

of affirming these predicates was to *avoid* any kind of substance metaphysics.[14] Traditionally, Christian theology has emphasized as a corollary of the creator-creature distinction God's independence, expressed by a cluster of predicates such as simplicity (i.e., not a composite being made up of various parts), immutability (unchangeableness), impassibility (immunity to suffering), and aseity (independence).

In some biblical passages the doctrinal gold is lying on the surface of the text. Interestingly, this occurs often in doxological passages such as 1 Tim 6:15-16: "who is the blessed and only Sovereign, the King of kings and Lord of lords, who alone has immortality, who dwells in unapproachable light, whom no one has ever seen or can see. To him be honor and eternal dominion. Amen." More often, we draw necessary conclusions from God's characteristic behavior in biblical narratives. From throbbing verbs emerge consistent adverbs and stable nouns.

Taking the "strong verbs" disclosed in the narrative of the covenant trial as our starting point, nothing could be clearer to the covenant people in both testaments than God's self-existence, independence and uniqueness. It is basic to the transcendence of YHWH in contrast to the idols of the nations. Psalm 115:3 is typical: "Our God is in the heavens; he does all that he pleases." Hence, the recurring polemic against the idols: "To whom will you liken me and make me equal, and compare me, that we may be alike?...Remember this and stand firm, recall it to mind, your transgressors, remember the former things of old; for I am God, and there is no other; I am God, and there is none like me, declaring the end from the beginning, and from ancient times things not yet done, saying, 'My counsel shall stand and I will accomplish all my purpose...'" (Is. 46:5, 8-10). YHWH is in a class by himself. There is no genus of "deity" to which he belongs, a *whatness* of which God is an instance.

To whom will you liken God, or what likeness compare with him?...It is he who sits above the circle of the earth, and its inhabitants are like grasshoppers; who stretched out the heavens like a curtain, and spreads them like a tent to live in; who brings princes to naught, and makes the rulers of the earth as nothing...Have you not known? Have you not heard? The LORD is the everlasting God, the Creator of the ends of the earth. He does not faint or grow weary; his understanding is unsearchable. He gives power to the faint, and strengthens the powerless (Is. 40:21-23, 28-29).

---

14   William P. Alston, "Substance and the Trinity" in Gerald O'Collins et al., eds., *The Trinity: An Interdisciplinary Symposium* (Oxford: Oxford University Press, 1999), 179-201.

It is precisely because God—and only God—has life and sovereignty in himself that the weak and powerless can cry out to him in their distress. Evil powers never have the last word.

While Exodus 3:14 is inconclusive for drawing sophisticated doctrines of aseity and eternity, Revelation 1:4 (drawing, no doubt, on the LXX translation of Ex 3:14) at least points in the direction of something like aseity and eternity, referring to the Son as "the one who is, and was and is to come (*ho on, kai ho en, kai ho erchomenos*), the Almighty." Being is not antecedent to God or a predicate shared with creatures: "Just as the Father has life in himself, so he has granted the Son also to have life in himself..." (Jn 5:26). Scripture repeats the constant refrain that the world is dependent on God, while God is dependent on no one and no thing. Surrounded by Epicurean deists and Stoic pantheists, Paul glosses Isaiah 40 along with some Greek poets (Ac 17:24-28). In this passage divine transcendence is not set against immanence, but is the very presupposition for it. The distinction between creator and creature is not an ontological opposition: it is precisely in God's independence and freedom from contingency that a habitable space is opened for the freedom of contingent reality. If the world is not God's body, it is certainly God's house. This reverses panentheism: "God indwells all," not "all indwells God"; thus God is necessarily independent and yet contingently related to the world. The necessary relations of the Trinity cannot be univocally applied to the God-world relationship.

Perhaps among the most conclusive arguments for God's infinite perfection and independence is the fact that nothing can be given to him or done for him by a creature that demands reimbursement: "For from him and through him and to him are all things. To him be the glory forever. Amen" (Ro. 11:34-6). The human analogy here is once again the suzerainty treaty: the suzerain owes nothing to the vassal but freely and sovereignly establishes a relationship of genuine, if hierarchical, mutuality. To assert absolute perfection, then, is to recognize that God is free of all limitations and containments (1 Kings 8:27). It is not even that he is infinitely *extended* in space (pace Spinoza) but that he *transcends* space (and, as we will argue, time)—even as God *indwells* both more fully (repletively) than any creature. This is one of those mysteries that we are expected to accept without demanding philosophical resolution or synthesis.

All created reality is contingent upon the necessary existence of God without being swallowed up in that necessity. As Herman Bavinck notes, this "unbounded, limitless, absolutely undetermined, unqualified" view of God is irreconcilable with pantheism ancient and modern: Babylonian, Hellenistic, Neo-Platonist, kabbalistic and Spinozistic.[15] Possessing every virtue in an absolute degree, perfect, God's infinitude is qualitative, not quantitative; intensive, and extensive; positive, not negative.[16] God's infinity cannot mean that he can be anything or everything (pace Ockham and Hegel), unbounded and absolutely undetermined, because his attributes are descriptive of his being itself. In other words, God is bound by his nature, but only by his nature. But just so, God is bound to us (better, has bound himself to us) by a free decision to enter into covenant with us and with the whole creation. God is not free to act contrary to such covenantal guarantees because doing so would entail the violation not only of his decision but of his nature, particularly his faithfulness. God's infinite perfection is his greatness: "Great is the Lord, and greatly to be praised, and of his greatness there is no end" (Ps. 145:3). And all of these biblical references to God's incomparable perfection have concrete historical events as their frame of reference. In the prophets, for example, YHWH invites the covenant people to a trial of the gods: can they speak and act as YHWH has done? "Their idols are like scarecrows in a cucumber field, and they cannot speak; they have to be carried, for they cannot walk. Do not be afraid of them, for they cannot do evil, nor is it in them to do good. There is none like you, O LORD; you are great, and your name is great in might" (Jer. 10:5-6).

God can be wholly identified with his revelation without being entirely reduced to it: this is the point of analogy and incarnation, and it is the point of the doctrine of aseity. In every identification, God is always *that and yet not that*. While the absolute and the personal are antithetical concepts in ancient Greek paganism and in modern (idealist) philosophy, they find their unity in the God of Israel.[17]

Since there is no predicate of being univocally shared by God and creatures, God's freedom is qualitatively and not simply quantitatively different from our own. This is where Barth's affirmation of both freedom *from* (transcendence) and freedom *for* (immanence) is so crucial: "But freedom in its positive and proper qualities means to be grounded in one's being, to be determined and moved by oneself."[18] This once more affirms God's self-determination and aseity.[19] But it must not be defined only negatively (independence *from* conditions), but positively—as God's

---

15   Herman Bavinck, *The Doctrine of God*, tr. William Hendriksen (Grand Rapids: Baker, 1951), 152.
16   Ibid.
17   I. A. Dorner, op.cit., 84-85.
18   Karl Barth, CD 2/1, 300-301.
19   Ibid., 302.

unique freedom to enter into fellowship and so freely will to be conditioned.[20] The purely negative likely originates in a neo-platonism in which to enter into such fellowship is a sign of less being.[21] It is not a generic freedom that we then apply to the gods or God, but the freedom proved in Jesus Christ.[22] To say that God is a se, "we say that (as manifest and eternally actual in the relationship of Father, Son and Holy Ghost) He is the One who already has in Himself everything which would have to be the object of His creation and causation if He were not He, God. Because He is God, as such He already has His own being."[23]

On no point is the challenge to a traditional understanding of divine perfection more forcefully elaborated today than the concept of *impassibility*. Traditionally regarded as an implication of divine perfection, the notion of God's immunity to suffering is now frequently seen rather to be an implication of a certain presupposition of perfection defined by Greek metaphysics rather than by scripture.

T. E. Fretheim's *The Suffering of God* was formative in raising this question in biblical theology. The biblical writers, he argued, used the metaphor not only in an emotive sense but as "reality depicting."[24] (The contrast of metaphor with "reality-depicting language" already assumes a fundamental misunderstanding of language, we would argue.)[25] Fretheim recognizes the twin dangers of agnostic equivocity and rationalistic univocity. The metaphors are metaphors or analogies, he realizes. Nevertheless, they need to be taken seriously as revealing something important about God's very nature; otherwise, why call them revelation at all?[26] But, as Childs observes, Fretheim assumes "that a biblical metaphor always arises from the projection of human experience to a depiction of the divine...A. Heschel (*The Prophets*, II, 51f.) correctly senses the problem when he writes: 'God's unconditional concern for justice is not an anthropomorphism. Rather, man's concern for justice is a theomorphism.'" While in the history of religions, Fretheim might be right, "according to Israel's scriptures this is blasphemy. God, not man, is the only creator."[27] Second, Childs judges that Fretheim's "organismic

---

20   Ibid., 303.
21   Ibid.
22   Ibid.
23   Ibid., 306.
24   T. E. Fretheim, *The Suffering of God: An OT Perspective* (Philadelphia: Fortress Press, 1988), 7.
25   In addition to the many sources to which I appeal in the hermeneutical discussions in *Covenant and Eschatology*, I would single out Colin Gunton, *The Actuality of Atonement: A Study of Metaphor, Rationality and the Christian Tradition* (Grand Rapids: Eerdmans, 1989).
26   As we see below, this argument is prominent in what has come to be called "open theism" in evangelical theology, especially in its critique of immutability.
27   Childs, 357.

image" of the mutual interdependence of God and humans is more indebted to process thought than to the dynamic movement of revelation.

God is self-contained: 'I am Yahweh' (Ex. 6.2). 'I am who I am' (3.14). There is none like him (Ex. 8.10; 15.11; Ps. 86.8). He is God alone (Deut. 4.35; II Kings 19.15). His love is everlasting (Jer. 31.3). God does not from necessity need Israel (Ps. 50.10ff), but rather willed not to exist for himself alone. In full freedom for his own purpose, God loves unconditionally with an utterly sovereign love. James' witness is fully Jewish in depicting God as 'the Father of lights with whom there is no variation or shadow due to change' (1.17; cf. Job 28.24; Ecclus. 42.18-20; Wisd. 1.5ff).[28]

Although as "Living God" and not a static concept, God suffers with and for his people (Is. 63:9), the fact remains that "God is God and not human (Hos. 11.9), yet he has become 'God with us' (Isa. 8.10)."[29] And he is God-with-us not only in the incarnation, but already in anticipation of the incarnation as creator, sustainer, liberator and Lord.

On the one hand, the true God is not different from the God we meet in Jesus Christ. On the other hand, we must not simply collapse God into Jesus—or, for that matter, God's incomprehensible being and his being with us in the historical economy. One of the reasons Philippians 2 is so revolutionary is that a person of the Trinity humbles himself to assume our humanity, though without any change in his divine nature. The *incarnation* is where God becomes weak for us in our humanity even while remaining immune to suffering in his divine nature. We should beware of views that render the incarnation merely an instance of a general phenomenon that goes on quite well without it. Furthermore, they fail to take into account the fact that as *covenantal*, God's relation to the world is just as much an ontological fact as it is in rival accounts, but as such it underscores the important truth that God *enters into* covenants rather than being *constituted* in his very being by them.

No one has provided a more thorough criticism of impassibility in systematic theology along these lines of a general divine kenosis than Jürgen Moltmann. He asks, "How can Christian faith understand Christ's passion as being the revelation of God, if the deity cannot suffer?...If God is incapable of suffering, then—if we are

---

28   Ibid.
29   Ibid., 358.

to be consistent—Christ's passion can only be viewed as a human tragedy"[30] "If, in the manner of Greek philosophy, we ask what characteristics are 'appropriate' to the deity, then we have to exclude difference, diversity, movement and suffering from the divine nature," he writes.[31] "The absolute subject of Nominalist and Idealist philosophy is also incapable of suffering; otherwise it would not be absolute," so we are working with Greek, nominalist and idealist philosophy as the conceptual fund for the traditional doctrine.[32]

Yet however impassibility (along with simplicity and aseity) might have been formulated in nominalism and idealism, the fact of the matter is that these affirmations were strenuously maintained by the ecumenical church until recently, quite apart from these modern developments. In fact, the demise of this consensus occurred with the *advent* of absolute idealism. Moltmann argues that the patristic theology clung to impassibility in theory (contrary to its liturgical and devotional praxis) "for two reasons": to protect the creator-creature distinction, and to hold out salvation as conferring "immortality, non-transience, and hence impassibility too" by participation in his eternal life.[33] The ancient formulation knew only the false choice between "essential incapacity for suffering" and "a fateful subjection to suffering."

But there is a third form of suffering: active suffering – the voluntary laying oneself open to another and allowing oneself to be intimately affected by him; that is to say, the suffering of passionate love. In Christian theology the apathetic axiom only really says that God is not subjected to suffering in the same way as transient, created beings. It is in fact not a real axiom at all. It is a statement of compassion. It does not exclude the deduction that in another respect God certainly can and does suffer. If God were capable of suffering in every respect, then he would also be incapable of love.[34]

Moltmann approaches here what I am calling the analogical proviso, even allowing that the "apathetic axiom only really says that God is not subjected to suffering in the same way as transient, created beings," which he is quite willing to accept. "God does not suffer out of deficiency of being, like created beings. To this extent he is 'apathetic.' But he suffers from the love which is the superabundance and

---

30   Ibid., 21-2.
31   Jürgen Moltmann, *The Trinity and the Kingdom,* 21.
32   Ibid.
33   Ibid., 23.
34   Ibid.

overflowing of his being. In so far as he is 'pathetic.'"[35]

But is Moltmann consistent with this analogical proviso or qualification? He develops his account out of the relationship in which God "makes himself a partner in a covenant with his people."[36]

Creation, liberation, covenant, history and redemption spring from the pathos of God. This therefore has nothing to do with the passions of the melody, envious or heroic gods belonging to the mythical world of sagas. Those gods are subject to destiny because of their passions. But the divine passion about which the Old Testament tells us is God's freedom. It is the free relationships of passionate participation...Of course the images of Yahweh as Israel's friend, or father, or mother, or her disappointed lover are just as anthropomorphic as the notions of an ardent, jealous, angry, or erotically craving God. But what these images are trying to express is missed by the person who holds 'apathy' to be the only characteristic that is 'appropriate' for the deity.[37]

Appealing to the mystical, kabbalistic and speculative traditions, Moltmann almost treats the incarnate Christ as a cipher for God's eternal kenotic being: "If Christ is weak and humble on earth, then God is weak and humble in heaven. For 'the mystery of the cross' is a mystery which lies at the centre of God's eternal being"—and not simply at the center of God's eternal plan.[38] Moltmann so identifies revelation (the economy) with God's being (in himself) that despite his criticisms of Barth for substituting an absolute Subject for the three persons, his own move is strikingly similar. According to Sabellianism (modalism), it is the Father (as the only divine person) who suffers. While Moltmann is not a modalist, the same question could be put to his project: What is it that the *Son* uniquely brings to the God-world relationship?

The historical passion is not so much the culmination of a divine plan as it is a window through which we see what is in fact an eternal event—this despite Moltmann's otherwise persuasive and pervasive critique of Parmenides and Plato. "If we follow through the idea that the historical passion of Christ reveals the eternal passion of God, then the self-sacrifice of love is God's eternal nature."[39] In fact, the Christ event does not seem to be a contingent (and therefore genuinely

---

35   Ibid.
36   Ibid., 25
37   Ibid., 25-6.
38   Ibid.
39   Ibid., 32.

historical) eschatological intrusion, but is necessary to God's inner being. It is not simply that God's mercy, grace, compassion and kindness are eternal attributes: the cross itself, or at the very least, the event (not just the possibility) of suffering and self-sacrifice are predicates of God's nature. The cross is not something that might not have happened: "Self-sacrifice is God's very nature and essence."[40]

While we cannot explore this point more fully, one wonders if the theodicy represented here can be correlated not only with scripture but with the experience of suffering that Moltmann himself has known quite closely. How can a victim of the Holocaust, for example, concede, "Suffering love overcomes the brutality of evil and redeems the energy in evil, which is good, through the fulfillment which it gives to this misguided passion"?[41] Moltmann says that "the process of evolution is the process of redemption through suffering love."[42] This requires us to regard God's love in the creation and sustenance of the world as *suffering* love" rather than unconditional love. And it therefore calls into question, as much as the pagan view Israel opposed, not only the goodness of God but the goodness of creation as creation. What is the source of suffering in creation (and thus in God)? The Son, the Spirit—eventually the other that is the world? Moltmann speculates that "if God is already in eternity and in his very nature love, suffering love and self-sacrifice, then evil must already have come into existence with God himself, not merely with creation, let alone with the Fall of man."[43] Rather than embrace a dualistic cosmology such as Manichaeism, with good and evil grounded in two opposing gods, Moltmann synthesizes these oppositions within the very being of God himself.[44] Again we should be aware that in the history of metaphysics dualism and monism often depend on each other for their strength. Thus Moltmann approves G. A. Studdert Kennedy's conclusion: "God, the Father God of Love, is everywhere in history, but nowhere is He Almighty."[45] A God who does not suffer does not really live.[46] It would seem that the categories provided by nineteenth-century speculative philosophy press Moltmann to choose between the "absolute" and the "personal." Given the interdependence of God and the

---

40 Ibid.
41 Ibid.
42 Ibid.
43 Ibid., 34.
44 Ibid.
45 Ibid., 35 G.A. Studdert Kennedy—*The Hardest Part*—received more attention than Barth's *Epistle to the Romans*, which came out at the same time. "In fact," Moltmann judges, "it deserved even greater attention than Barth's book, for the theology of the suffering God is more important that the theology of the God who is 'Wholly Other.'"
46 Ibid., 38.

world via the history of suffering, "It is not only that we need God's compassion; God also needs ours...The deliverance of the world from its contradiction is nothing less than God's deliverance of himself from the contradiction of his world."[47]

In recent discussions of impassibility (as other incommunicable attributes), readers are pressed to make a decision between false alternatives. This point comes into sharper focus in open theism's treatment of the classical doctrine of divine impassibility, which it incorrectly defines as the inability to experience or feel emotion. If God were exactly identical to every representation we come across in scripture, could we not justly conclude that he is, for instance, capricious: "Kiss the Son, lest he become angry and you perish in the way, *for his wrath can flare up in an instant*" (Ps. 2:12, emphasis added)? As we have seen above, Moltmann seems more aware of the dangers in entirely rejecting the analogical proviso just at this point.[48] In this Psalm, God is depicted as mocking his enemies with sardonic laughter. But do we really want to ascribe this univocally to God's being rather than to recognize it as a sober comparison of a great king undisturbed by the pretenses of human power? We have yet to discover among open theists an argument in favor for God's rage being understood in the same univocal terms as his repentance.

There is also enough similarity to what we experience as love to say "God is love" (1 Jn. 4:8), but love is obviously different in the case of the one who loves in absolute freedom than for creatures whose experience of love is always related to some form of dependence and reciprocity. This very point seems implied in the same chapter: "In this is love, not that we loved God, but that he loved us and sent his Son to be an atoning sacrifice for our sins...We love him because he first loved us" (1 Jn. 4:10, 19). In other words, here God's love is the ultimate reality and human loves analogies: *human love is a theomorphism*.

Surely this dialectic play of analogies is comparable to the narrative representation of God as repenting and yet affirming, "I am not a mortal that I should repent" (1 Sam.15:29). Jealousy is praised in God (Ex. 20:5; 34:14; Dt. 4:24), while it is condemned in creatures (1 Cor. 3:3; Gal. 5:20), so clearly "jealousy" cannot mean exactly the same thing in God and creatures. God is described as uprooting the

---

47   Ibid., 39.
48   Moltmann, *Trinity and the Kingdom of God*, op.cit.: "God experiences people in a different way form the way people experience God. He experiences them in his divine manner of experience" (4). It is interesting that Moltmann approaches the analogical proviso most nearly whenever he is faced with the representations with which he is uncomfortable (viz., anger, wrath, impatience, jealousy) but loses sight of it whenever elaborating more sympathetic divine outbursts.

Israelites "in furious anger and great wrath" (Dt. 29:28), and yet "his anger lasts only a moment, but his favor lasts a lifetime" (Ps. 30:5). All of these diverse analogies must be taken seriously within their specific redemptive-historical context and then interpreted in the light of the rest of scripture. The anger that God condemns in us (Prov. 29:11, 22; 22:24; 1 Cor. 13:5) is different from the anger that fills him with holy wrath, whatever similarities there may be. Neither Moltmann nor the representatives of openness theology give any significant space to the wide range of divine pathos. Even if we were to adopt their univocal attribution of emotion to God, we would be left with a monopathetic deity whose only pathos is suffering love or, in Pinnock's expression, creative love. But can this do justice to the scores of passages in which God not only feels our pain but inflicts it? What of God's hatred, vengeance, jealousy and wrath? Even if they were to make a serious appearance in these proposals, such predications would be quickly absorbed into the higher synthesis. John Sanders, an advocate of open theism, judges,

> The desire not to speak about God anthropomorphically simply seems correct. After all, just about everyone takes the biblical references to the 'eyes,' 'arms' and 'mouth' (anthropomorphisms proper) of God as metaphors for divine actions, not assertions that God has literal body parts. But some go further, claiming that the anthropopathisms (in which God is said to have emotions, plans or changes of mind) are not actually to be attributed to God.[49]

Yet it is precisely the desire to speak anthropomorphically and to recognize it as such that defines an analogical approach. But further, why would we make an arbitrary distinction between analogies of being and analogies of feeling? This is not to reject predications of emotion to God (as classical theism has tended to do), but it is also not to say that emotions are predicated univocally of God and humans. If all predicates applied to God and creatures must be regarded as analogical, that would include references to God's sardonic laughter at his enemies in Psalm 2 or his grief at the disobedience of covenant partners. Perhaps, to attain consistency, one should speculate with Moltmann that God has tear ducts.[50] Pinnock does in fact take this next logical step, speculating concerning God's embodiment beyond the incarnation.[51] This is a good example of how God's transcendence itself is at

---

49   John Sanders, *The God Who Risks: A Theology of Providence* (Downers Grove, IL: IVP, 1998), 20.
50   Moltmann, *The Crucified God* (New York: Harper & Row, 1974), 222.
51   Pinnock, *Most Moved Mover*, op.cit., 33-4. He cites Mormon theologian D. Paulsen, among others,

stake in these debates, and how the denial of divine simplicity easily leads to a rejection of divine spirituality. But short of making the move to affirm divine corporeality, there seems to be no theoretical reason to separate attributions of particular emotions from attributions of particular limbs and organs.[52]

We do not have the space here to pursue this important point further.[53] Nevertheless, renewed attention to this particular formulation of divine impassibility would seem to be called for on both sides of this debate.

B. B. Warfield's treatment of divine emotion contrasts sharply with the picture that one obtains from many of the recent caricatures especially of Reformed orthodoxy and also warns us against formulations of the traditional view that begin with philosophical presuppositions of what is appropriate for God rather than attending closely to the biblical narrative. We are told, Warfield says, "that God is, by the very necessity of His nature, incapable of passion, incapable of being moved by inducements from without; that He dwells in holy calm and unchangeable blessedness, untouched by human sufferings or human sorrows forever—haunting

> The lucid interspace of world and world,
> Where never creeps a cloud, nor moves a wind,
> Nor ever falls the least white star of snow,
> Nor ever lowest roll of thunder moans,
> Nor sound of human sorrow mounts to mar
> His sacred, everlasting calm."

But Warfield replies,

> Let us bless our God that it is not true. God can feel; God does love. We have Scriptural warrant for believing that, like the hero of Zurich, God has reached out loving arms and gathered

---

for support and appeals to Mormon criticisms of divine incorporeality as well as other classical attributes (ibid., 35, fn 31 and 68fn.11).

52   Marylin Adams has observed, in a written response as part of a seminar with Professors Nicholas Wolterstorff and Marylin Adams on Divine Impassibility at Yale University in 1997: "It seems to me that human suffering could be a reason for Divine compassion without being an efficient cause of it." Adams captures what is really at stake here: "If something other than God causally affects God, however, God can't be the first cause of every change, unless Divine passibility is just an indirect approach to Divine self-change...If God could be totally or even nearly overcome by grief within God's Divine nature, God would not only fail to have an ideal Stoic character (which those of us who flirt with passibility can live with), God's providential control might be jeopardized. Do crucifixion, earthquakes, and eclipses signal that God has 'lost it' in Divine rage and grief?"

53   See Paul Helm, The Impossibility of Divine Passibility," in *The Power and Weakness of God* , ed. Nigel Cameron (Edinburgh: Conference in Christian Dogmatics, 1990), 123, 126.

into His own bosom that forest of spears which otherwise had pierced ours. But is not this gross anthropomorphism? We are careless of names: it is the truth of God. And we decline to yield up the God of the Bible and the God of our hearts to any philosophical abstraction....We may feel awe in the presence of the Absolute, as we feel awe in the presence of the storm or of the earthquake...But we cannot love it; we cannot trust it...Nevertheless, let us rejoice that our God has not left us by searching to find Him out. Let us rejoice that He has plainly revealed Himself to us in His Word as a God who loves us, and who, because He loves us, has sacrificed Himself for us.[54]

At the same time, Warfield can only testify to these wonderful truths because God freely assumed our humanity without ceasing to be God. The sixth-century Syrian monk we know as Pseudo-Dionysius put it this way: "Marvel at this incomprehensible mystery: the simple became complex, the immutable and impassible became subject to change and suffering like us in all respects but sin—without ceasing to be simple, immutable, and impassible."

If God were *merely* absolute—without relation—he could not be the Father who "so loved the world that he gave his only-begotten Son." Yet if he were *not* absolute, he would be part of the problem rather than the savior from it. The key distinction that emerged all the way back in the Cappadocian fathers was that while God is not related to creation, he freely relates his creation to himself. Instead of making God in our image, God makes us in his image. God is not like us; rather, he created us to be like him according to his moral character. Whatever weaknesses that might attend criticisms and counter-proposals, there can be little doubt that some traditional interpretations of God's otherness have been freighted with assumptions that are alien to the biblical canon.

The Stoic doctrine of *apathes / apatheia* is flatly denied by the Christian tradition wherever the latter asserts God's free involvement in the world. Moltmann is right when he says that we cannot read the passion narratives and conclude that God is aloof and unaffected by us. While some ancient and medieval writers evidence a wariness toward attributing emotion to God, in etymological terms

---

54   B. B. Warfield, *The Person and Work of Christ*, ed. Samuel G. Craig (Philadelphia: The Presbyterian and Reformed Publishing Company, 1970), 570-1. I am grateful to Professor John Frame for pointing out this reference.

at least God's impassibility referred not to an inability to relate or to feel, but to *suffer*. For the ancients, "emotions" referred mainly to the temperamental moods of the gods, not to feeling or experience per se. This is one of those cases in which the English cognate does not match the Greek or Latin. We assume that *passio* is simply passion, but *suffering* was the precise definition in antiquity.[55] This is true even for John of Damascus, whose citations above might make us skeptical. As Gerald Bray points out, "Apatheia, as John of Damascus understood it, meant the inability to suffer, i.e., impassibility in the strict sense. The emphasis was not on tranquility in a state of indifference, but on the sovereignty of God."[56] Moreover, impassible does not mean without affections but rather immunity to being the passive victim of creatures. Immutability does not mean immobility; on the contrary, God is the self-moved mover, ever-living, ever-active, ever-moving all things toward his goodness. However much in this respect the Christian doctrine *sounds similar* to Aristotle's Unmoved Mover, the differences are greater. Charles Hodge, for example, reminds us that in the classical view God is immutable, "but nevertheless that He is not a stagnant ocean, but an ever living, ever thinking, ever acting, and *ever suiting his action to the exigencies of his creatures,* and to the accomplishment of his infinitely wise designs" (emphasis added). Far from speculating *how* this is so, which extreme representations on both sides of this debate are often tempted to do, he adds,

> Whether we can harmonize these facts or not, is a matter of minor importance. We are constantly called upon to believe that things are, without being able to tell how they are, or even how they can be. Theologians, in their attempts to state, in philosophical language, the doctrine of the Bible on the unchangeableness of God, are apt to confound immutability with immobility. In denying that God can change, they seem to deny that He can act.[57]

Immutability must not be confused with immobility, and there is unanimity here among the various Reformed dogmatics.[58] In a similar vein, Cornelius Van Til writes,

---

55 Richard Muller, "Incarnation, Immutability, and the Case for Classical Theism," *Westminster Theological Journal,* 45 (1983), 27: "The scholastic notion of God as immobile does not translate into English as 'immobile'—as one of the many cases of cognates not being fully convertible—but as 'unmoved.'"
56 Gerald Bray, *The Doctrine of God*, 98.
57 Hodge, *Systematic Theology*, vol. 1 (Grand Rapids: Eerdmans, 1946), 390-1.
58 Ibid., 392. Here Hodge criticizes in particular some statements of Augustine to that effect, charging that he speculated beyond the limits of exegesis. But modern theology is far more indebted to philosophical assumptions, he charges. "We must abide by the teachings of Scripture, and refuse to subordinate their authority and the intuitive convictions of our moral and religious nature to the arbitrary definitions of any philosophical system." Bavinck concurs: "The fact that God is immutable does not mean that he is inactive:

> Surely in the case of Aristotle the immutability of the divine being was due to its emptiness and internal immobility. *No greater contrast is thinkable than that between the unmoved noesis noeeseoos of Aristotle and the Christian God.* This appears particularly from the fact that the Bible does not hesitate to attribute all manner of activity to God....Herein lies the glory of the Christian doctrine of God, that the unchangeable one is the one in control of the change of the universe (emphasis added).[59]

Kevin J. Vanhoozer offers a suggestive way forward. He begins by summarizing the traditional account. Although Augustine moved beyond the Platonic view that the gods, lacking nothing, cannot love (referring to God's love as "gift-love: agape"), he nevertheless held with the Stoics the belief that *"pathos*—any emotional event that 'disturbs' reason and joy—has no place in the life of the only wise God."

Importantly, Aquinas does not believe that God *responds* to the good in a thing by loving it, but rather that God's love for a thing is the *cause* of its goodness. On the traditional view, then, God metes out good but takes neither joy nor delight in the good he brings about (for this would make God's joy conditional on something in the world). That in which God takes delight turns out to be his own exercise of benevolence... Similarly, we may experience God's mercy or his wrath, but it is not God who changes, only our relation to him. 'What changes is the way we experience the will of God' (Richard Creel)...This is a most important analytic point: impassibility no more means impassive than immutability means immobile. God may be unmoved (transcendent: unsusceptible to worldly causes), but he is nevertheless a mover (immanent: active and present in the world).[60]

Furthermore, because God is the Father, the Son, and the Spirit, there is no question of brute force operating on a passive object. The characteristic method of God's creative, providential and saving operations is *speech*. The Father's word goes forth, mediated by the Son, made effectual in creatures by the Spirit. Because this word is not only above us but with us and within us, it is wins our consent and participation.

Even evil and sin are comprehended in God's eternal decree; therefore, not even these can be said to condition God's will or acts. Further, Vanhoozer's

---

immutability should not be confused with immobility," Herman Bavinck, *The Doctrine of God*, tr. William Hendriksen (Eerdmans, 1951; Baker, 1977), 151.

59   Cited by Muller, "Incarnation, Immutability and the Case for Classical Theism," op.cit., 30.

60   Kevin J. Vanhoozer, *First Theology: God, Scripture and Hermeneutics* (Downers Grove, IL: IVP, 2002), 74-6.

construction of this argument is trinitarian: "the Son and Spirit are means of the Father's communicative action."[61]

In the covenant God establishes with creatures, there is real partnership, but always in analogical rather than univocal relations. Recent criticisms of impassibility rarely succeed in challenging the dominant causal paradigm; they simply insist that the causal impact should run in both directions and often have difficulty resisting the temptation to see our acting upon God and God's causal action upon us in univocal terms. This is not to eliminate the category of cause from theological discourse, but to question its usefulness as an all-encompassing paradigm within which the divine-human relationship should be interpreted. Thus, we will be appealing to this communicative approach at a number of points throughout this volume.

Finally, what are we to make of the attribution of *immutability* to God? As with impassibility, a lot depends on the definition. According to critics of the doctrine, immutability is equivalent to immobility. In fact, in reducing the classic doctrine of God to Aristotle's "unmoved mover," Clark Pinnock simply calls it the "immobility package."[62] Ever since at least Dorner, there has been an attempt to forge a distinction between God's moral attributes, which cannot change, and God's being, which is conditioned to some degree by the world. Adherents of this thesis range from more conservative presentations (such as Dorner's) to more radical versions (such as process theology). But can a covenantal paradigm, underscoring the analogical character of all theological predication, avoid such a dualism between God's character and being?

What is it then exactly for God to be moved? If we knew the answer to that, would we not have univocal (archetypal) knowledge of God's being *in esse*? There is an appropriateness to analogies that must not be given short shrift in order to save God from his own revelation, and yet analogies are not an exact fit between sign and reference. In scripture, the virtue in not being "moved" lies in the assurance that God is trustworthy (Ps. 16:8; 21:7), while for the Greeks it meant that immobility—pure stasis, was a supreme mode of being.

How then might we build a doctrine of God with the timber of "strong verbs" leading to adverbs and nouns? In that narrated identity of God in scripture there

---

61 Ibid., 94.
62 Clark Pinnnock, *Most Moved Mover*, 78. Even in the most pristine expressions of "scholastic Calvinism," Aristotle's "unmoved move" is explicitly summoned for refutation. In addition to Warfield one could cite, for example, his colleague Charles Hodge, *Systematic Theology*, vol 1 (Grand Rapids: Eerdmans, 1946, from NY: Charles Scribner and Co., 1871), 391.

emerges a number of direct claims and legitimate inferences that justify at least the conclusion that despite the anthropomorphic analogies that render a real actor in a historical drama, God cannot be *overwhelmed* by *surprise*, since his knowledge is perfect and encompasses the past, present and future (Job 37:16; Ps. 139:1-6, 16-18), including the free acts of creatures (Ex 7:1-7, , 14; 8:15, 19; 9:12, 35; 10:1-2; 11:1-3, 9; 1 Sam 23:10-13; Is 42:9; Ac 2:23; Ro 8:28; 9:16; Eph 1:11). Although God can be opposed, ultimately he cannot be *overwhelmed* by *opposition* (Dan 4:17-37; Ex 15:1-23; 8:11; Ps 22:28-31; 47:2-8; 115:3; 135:5-21; Jer 27:5; Ac 17:24-6; Ro 9:17-21; Rev 11:15-19). And although God can be present in a particular place and time, he cannot be *overwhelmed* by such *circumscription* (Ps 139:7-12). The focus of the biblical testimony seems to be on the proscription of any limitations on God's attributes, not of God's capacity to genuinely relate.

Similarly, while God participates in the joy and sorrow of his people, without which the moral attributes of God would be empty, he is never *overwhelmed* by *distress*. Thus, narratives in which God is represented as impatient or enraged reveal the seriousness with which God takes transgression of his covenant, but they provide no univocal description of God's being in itself. God is never overwhelmed with distress because God is more unlike than like us. And this is treated as welcome news for those for whom God not only has compassion but also reserves anger: "I will not execute my fierce anger; I will not again destroy Ephraim; for I am God and no mortal, the Holy One in your midst, and I will not come in wrath" (Hos 11:9). The same is assured in Malachi 3:6: "'For I am the LORD, I do not change; *therefore you are not consumed*, O sons of Jacob.'" God's immutability is surely to be distinguished from any Greek concept of immobility, yet God's independence from the world is maintained precisely in and with his involvement in it. Only because God does not change, despite constant reprisals from his creation, can there be confidence to face each day without the threat of immanent disaster.

"To whom will you liken me and make me equal, and compare me, as though we were alike?" (Is. 46:5; 55:8-9; Num 23:19; 1 Sam. 15:29; Hos. 11:9). The fact is that *God* has compared himself to humans, as though we *were* alike—and yet (the analogical proviso), God retains his transcendence. Although *truly* known in his revelation, God cannot be *contained* by it (*finitum non capax infiniti*). To take analogies seriously is not to take them univocally. Scripture is no less analogical when it says that God does not repent than when it represents him as doing just that. Models are metaphors and rather than being alternatives to "reality depicting" language, they are the very means of indicating reality. This is as true in the natural sciences as in theology.[63]

Despite his incomprehensibility, God wills to enter into a relationship with his creatures. The covenant is the context in which that becomes possible. God enters into worldly relations, yet without simply collapsing Jesus into God, revelation into the divine essence, the immanent into the economic trinity, the eternal decree (things hidden) into its temporal execution (things revealed). Let us turn for a moment to examples of this covenantal (analogical) discourse, particularly as touching on this debate. Since we have raised the question of immutability as part of the constellation of attributes traditionally predicated of God (and under contemporary criticism), let us interact at this point especially with the claims of what has come to be called "open theism," especially within recent evangelical discussions. We have already referred to some of their representative writings.

The obvious examples have to do with God relenting and repenting. Both, open theists contend, demonstrate that God is *not* immutable, independent or omniscient—at least as these terms have been historically understood.[64] In 1 Samuel 15:11, for example, God regrets having made Saul king, and yet in verse 29 we read, "Moreover the Glory of Israel will not recant or change his mind; for he is not a mortal, that he should change his mind." Neither God's nature or his secret plan changes, and this is why believers can be confident that "if we are faithless, he remains faithful; he cannot deny himself" (2 Tim. 2:13; cf. Mal. 3:6, to the same point). So what changes if not God's secret plans? It is his revealed plans that change: the judgment that he has warned that he will bring upon the people is averted—precisely as God had predestined before the ages. The dynamic give-and-take so obvious in the history of the covenant must be distinguished from the eternal decree that scripture also declares as hidden in God's unchanging and inaccessible counsel (Eph. 1:4-11).

These are not two contradictory lines of proof-texts, one line pro-openness; the other pro-classical theism. Rather, there are two lines of analogy acting as guardrails to keep us on the right path. There is real change, dynamic interaction and partnership in this covenant (*Deus revalatus pro nos*). At the same time, God is *not like* the human partner in that he does not repent *the way the latter repents*: God transcends the analogies (*Deus absconditus in se*) even while revealing himself

---

63   See Janet Martin Soskice, *Metaphor and Religious Language* (Oxford: OUP, 1984).
64   According to open theists, God knows everything that can be possibly known, which excludes the decisions and actions of free creatures. I leave it to the reader to determine whether this stretches or breaks any identification with *omni*science.

in and through them. With scripture, we speak on one hand of the fall as contrary to God's revealed will and yet comprehended in God's secret plan (Ro 8:20-1). In this view, we need not have the difficulty with the "repentance" passages the way open theists seem, by their silence, to be burdened by the "non-repentance" passages. Against both hyper-Calvinism and openness theology, we need not reduce everything to either the eternal decree of the hidden God or the historical covenant of the revealed God.[65]

An analogical account provides a paradigm in which both God's independence from and relatedness to creaturely reality may be seriously affirmed without resolving the mystery in a false dilemma. Although Moltmann is an exception, Jenson, Pinnock and Sanders all reflect an impatience with paradox that goes hand in hand with their impatience with analogy.[66] This rationalistic tendency can be seen, ironically, on both sides of the debate, by both defenders and critics of classical theism, where certain predicates are either affirmed or denied in a univocal sense.

Yet, despite calls to trade abstract for concrete description of God, many of the critics of traditional affirmations of God's independence do end up speaking of transcendence and immanence in quite abstract, static, and general terms. Some of their expressions appear to be timeless ideas drawn from the familiar antitheses of ancient and modern dualism (and dualistic monism) and this often leads to false dilemmas. Either we worship a God who does not want to "control everything, but to give the creature room to exist and freedom to love," or "...an all-controlling despot who can tolerate no resistance (Calvin)," giving the false impression that Calvin actually held this position attributed to him.[67] Further, we must choose between a God who is "immobile" (a "solitary monad") and the "Living God" who is dependent on the creation for his happiness.[68] That is important, since the very title of Pinnock's book suggests that the position he is criticizing is little more

---

65   Pinnock and his colleagues may not approve the Reformed account of double agency, but their repeated misrepresentation of this tradition as "omnicausality" and the elimination of human partnership in the covenant is a perennial weakness of their rhetoric. This notion of double agency is not the incursion of philosophy, but is a good and necessary inference from such numerous passages. In the familiar Joseph narrative, the same event—Joseph's cruel treatment by his brothers—has two authors with two distinct intentions: "You meant it for evil, but God meant it for good" (Gen. 50:19-20). Peter offers precisely the same rationale for the crucifixion: "You with you wicked hands...But he was delivered up according to God's foreknowledge" (Acts 2).

66   For example, Hunsinger notes concerning Jenson, "Again and again, throughout his career, he has vilified paradox as a 'pious mystery-mongering of the vacuity'; by means of paradox, he believes, 'we communicate nothing whatever' [*The Triune Identity*, 126]...This criticism, it seems, underlies Jenson's resort to rationalistic metaphysics" (Hunsinger, "Review essay," op.cit., 199).

67   Pinnock, *Most Moved Mover,* op.cit., 4.

68   Ibid., 6

than a religious gloss on Aristotle's "Unmoved Mover." But since we have already seen that immobility is in no way required by immutability, we need not repeat those arguments here.

YHWH is therefore not a solitary monad lost in self-contemplation, a Buddha-like figure who closes his eyes to the world in order to contemplate his own bliss. But he is also not a creature contained in and circumscribed by the reality that he has created apart from himself. Douglas Farrow puts it well: "It is an imposition on the biblical narrative, as on dogmatic tradition, to suggest that the God who has decided not to be God without us is therefore only God by being God with us."[69]

In contrast to both Parmenidean permutations of divine bliss and Heraclitean versions of divine flux, biblical hope inserts the eschatological category of *Shalom*. While this is certainly not Stoic immobility and *apatheia*, it is nevertheless peaceful existence, but the kind of peace defined by God in the analogy of Israel and its theocratic laws and supremely in Christ's proclamation of the kingdom: the absence of strife, suffering, evil, and unrighteousness. It is even named sabbath *rest*, not because there is no *movement* but because there is no *departure from* the proper relation to God; not because there is no passion, but because the passion of God's own abundant life and joy constantly revitalizes and refreshes its inhabitants. If God indwells the Sabbath (and if he doesn't, how can he bring us into it?), then he is already enjoying everlasting peace, joy, and righteousness in the triune fellowship of perfect giving and receiving, loving and being loved. God not only enjoys this sabbath reality in its fullest measure already but is working to bring it about for us. In answer to criticism for healing on the Sabbath, Jesus replied, "My Father is still working, and I also am working" (Jn 5:17). Yet this working is also a resting in which the ultimate purposes of the Triune God, though opposed, are never thwarted. It is precisely because God is independent and unconditioned in his Sabbath reign that he is *able* to bring hope to victims and victimizers and it is precisely because God has freely entered into a covenantal relation with the creatures that we can trust that he is *willing* to do so.

---

69   Douglas Farrow, "Robert Jenson's *Systematic Theology*, Three Responses," *International Journal of Systematic Theology* 1.1 (1999): 91.

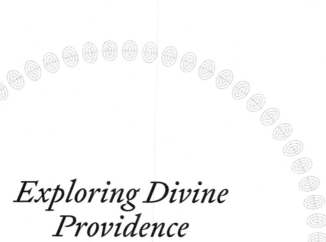

Exploring Divine Providence
Reason, Scripture, Free Will, and the Reality of Suffering

DR. SHERIF A. FAHIM
Professor and New Testament Chair,
Alexandria School of Theology
General Director of El-Soora Ministries
Egypt

Theologians identify two external actions of God whereby something outside of Himself is either produced, which is called creation, or is preserved or governed while it exists, which is called providence. This article principally treats with the latter. As Francis Turretin introduces his teaching on God's providence, "There is a providence in the world by which all things (even the smallest) are not only at the same time most wisely and powerfully directed but also so connected with the divinity that it cannot be wholly denied without at the same time denying God."[1] This simple definition challenges two views about the relation between God and the universe: pantheism and deism. In pantheism, the universe is God. Thus, there is no distinction between God and the universe. The other view is deism, which is more popular and influential. According to deism, God created the universe in accordance with certain laws and inherent powers so that the universe is running by itself according to these laws, independent of God. Contrary to pantheism, in deism, the distinction between God and the universe is overstated.[2]

According to Christian theism, the divine providence means that God is not merely the Creator of creation or merely the setter of its laws: he is also the one who preserves, regulates, and leads it to fulfill his purposes, which he intended in Himself with the utmost freedom from before the foundation of the world. Creation depends on God not only for its origin but also for its survival and continuation. There is no internal force in creation that enables it to survive on its own. The Apostle Paul says, "For in him we live and move and have our being" (Acts 17:28), and about Christ, the writer of Hebrews says that he "upholds all things by the word of his power" (Hebrews 1:3). In fact, the meaning of divine providence goes beyond merely preserving creation. Rather, as the Westminster Confession of Faith (WCF 5.1) says: "God, the great Creator of all things, doth uphold, direct dispose, and govern all creatures, actions, and things, from the greatest even to the least, by his most wise and holy providence, according to his infallible foreknowledge, and the free and immutable counsel of his own will, to the praise of the glory of his wisdom, power, justice, goodness, and mercy."

This definition emphasizes that providence includes everything without exception. This providence is always consistent with the character of God, who

---

1 Francis Turretin, *Institutes of Elenctic Theology*, ed. by James T. Dennison, trans. by George Musgrave Giger, vol. 1 (Phillipsburg, N.J: P&R Pub, 1992), 489.
2 For further discussion of these two competing views, see Paul Helm, *The Providence of God*, Contours of Christian Theology (Downers Grove, Ill: InterVarsity Press, 1994), 72–74.

is perfect in his wisdom, goodness, and holiness. God did not create creation and then remain a spectator. Instead, he created it for a specific purpose that he intended in eternity. he takes care of this creation, directs it, and organizes it to achieve his eternal purposes. It is this providence that makes the psalmist praise God, saying: "Whatever the Lord pleases, he does in the heaven and in the earth, in the seas and all deeps" (Psalm 135:6) and "Our God is in heaven. he does all that he pleases" (Psalm 115:3). This is the same meaning that Nebuchadnezzar expressed in Daniel 4:35: "And he does according to his will among the host of heaven and among the inhabitants of the earth, and none can stay his hand or say to him: What have you done?

In this article, we begin by discussing the interplay between human reason and divine revelation as we approach the profound topic of God's providence. Next, we explore the theological question of whether God takes risks by endowing human beings with free will and how this autonomy aligns with divine sovereignty. This risky position will be analyzed in relationship to God's omniscience, God's omnipotence and God's goodness. Finally, the concept of concurrence, where God's will and human actions intersect, is examined to provide a deeper insight into divine governance.

I. HUMAN REASON AND DIVINE REVELATION

Where do we get our information about God's providence from? On what basis do we build our understanding of God's providence? These questions are important because many times the discussion of this matter begins from the Bible but then the discussion drifts to the arena of reason, shifting the question to: what is the most logical view of providence? This is not to say that the Bible is against reason, but first, we must ask: what is reason, and how do we determine if something is reasonable? What is the correct relationship between divine revelation and reason? We cannot put these two things on an equal footing, especially considering what the Bible says about human thought and human reason.

Being created in God's image implies that humans can understand God's revelation. One of the special capacities given to humans in creation is intellect or reason. Reason is the God-given faculty by which human beings can think and act according to logical forms. Through reason, they can also form beliefs, draw inferences, and formulate arguments. However, humans are dependent on God's revelation to gain knowledge. Cornelius Van Til explains this principle by saying that human knowledge is essentially a reinterpretation of God's interpretations.[3] Van Til contends that "the self-existent God is the original of which man is the derivative."[4] In addition to this Creator-creature distinction, Scripture teaches that human capacities have been dramatically distorted by the Fall. As Van Til asserts "the human mind as it exists today should not only be thought of as derivative but should also be thought of as ethically depraved."[5] The Bible assumes that humans by nature became corrupt after the Fall, meaning that they reject the things of God. After the Fall, humans became enemies of God and did not accept to be subject to God and under his authority. The Fall, in essence, represents a desire to be independent from God and to even to take his place. We must keep these facts in mind as we think about how human beings perceive God's providence.

Given this description of the human reason, is there any room for it as we approach divine revelation? Of course, yes. How can we understand divine revelation without thinking? We use our minds to understand the words in the Bible and their relationship to each other. However, the human problem is not merely intellectual; it is also spiritual and moral. This affects the way we discuss the biblical doctrine of the divine providence. As we approach the Bible and begin to understand what it teaches about providence, objections rise. These objections do not aim to provide an interpretation that contradicts the biblical text, but stem from the biblical teaching no longer being pleasing to our human reason. Examples of these objections include, "But this means we are not free?" Or "This means we are puppets?" These objections here are not necessarily based on biblical ground but rather depends on human experience, which certainly shows that we are not puppets. In other words, according to the biblical teaching on providence, God is completely in control of human beings including all their decisions. Many see this as inconsistent with their experiential freedom, leading to the rejection of this teaching.

Ironically, this rejection of the biblical teaching on divine providence does not necessarily come from non-Christians or those who deny the authority of the

---

3   Cornelius Van Til, *An Introduction to Systematic Theology* (Phillipsburg, N.J: Presbyterian and Reformed Pub. Co, 1974), 24.
4   Van Til, *An Introduction to Systematic Theology*, 31. Van Til explains this idea in more detail as he says, "God is self-contained God. This God as self-contained makes every fact to be what it is. Therefore, man's study and understanding of any fact is an understanding of something of the ways of God in the world. Man's system of truth, even when formulated in direct and self-conscious subordination to the revelation of the system of truth contained in Scripture, is therefore not a deductive system." Cornelius Van Til, *A Christian Theory of Knowledge* (Philadelphia: Presbyterian and Reformed Pub. Co, 1969), 38.
5   Van Til, *An Introduction to Systematic Theology*, 24–25.

Scripture. In fact, many who profess that the Bible is the authoritative word of God and that they believe in God's sovereignty still struggle with this concept. The question is: what do they mean by God's sovereignty? Delving deeper into more detailed questions about divine providence often reveals that their belief in God's sovereignty does not align with the teachings of Scripture. Even more perplexing is that different people, all claiming to believe in God's sovereignty, can provide varying answers to these detailed questions. Therefore, to correctly understand God's providence and sovereignty, we must derive these meanings from God's revelation of Himself in the Bible, even if this challenges our preconceived notions. There is a significant difference between understanding what the Bible says about God and trying to make the Bible say what we want about God.

II. TWO DANGERS

Before going further, it is necessary to adhere to the revelation that God gives through his word. There are two dangers we need to be aware of as we approach God's revelation on any doctrine in general, including divine providence. On the one hand, one must not go beyond the limits of the divine revelation of Himself in the Holy Scriptures and describe God in ways far beyond what he says about Himself. Sometimes Christians reach certain limits that they cannot cross in terms of divine revelation, encountering seemingly contradictory information that they cannot fully understand or reconcile. When this point is reached, the temptation is to sacrifice one piece of information so that the big picture may seem more logical. Most of the time, God's sovereignty is sacrificed on the altar of human freedom.

On the other hand, Christians sometimes fall into an opposite error of claiming not to be able to know anything about God's character. This claim presents itself in the guise of humility, suggesting that because God is transcendent, we cannot know or speak about him clearly, and it is better to say we do not know. This uncertainty has become a hallmark of post-modernism, which posits that truth is fluid or relative and there is no such thing as absolute truth. The problem with this view is that it downplays the objectivity of divine revelation. God revealed Himself to human beings not so that they would remain in ignorance, but so they would know him. One must neither ignore what the Bible teaches nor claim that it is not clear enough or subject to different interpretations. Such strategy is against the very concept of revelation. God revealed himself to us in the Bible so that we may know him and know ourselves, providing comfort and encouragement to his people. Ignoring what God says about Himself or convincing people that no one can understand the Bible deprives them of knowing God. Often, the reason for claiming one cannot know what the Bible says is a rejection its teachings. While open rejection is a violent reaction to the Bible, claiming unknowability seems more humble and acceptable, but ultimately results in the same outcome: denying or rejecting a truth that God has clearly revealed. With this background in mind, it is time to delve deeper into the meaning of divine providence, especially considering the suffering and evil that exist in the world created and sustained by God.

III. DOES GOD RISK?

Why is there suffering? If God is sovereign and he is good, then why is there so much suffering in the world? Many people attempt to answer this question by trying to protect God from being responsible for pain or suffering. Their answer often goes like this: "God created human beings free and responsible for their decisions. They choose what they want. God cannot interfere in our decisions, otherwise we become like puppets in his hands. We decide whether to follow him or not, whether to be good or evil. Our free will determines what will happen. God respects our free will and does not interfere in our decisions. Unfortunately, we have abused this freewill, and the result is the pain and evil we see around us. God has accepted this risk, meaning the possibility of misusing our freedom, because he wants human beings to love him freely and not by compulsion, and the result is what we see now."

Let us think about this statement, which we may have often heard or even believed. According to this statement, life and creation can be described as a divine risk.[6] What is meant by the "risk" here is the following: Although God has an eternal purpose for creation and a final scene that he wants to see, this purpose can only be achieved through the free will of humans and angels, that is, all moral beings. Without these rational creatures carrying out their roles, the scene will not end as God intended. Based on this way of thinking, creation becomes a divine risk dependent on the decisions of creatures. Because of the freedom of creatures, the events of history can change and not follow the path God intended, and thus the

---

6 I owe a lot in this section to one of Paul Helm's chapters in his book *The Providence of God*. Helm discusses the doctrine of the providence of God in the light of the Augustine-Pelagius conflict. The writer named the views that lean to Augustine as risk-free views in which God does not tolerate the changing of his decreed plan because of man's free will. On the other hand, Helm called the other views which lean towards Pelagius as risky views in which God starts something not knowing how it will turn out. The uncertainty of the second group is due to human freedom which may change the ends of events; therefore, a risk exists. Helm, *The Providence of God*, 40–68.

endings may change. This view can be summarized as emphasizing the freedom of human will, and that man is the maker of history and events. According to this view, creation is a divine risk.

What are the repercussions of the idea of divine risk? This opinion is very widespread and seems to defend human freedom; its supporters believe that they are beautifying and glorifying God with this description. But is what they say true? Is the way they describe God consistent with God's description of Himself according to the Bible? what are the implications of such view on our understanding of the character of God? Three main attributes of God shall be discussed in light of the divine risk view: God's goodness, God's omniscience, and God's omnipotence.

VI. GOD'S OMNISCIENCE

Consistency with the view of the divine risk demands denying the fact that God is all-knowing. God created creation and gave man his freedom, and with all the existing human beings it becomes very complicated, as the end of things depends on the infinite possibilities of decisions that human beings make every day. God's risk means that he does not know how things will turn out, but that he acts as a spectator and, at best, can predict what might happen, but he cannot be certain how things will end. Richard Rice argues, "The idea that God interacts with a world where there is genuine creaturely freedom does not require us to deny divine foreknowledge. It requires only that we define the scope of foreknowledge with care...God knows a great deal about what will happen...All that God does not know is the content of future free decisions, and this is because decisions are not there to know until they occur."[7] Those who adhere to the freedom of the human will as the ultimate controlling factor of human history will inevitably go to what is called open theism in theology.

Open theism teaches that "the triune Creator cannot be absolutely sovereign or know the future because it must be open for loving relationships to exist."[8] This view argues that for humans to be truly free, God must be not omniscient.[9] For

---

7   Richard Rice, "Divine Foreknowledge and Free-Will Theism," in *The Grace of God, the Will of Man: A Case for Arminianism*, ed. by Clark H. Pinnock (Grand Rapids: Zondervan, 1989), 134.

8   Joel R. Beeke and Paul M. Smalley, *Reformed Systematic Theology: Revelation and God*, vol. 1 (Wheaton, Illinois: Crossway, 2019), 602.

9   Richard Swinburne argues that "For a person is not less worthy of worship if his knowledge is limited by what he has yet to decide, and if he limits it further voluntarily in order to allow some of his creatures to determine their

them, "exhaustive divine foreknowledge would destroy human responsibility."[10] This view is not new in church history; Augustine interacted with the same reasoning in Cicero's views of foreknowledge in relation to freewill. Augustine describes Cicero's view in the following words: "he (Cicero) attempts to accomplish by denying that there is any knowledge of future things, and maintains with all his might that there is no such knowledge either in God or man, and that there is no prediction of events."[11] Augustine understood that Cicero wanted to defend freewill with all his might and so he refused the foreknowledge of God;[12] a position that Augustine strongly rejected by saying: "For, to confess that God exists, and at the same time to deny that he has foreknowledge of future things, is the most manifest folly."[13]

This denial of God's omniscience was also held by the Socinians in the 16th and 17th centuries who "openly withdraw from God the knowledge of future contingencies as not being in the class of knowable things, saying either that he does not them absolutely or only indeterminately and probably."[14] Francis Turretin refuted the Socinians' views by arguing that, "the orthodox maintain that future contingent things fall under the infallible knowledge of God."[15] According to the latter view, all things, including the contingent, "fall under the infallible knowledge of God, not as knowing them only indeterminately and probably, but determinately, and most certainly."[16]

The question here is: How can God be perfect when his knowledge is not perfect? According to this view, God is not perfect, but he is growing in knowledge. God becomes instead of God is. In this scenario, God created the world without knowing where it would go, and it may not turn out well in the end. Those who lead history here are human beings with their own free will. This is the risk. God decided to limit Himself, his knowledge, and even his freedom. The most he can do is anticipate their reactions because of his knowledge of the circumstances surrounding them.

---

own destiny. The latter is a limitation which he can at any moment abandon by withdrawing from humans their free will." Richard Swinburne, *The Coherence of Theism* (Oxford: Clarendon Press, 2010), 183.

10   Beeke and Smalley, *Reformed Systematic Theology: Revelation and God*, 1:743.

11   Augustine of Hippo, "The City of God," in *St. Augustine's City of God and Christian Doctrine*, ed. Philip Schaff, trans. Marcus Dods, vol. 2, *A Select Library of the Nicene and Post-Nicene Fathers of the Christian Church*, First Series (Buffalo, NY: Christian Literature Company, 1887), 5.9.

12   Augustine argues that Cicero held to his position "in order that he may not grant the doctrine of fate, and by so doing destroy free will. For he thinks that the knowledge of future things being once conceded, fate follows as so necessary a consequence that it cannot be denied." "The City of God," 5.9.

13   Augustine of Hippo, "The City of God," 5.9.

14   Turretin, *Institutes of Elenctic Theology*, 1:208.

15   Turretin, *Institutes of Elenctic Theology*, 1:208.

16   Turretin, *Institutes of Elenctic Theology*, 1:209.

However, this also does not mean being certain about what will happen because, in the end, a person may do something unexpected of his own free will. Additionally, the circumstances surrounding each human being include other human beings with other own free wills, which makes the matter even more complicated.

People of this thought sometimes claim that God knows events without being in control of them. However, it is not possible to separate God's foreknowledge from his control over everything. If God knows in detail everything that will happen in the future, then nothing can change. How could God know exactly what will happen while remains a possibility to change the things that he knows will happen? If God knows for sure what will happen, then there is no possibility that this could change, even if humans were free.

Some might argue that God does not know what will happen determinately but has a very high expectation of what will take place. However, does this perspective align with the biblical description of God's knowledge and understanding? Doesn't the Bible present God as omniscient? How then can we read Psalm 139? How can we understand Isaiah 46:9-10 "Remember the former things of old, for I am God, and there is no other, I am God and there is none like me, declaring the end from the beginning and from ancient times things not yet done, saying, 'My counsel shall stand, and I will do all that I please." The very concept of prophecy contradicts the idea that God does not know the future! The same applies to the teaching of the New Testament? For instance, how could Jesus know that Peter would deny him three times? Was there a chance that Peter would not deny Christ? Could Peter deny Christ once and then by his own free will change his mind and stop the denial act? How can we understand all the prophecies about the Second Coming, the New Heaven, and the New Earth? How can we know that the ending will be good? How can we confidently proclaim the promise: "All things work together for good to those who love God" (Romans 8:28)?

V. GOD'S OMNIPOTENCE

Holding to the concept of divine risk in relation to providence introduces a god who desires many things but is unable to implement them. his will may be good, but it is ineffective or incapable. The Bible teaches about many things that God wants which do not happen in creation. For instance, God wants all people to be saved and we know that this desire will not be fulfilled. But on the other hand, the Bible tells us that God does whatever he pleases (Psalm 115:3, Psalm

135:6), and there is no one who can withhold his hands (Daniel 4:35), and in the New Testament it says that he does all things according to the counsel of his will (Ephesians 1:11). The Lord confirms that his purpose will stand and that he will do all his good pleasure (Isaiah 46:10).

If God's will is limited by our personal freedom, this implies that all of God's promises to sanctify and glorify us (Romans 8:30) are empty promises that he cannot keep. How can he promise us something that is ultimately dependent on our freedom of will apart from him? This also suggests that he is not omnipotent, as something outside of Himself—the freedom of human will—limits God's power.

Therefore, we must be careful when we talk about God's will and ability, as the Bible distinguishes between God's will in relation to his commands and God's will in relation to his decrees. Regarding his commands, God's will may be broken; this is evident in the Ten Commandments which humans break daily. The Ten Commandments are an expression of God's will, yet they are always followed. However, when it comes to God's decrees, they cannot be thwarted. God works all things according to the counsel of his will (Eph 1:11). When a person breaks a commandment, this act itself is part of the divine decrees. In this sense, the decrees cannot be thwarted. The greatest example for this reality is the death of Christ. John Piper explains: "The betrayal of Jesus by Judas was a morally evil act inspired immediately by Satan (Luke 22:3). Yet in Acts 2: 23 Luke says, 'This Jesus was delivered up according to the definite plan (boule) and foreknowledge of God.' The betrayal was sin, and it involved the instrumentality of Satan; but it was part of God's ordained plan. That is there is a sense in which God willed the delivering up of his Son, even though the act was sin."[17] Therefore, the wicked, in their evil and rebellion against God, while breaking God's moral or perceptive will, are simultaneously implementing the divine decretive sovereign will precisely.

An objection may rise that speaking of two wills of God that contradict each other presents unsolvable dilemma that should be avoided. Refuting the Calvinistic position on the divine sovereignty and the principle of the two wills in God, Randall G. Basinger contends, "while it is hard (if not impossible) to imagine Calvinism without the distinction between God's sovereign will and his moral will, it is harder still to coherently conceive of a God in which this distinction

---

17   John Piper, "Are There Two Wills in God?" in *Still Sovereign: Contemporary Perspectives on Election, Foreknowledge & Grace*, ed. by Thomas R. Schreiner and Bruce A. Ware (Grand Rapids: Baker Books, 2000), 111.

really exists."[18] However, the biblical data challenges this objection.Sometimes we see that God is all-knowing and all-powerful, and no one can thwart his purposes; his grace is effective and succeeds in changing evil people into saints (cf. 1 Cor. 15:10). Other times, we see God regretting and backing down from doing certain things that he had intended to do, and we see people resisting God's grace and rejecting the Gospel, as Christ says, "How often would I have gathered your children together as a hen gathers her brood under her wings, and you were not willing!" (Mat. 23: 37). How can we reconcile these facts together? There are three possible solutions:

> The first solution is to say that the Bible contradicts itself and does not provide a consistent understanding of the will of God, and therefore there cannot be any true knowledge about God. This opinion is adopted by some liberal thinkers who reject the fact that the Bible is the word of God and do not see, or rather do not want to see, another solution to reconcile the data found in Scripture.

The second solution is to understand the descriptions of God as all-knowing, all-powerful in light of the parts that talk about God's remorse and unfulfilled desires. In this view, statements about his immutability, unchangeableness, and omniscience are seen as exaggerated formulas and not necessarily true. Accordingly, as Helm describes this solution, "we should be committed to maintaining that God is at times ignorant, that he changes his mind, that he is open to persuasion, that his purposes of goodness are thwarted, and so on."[19] In this case, we greatly diminish God, making him just a human being like us, albeit an immortal with some abilities higher than ours.

The third solution is to understand the words about God's remorse and unfulfilled desires in light of the parts that speak about God's supremacy, great power, fulfillment of his purposes, and omniscience. In other words, the statements about the intensity of God's power and knowledge must control the anthropomorphic statement and not vice versa. In this case, the parts about God's remorse and unfulfilled desires must be understood as a condescending language through which God communicates with us as finite beings to confirm our responsibility

---

18 Randal G. Basinger, "Exhaustive Divine Sovereignty: A Practical Critique," in *The Grace of God, the Will of Man: A Case for Arminianism*, ed. by Clark H. Pinnock (Grand Rapids: Zondervan, 1989), 203.
19 Helm, *The Providence of God*, 51.

before him. Calvin explains this line of thought as follows: "For because our weakness does not attain to his exalted state, the description of him that is given to us must be accommodated to our capacity so that we may understand it. Now the mode of accommodation is for him to represent himself to us not as he is in himself, but as he seems to us.[20]" God wants us to respond to him in a real relationship, so he condescended to us in a language that we understand. Rather, he spoke to us within the framework of time and place, as these are the frameworks through which we can relate. But all these real interactions are within a broader circle of divine sovereignty and providence that meticulously implements God's plan. Calvin affirms this understanding by saying, "Therefore, since every change among men is a correction of what displeases them, but that correction arises out of repentance, then by the word "repentance" is meant the fact that God changes with respect to his actions. Meanwhile neither God's plan nor his will is reversed, nor his volition altered; but what he had from eternity foreseen, approved, and decreed, he pursues in uninterrupted tenor, however sudden the variation may appear in men's eyes."[21] According to this view, God does not take risks. History follows the path carefully drawn by God. This view does not deny the freedom of man's will, but it holds that what man does with his free will is precisely what God intended in eternity.

VI. GOD'S GOODNESS

The last attribute strongly related to the divine risk view is God's goodness. Generally, one of the most difficult questions we face as we study God's providence and sovereignty is the existence of evil. A comprehensive study of the relationship between God's providence and evil is beyond this lecture. However, in relation to the discussion of God's goodness, if God is all-knowing, all-powerful, and all-good, then why did he intend for evil to exist in this life? Didn't he know from the beginning that this would happen? This may be the most common question I have been asked by children: why did God put the tree of the knowledge of good and evil in the Garden of Eden? Didn't he know that Adam and Eve would eat from it?

The famous response to this question from the risky position is: The freedom of the human will. God created man with free will, which explains the existence of

---

20   John Calvin, *Institutes of The Christian Religion*, The Library of Christian Classics v. 20-21 (Philadelphia: Westminster Press, 1960), 1.17.13.
21   Calvin, *Institutes of The Christian Religion*, 1.17.13.

evil in the world. But didn't God know that this would happen? According to the idea of the divine risk, God knows with great probability what the human race will end up with because of their free will. Yet, out of respect for this freedom, he lets them follow this path, saying: This is what they want, so be it, no matter what end this will be. God even knows what will happen to the children and the powerless, and he knows that evil people will exploit them, oppress them, and rob them of everything precious and valuable. Yet he stands by and watches without intervening because he is committed to the law of free will. Let's think about this idea. This means that God loves and respects this law more than he respects all the victims in history. He can sacrifice them, but he cannot sacrifice the freedom of the will. Is this love and is this goodness? Imagine a small child letting go of his father's hand and running towards a road full of speeding cars, and his father leaves him in order to assure him that he respects his child's freedom. What kind of father would do this?

In fact, the risky position does not solve the problem of evil properly and consistently with the goodness of God. While it portrays a blind God when it comes to knowledge, it presents a careless God when it comes to goodness. God's goodness, according to this view, is reduced to mere wishful thinking. Yes, God is good, but his goodness means that he only desires good for the people, it does not go beyond that. This perspective limits God's goodness to offering goodness, salvation, and grace to his creation, but asserts that he can accomplish none of them. God cannot do good to anyone without their approval.

While the risky position does not provide a satisfactory answer to the problem of evil, the issue still demands an explanation. How could moral evil or physical evil be consistent with a providential order established by an all-good, all-powerful God? One possible explanation is punitive: God is holy, and the suffering and evil we see around is an expression of his judgment against sin (cf. Romans 1:18-32; Rom. 8:23; Lamentations 3:38). However, as Paul Helm contends, this punitive view "can offer no explanation of why evil was permitted in the first place."[22] Accordingly, Helm goes further to argue for what is called the greater good. he says, "evil, moral evil, is necessary for a greater good...without the occurrence of moral evil certain other goods could not, logically speaking, arise. Without weakness and need, no compassion; without fault, no forgiveness, and so on."[23]

---

22 Helm, *The Providence of God*, 213.
23 Helm, *The Providence of God*, 213.

There was no way we could understand what God's forgiveness, restoration, renewal and new creation without the Fall. The existence of the Tree of Knowledge of Good and Evil was not only to highlight the importance of freedom of will and Adam's responsibility, although this is true. There was a bigger and deeper goal: that one day we may see a more glorious tree, which is the tree of the cross. This is what made Paul say in Ephesians 1:5-6 that the great purpose of the story is to praise the glory of his grace in Jesus Christ. The praise of his grace that is in Christ Jesus is the ultimate goal of the story from the beginning. The praise of God's grace was not possible apart from the Fall. John Piper explains this line of thought as follows, "God's ultimate purpose in creation and providence was not that his glory would be displayed and praised through means that did not involve the suffering of his Son. The cross was not an afterthought. It was part of the plan from before the foundation of the world (cf. 2 Tim. 1:9; Rev. 13: 8)."[24]

This question about God's providence and his goodness also, and most importantly, deals with God's saving grace. In other words, the issue that at stake is not only God's goodness in general, but also the intensity of this goodness. The question about God's goodness and how far it can reach "has been at the centre of a controversy about divine saving grace. Is that grace merely enabling, or is it effective?"[25] How many times has God shown kindness to people who reject it, only to make this kindness effective in their lives? As they hurried away from him, even trying to persecute his people and openly rebelling against him, he sovereignly converts them to be his beloved servants. Isn't this what God did with the Apostle Paul? Didn't he do that to the Samaritan woman? Did Lazarus ask him to raise him from the dead? God gave his people covenantal promises that are clear manifestations of his goodness: "I will make with them an everlasting covenant, that I will not turn away from doing good to them. And I will put the fear of me in their hearts, that they may not turn from me" (Jer. 32:40)? God's grace does not stop at offering salvation and goodness; it is effective and succeeds in its goal of bringing goodness and salvation to whomever God wants to save and bless. God's goodness does not stop at offering goodness, waiting for people to respond of their own free will until they enjoy it. Rather, goodness goes beyond that, as God in his providence saves irresistibly and irrevocably those who are wicked and transforms them to be conformed to the image of his beloved Son.

---

24   John Piper, *Providence* (Wheaton, Illinois: Crossway, 2020), 171.

25   Helm, *The Providence of God*, 50.

VII. CONCURRENCE

As shown above, the main issue the risky position wants to defend is human free will. Is a person truly free and able to do what he wants if God is totally sovereign, even over human choices? The Bible emphasizes man's responsibility for whatever he does or chooses, and accordingly every person will give an account for his actions and choices. A person is morally responsible and has the ability to do many things. However, it can be said that man is a secondary cause of whatever happens. Since Thomas Aquinas, theologians distinguish between God as the "primary cause" and creatures as the "secondary causes."[26] Behind all human choices and decisions is God's providence, a position that both Pelagians and Socinians deny. Both the Pelagians and the Socinians "do admit an influence upon natural things, but upon free things, at least with respect to their predetermination, they deny it, so that they may have an independent indifference of choice."[27] In contrast, the Reformed view argues that God carries out his good, pleasing, perfect, and inevitable will through the free will and free decisions of human beings. Petrus Van Mastricht explains this concurrence as follows:

> Second causes, whatever they may be, are first aroused and predetermined, insofar as this arousing and predetermining (besides the communication of strength and its preservation) is entirely necessary in order to bring forth into action what was previously in the potency of the creature. This is so in causes acting not only naturally, but also freely, and moreover, in the latter causes, it happens not only morally, by persuading, but also physically, by turning (Prov. 21:1; Phil. 2:13).[28]

Examples of this synchronicity or concurrence in the Bible are very numerous. For instance, consider the story of Joseph and his brothers in the Book of Genesis, the king of Assyria in Isaiah 10, and the climax of all examples: the cross of our Lord Jesus Christ. Christ's death was not a coincidence or merely the result of a conspiracy by Judas, the Jewish leaders, Herod, and Pilate. While these individuals decided and acted according to their evil desires, everything they did—and for which they will be held accountable—was part of God's eternal, inevitable plan to redeem his people and restore creation (cf. Acts 4:27-28).

---

26 Beeke and Smalley, *Reformed Systematic Theology: Revelation and God*, 1:1071.
27 Peter van Mastricht, *Theoretical-Practical Theology*, vol. 1 (Grand Rapids: Reformation Heritage Books, 2018), 327.
28 Mastricht, *Theoretical-Practical Theology*, 1:315.

VIII. CONCLUSION

We should not dilute the teaching of God's providence to uphold human responsibility. As Augustine argues, "let these perplexing debates and disputations of the philosophers go on as they may, we, in order that we may confess the most high and true God himself, do confess his will, supreme power, and prescience. Neither let us be afraid lest, after all, we do not do by will that which we do by will, because he, whose foreknowledge is infallible, foreknew that we would do it."[29]

Contrary to the risky position, the Bible teaches that God's providence encompasses everything that happens in this life, whether big or small, natural or moral. he makes the rain fall, the sun shine, and the flowers grow (cf. Psalm 147). Not a sparrow falls to the ground, nor a single hair from anyone's head, without his permission (Matthew 10:29-31). In the Christian faith, there is no such thing as chance or luck. "The lot is cast into the bosom and all its judgment is from the Lord" (Proverbs 16:1). Perhaps what happened to the prophet Jonah is an example of God's control even in the casting of lots (Jonah 1:7). While chance and luck imply randomness, God is a person with a clear purpose he is fulfilling. Chance is blind, but God sees everything. Chance is weak, but God is able. Chance is careless, but God is good. History is not guided by purposeless forces or a random system without intention. Rather, it is the wise, holy, all powerful, good and righteous God who leads history in all its details to an end that he intended from eternity.

What is striking about the definition of providence in the Westminster Confession is that it speaks not only of God's sovereignty over all things but also of the wisdom and holiness of God in exercising this control. Here we must distinguish between God's sovereignty and God's providence. God's sovereignty is his right and ability to do what he wants, whenever he wants. God has complete freedom and ability to accomplish his will as expressed in Job 42:2: "I know that you can do all things, and that no purpose of yours can be thwarted." This is the sovereignty of God. If it stopped there, it might be frightening, for if this God were evil or not good, the situation would be terrifying. But God is all good, all wise, and all holy. Therefore, the Bible teaches us about God's providence, which means that God uses his sovereignty to accomplish his purposes that are consistent with his wisdom, holiness, and righteousness. God's providence is the triune God's wise use of his sovereignty to accomplish the purposes that he intended in eternity.

---

29   Augustine of Hippo, *The City of God*, 5.9.

Holding to the risky position in order to defend human responsibility jeopardizes God's wisdom, power and goodness. The doctrine of God's providence, as taught in Scripture provides us with a caring, wise, loving, powerful and all-knowing God whose purposes can never be thwarted. This reality is well expressed by Turretin, "If God does not care for the world, it is either because he does not know or because he cannot or because he does not wish to. But how can this be said without the greatest blasphemy against him, since he is most wise (foreseeing all things and for all) and most powerful (with whom nothing is impossible) and the best (who as he created the world at first with the highest goodness, so he cannot but conserve and govern it when created by the same)."[30]

---

30   Turretin, *Institutes of Elenctic Theology*, 1:491.

God's Sovereignty Amidst Suffering

DR. KENETH PERVAIZ
Assistant Professor, Forman Christian College
Pakistan

Suffering, pain, hardships and trials are inevitable realities of life. As D. A. Carson, writes in his book, How Long, O Lord?, "...all we have to do is live long enough, and we will suffer."[1] When we experience the death of someone whom we love the most; when we see war, corruption, racism, genocide, poverty, starvation, injustice. . . it makes us wonder: 'Where is God?' The experience of bitter suffering makes some even question the existence of God. Then theo-philosophical questions are raised: "If God is omnipotent, if he is sovereign and perfectly good, then why does he allow suffering, pain, and evil in the world?"

I. THE UNDERSTANDING OF DIVINE ATTRIBUTES

The knowledge of the attributes/characteristics of our parents is not limited to merely intellectual beliefs. It impacts our relationship with them. Likewise, the knowledge of God's attributes (the character/person of God) is not merely restricted to intellectual beliefs. Rather the true Bible-based knowledge of who God is (i.e. his attributes) affects how to relate to him. The true biblical understanding/knowledge of God's character/his attributes is directly proportional to our deeper relationship with him. For example, Islam's understanding of the divine being—i.e. "Who God is"—hugely impacts how they relate to him.

The attribute of God's sovereignty expresses the fact that God is the Almighty, the possessor of all power in heaven and earth, so none can defeat his counsels, hinder his purpose, or resist his will (Psalm 115:3). As Pink states,

> The sovereignty of God. What do we mean by this expression? We mean the supremacy of God, the kingship of God, the godhood of God. To say that God is sovereign is to declare that God *is* God. To say that God is sovereign is to declare that He is the Most High, doing according to His will in the army of heaven, and among the inhabitants of the earth, so that none can stay His hand or say unto Him what doest Thou? (Dan. 4:35).[2]

In his sovereignty, God maintains and upholds the whole creation (Ps 147:8–9); he controls all life (Isaiah 45:6–7); he does whatever pleases him (Psalm 115:2–3); he directs all events, small and great, towards the goals that he has determined (Psalm 135:6; Isa 46:9–11).

---

1 D.A. Carson, *How, Long, O Lord?*, 2nd edition (Grand Rapids, MI: Baker Academic, 2006), 9.
2 A.W. Pink, *The Sovereignty of God*, (Ann Arbor, MI: Cushing-Malloy 1970), 23. Emphasis original.

II. GOD'S SOVEREIGNTY AND THE PROSPERITY GOSPEL.

The Prosperity Gospel offers a mistaken view of God's Sovereignty. Unfortunately, the supporters of 'Prosperity Gospel' understand the attribute of God's Sovereignty as something wherein human pain, hardships and suffering cannot be a part of God's good plans for his people. In other words, in their view, if God is a merciful, powerful, omnipotent agent, how can his people experience pain and suffering?

It is assumed that if God is good, then he will only let good things happen to his people. Suffering cannot be God's will for believers. In this ideology, believers are promised unconditional healing and wholeness if they have enough faith. In the prosperity gospel, suffering, pain, grief, sorrow are not part of God's plan because God is a good heavenly father who not only protects his children from harm and suffering but also delights in prospering them in all areas of their lives. For this reason, when the advocates of the prosperity gospel find believers experiencing pain, hardships, and suffering, they blame believers for not having sufficient faith or not having sufficient faith/trust in God's goodness and sovereignty to justify their ideology. Refuting such a mistaken view of God's Sovereignty, D. A Carson writes:

> Despite the best efforts of the proponents of the health and wealth gospel, the fact is that Christians get old and wrinkled. They contract cancer and heart disease, become deaf and blind, and eventually die. In many parts of the world, Christians have to face the blight of famine, the scourge of war, and the subtle coercion of corruption. This is not to say that God does not sometimes intervene on behalf of his people in remarkable ways. It is to say, rather, that we too live in a fallen world and cannot escape participation in its evil and suffering. If you doubt this, you are (1) ignorant of what many Christians around the world have to face daily; (2) not old enough yet, for certainly if you live long enough you too will suffer; (3) kidding yourself; or (4) some combination of the above.[3]

---

3   Carson, 63.

III. SUFFERING OF GOD'S PEOPLE AS THE COST OF DISCIPLESHIP

The theme of the suffering of God's people in the NT writings is evident. Biblical references in the NT explicitly demonstrate the fact that followers of Jesus will experience suffering and persecution for the sake of their faith. In the Bible, believers are clearly informed that they should not expect an easy, comfortable, and problem-free life. Instead, they are forewarned that they should expect an ongoing spiritual warfare (1 Peter 5:8–9; Ephesians 6:12) which is declared upon them by their enemy, Satan (1 Peter 5:8–9). Believers' suffering, adversaries, hardships, and persecution are part of that spiritual warfare. In the Christian faith, suffering and persecution are not optional. Rather, they are a significant component of their faith: "In fact, everyone who wants to live a godly life in Christ Jesus will be persecuted (2 Timothy 3:12);" "Remember what I told you: 'A servant is not greater than his master.' If they persecuted me, they will persecute you also. If they obeyed my teaching, they will obey yours also" (John 15:20)."

God's Sovereignty in the Midst of Suffering: Exegesis of Selected Scripture Passages

Christians express God's omnipotence by proclaiming, "God is sovereign over everything." What we mean by this is that God is all-powerful, he knows everything, and he is always in control. And since God is omnipotent, he makes Christians victorious and he is able to protect and uphold them in all circumstances.

However, does God's sovereignty reflect only when believers are leading victorious lives? Does it reflect only when believers enjoy God's blessings in different aspects of life? Or is God sovereign in the midst of believers' suffering as well?

In the following biblical passages, we will explore: (1) how God's sovereignty functions when his people go through suffering and persecution, and (2) how believers should respond in the midst of suffering in the present age.

a. Genesis 45:4–8; 50:19–20

> Then Joseph said to his brothers, "Come close to me." When they had done so, he said, "I am your brother Joseph, the one you sold into Egypt! And now, do not be distressed and do not be angry with yourselves for selling me here, because it was to save lives that God sent me ahead of you. For two years now

> there has been famine in the land, and for the next five years there will be no plowing and reaping. But God sent me ahead of you to preserve for you a remnant on earth and to save your lives by a great deliverance. "So then, it was not you who sent me here, but God. he made me father to Pharaoh, lord of his entire household and ruler of all Egypt.

> But Joseph said to them, "Don't be afraid. Am I in the place of God? You intended to harm me, but God intended it for good to accomplish what is now being done, the saving of many lives.

After Jacob's death, Joseph's brother approached him fearing that he may have been awaiting their father's death to take revenge upon them. They were aware of what they had done to him. Joseph was sold into slavery, lived as a prisoner for many years; he had faced false accusations because of his integrity. Joseph's suffering wasn't light and short. What would he do to his brothers? How would he respond to this situation?

It's not that Joseph is in a denial mode and ignores the suffering he had endured. Instead, he chooses to respond to this situation with a divine perspective. Joseph assures his fearful brothers that he does not want to put himself in the place of God.

Notice, Joseph does not say that his brothers cruelly sold him into slavery and then God turned this situation around. Neither does he say that God planned to bring him to Egypt with first-rate protocol but then his brothers messed up God's plan. No! Joseph's response implies that God was working sovereignly in his suffering, trials, and hardships. The understanding of God's sovereignty shaped the way Joseph viewed his suffering.

b. Acts 4:23–31

> On their release, Peter and John went back to their own people and reported all that the chief priests and the elders had said to them. When they heard this, they raised their voices together in prayer to God. "Sovereign Lord," they said, "you made the heavens and the earth and the sea, and everything in them. You spoke by the Holy Spirit through the mouth of your servant, our father David: "'Why do the nations rage, and the peoples plot in vain? The kings of the earth rise up, and the rulers band together against the Lord and against his anointed one. Indeed

> Herod and Pontius Pilate met together with the Gentiles and the people of Israel in this city to conspire against your holy servant Jesus, whom you anointed. They did what your power and will had decided beforehand should happen. Now, Lord, consider their threats and enable your servants to speak your word with great boldness. Stretch out your hand to heal and perform signs and wonders through the name of your holy servant Jesus." After they prayed, the place where they were meeting was shaken. And they were all filled with the Holy Spirit and spoke the word of God boldly.

This chapter records the first time the Apostles encountered persecution from the Jewish authorities. Upon release, Peter and John went to other believers to tell them about what had happened. When believers heard the report from the Apostles, they "raised their voices together and prayed. The content of their prayer is very interesting; most of the prayer on this occasion consists of reflections on the sovereignty of God: "When they heard this, they raised their voices together in prayer to God. "Sovereign Lord," they said, "you made the heavens and the earth and the sea, and everything in them" (Acts 4:24). Notice that they addressed God as "Sovereign Lord" here, but the word in Greek is not kurios but despotes—which is not the usual word used for the word Lord. The term despotes means "one who holds complete power or authority over another." Though the powers of the world were rising against them, they were affirming that the God they serve holds ultimate authority.

The implication is that God, the Creator of everything, is greater than the authorities who are now attacking them and trying to destroy their faith. It is significant that the early believers understood the significance of divine sovereignty from the Scriptures. The early church's key response to persecution was based on their understanding of God's sovereignty.

c. 2 Corinthians 1:8–10

> We do not want you to be uninformed, brothers and sisters, about the troubles we experienced in the province of Asia. We were under great pressure, far beyond our ability to endure, so that we despaired of life itself. Indeed, in our hearts we felt the sentence of death. But this happened that we might not rely on ourselves but on God, who raises the dead. he has

> delivered us from such a deadly peril, and he will deliver us
> again. On him we have set our hope that he will continue to
> deliver us.

In his writings, Paul did not consider his sufferings for Christ as his private matter. Rather, he wants his readers to be aware of his sufferings. He openly tells Corinthians about his and his companions' troubles, hardships, and sufferings which were "far beyond their ability to endure." After he describes his suffering, how does he respond to them? How does he view his suffering for the sake of his faith? Notice the text: he understands his suffering experience in light of God's sovereignty. Firstly, God uses Paul's suffering as a tool to make him rely upon him. Secondly, God is not unmindful of Paul's suffering and hardships; it's not as if things are out of his control. Paul confidently says that God has rescued him from such "deadly peril" in the past and, in his sovereignty, he will continue to do so. God's sovereignty offers secure hope to Paul and his companions in their suffering and hardships.

d. 1 Peter 4:19

> So then, those who suffer according to God's will should commit
> themselves to their faithful Creator and continue to do good.

The theme of suffering is prevalent in 1st Peter because Peter's audience was facing severe persecution. Verse 19 here in chapter 4 is a conclusion of verses 12-18. Peter's connection of believers' experience of suffering with God's will demonstrates the fact that all suffering of believers passes through divine will. In other words, believers' experience of suffering shouldn't strike or surprise them because they see God's sovereign hand amidst suffering. Peter instructs believers that when they experience suffering, they "should commit or entrust themselves to their faithful creator." Schreiner comments, "the reference to God as Creator (*ktistes*) implies God's sovereignty, for the creator of the world is also sovereign over it."

e. A Few Principles from Textual Observations

We may gather a few principles from these textual observations. First, the understanding of God's Sovereignty functions to assure us that things are never out of God's control. Second, the understanding of God's Sovereignty also informs us that God is not surprised when his people suffer and endure hardships. In the midst of that, however, he only expects us them to put their trust in him. Lastly, the understanding of God's Sovereignty also demonstrates that sometimes God does not choose to take away the suffering, hardships, and persecution. Instead, he empowers his people with grace and strength to persevere!

IV. CONCLUSION

In some regions of the world, we are witnessing a growing trend of persecution where believers are going through immense pressure, torture, discrimination, and hatred. As we see in the New Testament, the early church was not unfamiliar with such suffering and persecution. Suffering, hardships, trials, and persecution were in the DNA of the early church.

What motivated the early church to persevere in the midst of suffering and persecution and stand firm was God's attribute of sovereignty over Satan's hand in suffering and persecution. The early church firmly believed that God's sovereignty extends over all things, including the presence of evil, sin, and suffering in this world.

The attribute of God's sovereignty was a key response of the early church to suffering and persecution. We must believe that the suffering and pain of God's people is not an accident. Rather, we should be firm in our belief that God is sovereign over every kind of suffering we encounter.

The biblical response to our fear of suffering, pain, trials, and persecution is not to merely stand passively and wait for the storm to pass, but to remember that God is in control and he is good. This should be encouraging to the present churches which dwell in hostile contexts. Believers must know that even though the situation around us may look very bleak and discouraging, the Bible reminds us that God is always in control of history, and we are challenged to believe that even the present persecution will ultimately be used by God to carry out his great purposes.

Exploring God's Attributes in Dialogue
With the Hymnology of Eastern Women

DR. GRACE AL-ZOUGHBI

Assistant Professor,
Arab Baptist Theological Seminary
Accreditation Officer, Middle East and North Africa
Association for Theological Education
Palestine

I t is not a simple task to identify and define the theological contribution of Middle Eastern women. Traditionally, public theological spaces have been primarily masculine domains, and not a space where females easily find expression and belonging. While history does not record many Middle Eastern female-authored theological treatises, nor their significant leadership in public ecclesial spaces. However, this is not to say that women have not undertaken the key theological task of proclamation and witness to the triune God and his self-revelation through Christ and the Spirit, or that they have not undertaken profound acts of spiritual leadership.

Born and raised in the Middle East, one of my earliest memories about Christianity is the vibrant sound of the Syriac female choirs as I strolled down past the Syriac church in Star Street in my little town of Bethlehem. During my recent field research in the Middle East, I was equally struck by the voices of women in other Eastern traditions, heads endowed with a white lace, voices tuned, and hearts adorned as they sang together. These contemporary experiences draw on a rich theological history. Since the earliest days of the faith, Middle Eastern women have been Christian theologians. Their means of expressing, indeed proclaiming, theology have been contextualized in culturally appropriate roles. Historically, Eastern women not only 'sang' hymns, but their hymns were filled with theology—God's teaching. Based on biblical passages, the songs they sang were a 'vehicle of their theology,' as Sebastian Brock terms it. Their faith was no less 'living and active,' nor their theology less profound, than that of more well-known theologians.

In this paper, I will argue that there is significant potential to be found in identifying and listening to the theological voice as it has been given expression in alternative forms, specifically in the form of sung hymns, both individual and communal. This paper seeks to give an account of Eastern Christian women in the context of hymnology, but particularly Arab Christian women in conversation with Syriac women in a wider discourse within global Christianity. This contribution will also explore how Eastern women, made in the image and likeness of God, have witnessed to God's attributes, and how they help us understand that all theology is a finite, human response to the self-revelation of the infinite God. At its simplest, we might suggest, the attributes of God answer these two questions: "Who is God?" and "what is God like?" The pieces I highlight in this paper give us an answer.

We will begin with the Magnificat as Mary's dialogue with God using the tradition of poetry, and how women then consequently used this very distinctive style of doing theology. In reflecting on the song of St. Mary as an early biblical poetic writing from a female theologian, we shall consider how through her praise, she is uniquely describing the attributes of God. Moving from this consideration of an individual example, we will then consider St. Ephrem and how during the Syriac era, dedicated women monastics emerged, such as the Daughters of the Covenant or Bnāt Qyāmā, who chanted St Ephrem's hymns in public worship. St. Ephrem encouraged women in their hymnology endeavors, and so his hymns demonstrate a way in which God's attributes may be given new depth from a hymnal perspective. Hymns describe the attributes of God in sung poetry, including his love, justice, mercy and holiness—among others. Both Mary's song, the Magnificat, and my example text from St Ephrem's Hymns of the Nativity, particularly focus on God's attributes as they are revealed through the incarnation; in Christ, God makes himself known to us as he is in himself.

This progression of women engaging in theology, through the medium of hymnology, has led to exciting theological developments, with strong potential for a whole new dynamic and a revivalist context. I will suggest that by intentionally exploring the attributes of God through hymnology—and other less traditional ways of undertaking theological reflection—women will be given space to reimagine and reengage in theological reflection.

I. THE ORIGINS OF THE SYRIAC CHURCH

To begin, some important historical context will help us frame the matters which we will consider. The ecclesial, theological, cultural, and spiritual origins and development of the Syriac church are intensely complex and mirror its geographical spread from the West Syriac to the East Syriac tradition. The term Syriac Christianity refers to the various Middle Eastern and Indian churches which belong to the Syriac tradition. Since late antiquity they have divided liturgically and doctrinally into three main groups: First, the Syrian Orthodox Church sometimes known erroneously as the Jacobite Church, which has rejected the doctrinal definition of the council of Chalcedon (451), and insists on the oneness of humanity and divinity in the incarnate Christ. Second, the Church of the East, sometimes known wrongly as the Nestorian or Assyrian Church, which has on different grounds rejected the council of Chalcedon, essentially because it did not distinguish strictly enough between the two natures in Christ. Third, the Maronites of the Lebanon, who have come to accept the definitions of Chalcedon.[1]

---

1 Sebastian Brock. 'The Syriac Churches in Ecumenical Dialogue on Christology', in A. O'Mahony (ed.),

Cutting across this scheme has been the creation of eastern rite Catholic churches.[2]

Christians of the Syrian churches perished in large numbers through the genocide, slaughter and deportation of Syriac Christians by Ottoman forces during World War I. In the oral tradition of the Syrian Orthodox, 1915, which is known as *sayfo*, '(the year of) the sword' or *firmano*, '(the year of) the firman' (i.e. of the warrant to kill the Christian population),[3] large numbers of churches were destroyed, but are currently being resuscitated by the faith of the saints. This is taking place through the vital mission and evangelism of the living stones in these churches, as well as their contributions to theological scholarship.

Hymn singing is a well-established practice in the Eastern churches. It is a gift from Eastern Christianity and the Syriac tradition which has been extended to the Protestant Church, rather than the other way around. It has been adopted by the Protestant tradition, as evidenced by the "schools" or even "altars" of praise which are spread all throughout the modern Middle East. This signals the increasing openness in the Christian world to the great Syriac Christian tradition, and new willingness to engage in dialogue. My exploration of hymnology today is a practical example of how this might be undertaken and is of global relevance.

II. SONGS IN THE SCRIPTURES: THE MAGNIFICAT AS AN EXAMPLE

As a creative method of worship, poetic theology was part of God's intention throughout biblical history. All Middle Eastern Christian cults are sung. A read liturgy would be an exception.[4] Singing the liturgy is thus an integral part of the exercise of faith. Eastern women not only 'sang' hymns, but their hymns were filled with theology—knowledge of God.

Eastern Christianity. Studies in Modern History, Religion and Politics (London, 2004), 44.

2   The term 'Syrian' used to designate individual churches is thus much broader than the geographical area of modern Syria. There have long been Syrian churches in India, but they now spread over all five continents, with sizeable diaspora communities in western Europe, the Caucasian states, North and South America and Australasia.

3   The figures given by Bishop (later Patriarch) Ephrem Barsaum in 1919 put the figure for Syrian Orthodox losses alone at over 90,000, more than a third of its population in the Middle East. Eight out of the twenty dioceses in the Middle East were either totally, or very largely, wiped out, and whole areas which had formerly had a sizeable Syrian Orthodox population were now left with none, since those who had escaped the massacres had fled elsewhere.

4   Severine Gabry-Thienpont and Olivier Tourn, *Christian Music and Worship in the Middle East*, in *The Rowman & Littlefield Handbook of Christianity in the Middle East*, edited by Mitri Raheb and Mark A. Lamport, The Rowman & Littlefield Handbook Series, 387- 397, 395 Lanham: Rowman & Littlefield, 2020.

Mary, the mother of Jesus, features prominently in all the Syriac liturgical and literary traditions. A special commemoration day, the 'Praises of Mary,' devoted to her following the Nativity, is found in both Eastern and Western Syriac tradition, on the second Friday after the Nativity in the former, and on 26 December.[5] This is particularly demonstrated in her song, situated at the beginning of Luke's Gospel where we see Mary positioned as knowledgeable of the Scriptures, living out inspiring faith, and thus receptive to what God was saying to her. Mary's profound song strikes me as the earliest writing from a female theologian of the early church. The song of Mary is an example of early biblical poetic writing from a female theologian and her understanding of God's attributes. It includes the most developed understanding of Jesus, the incarnate God, in Luke's Gospel. The deeply theological words of the Magnificat are a revelation about God, the nature of God, and how God responds to humanity, and humanity to God. It is a song of hope, coming from a young Nazarene woman, a real yearning to experience God acting in the world.

As our starting point, it is helpful to reflect on the meaningful words found in the Magnificat. Here is the Gospel of Christ, Luke 1:46-55:

> And Mary said:
> "My soul glorifies the Lord
> [47] and my spirit rejoices in God my Savior,
> [48] for he has been mindful
>   of the humble state of his servant.
> From now on all generations will call me blessed,
> [49] for the Mighty One has done great things for me—
>   holy is his name.
> [50] his mercy extends to those who fear him,
>   from generation to generation.
> [51] he has performed mighty deeds with his arm;
>   he has scattered those who are proud in their inner most thoughts.
> [52] he has brought down rulers from their thrones
>   but has lifted up the humble.
> [53] he has filled the hungry with good things
>   but has sent the rich away empty.
> [54] he has helped his servant Israel,

---

5 Sebastian Brock, 'Mary in Syriac tradition', in *Mary's Place in Christian Dialogue*, ed. A. Stacpoole (1982), 182–91, 185.

remembering to be merciful
[55] to Abraham and his descendants forever,
    just as he promised our ancestors."

What strikes me in Mary's words is the juxtaposition between the sovereignty of God and his compassion to the poor and the lowly. he is a God of justice. he sees and he knows. he is mighty as the song reiterates (49, 51), yet rightly opposes the proud rulers and the rich (I think we can think of several of these in our own context—and in the global context too). On the contrary, God has not forgotten about the humble (48, 52) but has lifted them up. he remains their hope which is in contrast to human's worldly view of their self-sufficiency. I like how intimately Mary thinks of God, and how she addresses him as her own Savior.

These attributes provide profound insights into the nature and character of God. Mary articulates her song, particularly as one who has met God within human history. Her prophetic declaration in the Magnificat anticipates the way that Jesus reshapes humanity's knowledge of God as God is within himself. Here are some key examples:

1. Mindfulness and Mercy (Verses 48, 50, 54)
    a. *Mindful of the Humble:* God is attentive and caring towards the humble and lowly. Mary acknowledges that God has taken notice of her humble state.
    b. *Merciful:* God's mercy extends to those who fear Him, across all generations. he remembers to be merciful to his people.
        i. "his mercy extends to those who fear him, from generation to generation."
        ii. "he has helped his servant Israel, remembering to be merciful."

2. Holiness (Verse 49)
    a. *Holy:* God is inherently holy, set apart, and pure. Mary proclaims the holiness of God's name.
        i. "Holy is his name."

3. Power and Might (Verse 49, 51)
    a. *Mighty:* God is powerful and capable of doing great things. Mary refers to him as the Mighty One.
        i. "For the Mighty One has done great things for me."

b. *Performs Mighty Deeds:* God performs powerful acts and shows his strength.

    i. "he has performed mighty deeds with his arm."

4. Justice (Verses 51-53)
   a. *Scatters the Proud:* God is just and brings down those who are proud and arrogant.

    i. "he has scattered those who are proud in their inmost thoughts."

   b. *Brings Down Rulers:* God deposes the powerful from their thrones, showing his authority over earthly powers.

    i. "he has brought down rulers from their thrones but has lifted up the humble."

   c. *Lifts Up the Humble:* God elevates those who are humble and lowly.

    i. "But has lifted up the humble."

   d. *Provides for the Needy:* God satisfies the hungry with good things, indicating his provision and care for the needy.

    i. "he has filled the hungry with good things but has sent the rich away empty."

   e. *Faithfulness* (Verses 54-55)

   f. *Faithful to his Promises*: God is faithful and remembers his promises to his people, particularly the covenant made with Abraham and his descendants.

    i. "he has helped his servant Israel, remembering to be merciful to Abraham and his descendants forever, just as he promised our ancestors."

These attributes reflect a God who is both transcendent in his holiness and power, and immanent in his mercy and faithfulness to his people; the fact there is no tension between God as he is in himself and God who is towards us; the way God acts towards us in Christ is entirely consistent with his internal perfections. The Magnificat thus provides a rich theological portrait of God, celebrating his involvement in human history and his care for the lowly and oppressed. The Creator of the world has become part of his creation; he has come to dwell as God with us. Mary's hymn celebrates the history of God's actions in Israel and looks forward to the redemption that is made available in Jesus Christ.

Based on our reading of Mary's hymn, it would be interesting to think about the transformative or even revolutionary power of some of the divine attributes.

How does its nature as a "song of reversals" impact the view of God, or vice versa? All the more so since classic theology has often been accused of supporting patriarchy. An important comment here is that the Magnificat reminds us of the importance of the voices of women in Christian theology, and indeed serves as an encouragement to Christian women, particularly where they have experienced marginalization. In a sociological sense—and reflecting on my own context as a Palestinian woman—many women have felt powerless. They have felt powerless in a Patriarchal world, and as part of the Christian minority. In reality, the Magnificat reminds us that women have strength in God and are able to articulate his attributes to all.

Centuries later in the Middle East, women continue reflect on the Magnificat, which brings hope to what seems like a hopeless context... Mary's life included suffering, but her hymn of praise expressed hope for a better future. Hers is a triumphant song of reversals: the proud are brought low, the humble lifted up, the hungry are fed while the rich go without. While living in oppressive circumstances, Mary triumphed as she prophesied the future.

The power of this, is that we are reflecting on this hymn now, generations before have listened to this, coming generations will listen to it. This is an ongoing conversation, always embedded in the story of humanity in our complex world.

III. ST. EPHREM THE SYRIAN

We have explored how the Magnificat is a representative example of an individual hymn and its declaration of God's characteristics. We turn now to a communal example, how St. Ephrem the Syrian, Poet and theologian, contributed to the role of women in hymnology and understanding God's attributes.

Poetry serves as a much-needed antidote to that tradition of theologising which seeks to provide theological definitions.[6] Sebastian Brock writes: "It is probably the universal expectation today that a theologian will write in prose, and most people would be surprised to learn that poetry can also be an excellent vehicle for theology. Indeed, examples of this can readily be found in the history of both the Latin West and the Greek East but it is above all in the earlier writers of the Syriac Orient that one finds this tradition of using poetry as a vehicle for theology most

---

6   Gordon Wakefield, 'John Wesley and Ephraem Syrus.' *Hugoye: Journal of Syriac Studies 1.2* (1998 [2010]): 273–286, 282.

prominently."[7] Fourth-century theologian Ephrem of Nisibis, wrote lyric poetry that conveys to his audience a carefully thought-out theological vision of the relationship between creator and creation, of the course of salvation history, and of the ways by which human beings can come to the knowledge of God. In 1920, at a time when this aspect of St. Ephrem's poetry was barely recognised in the West, Pope Benedict XV proclaimed St. Ephrem a doctor of the universal church.

Ephrem, known as the "Harp of the Spirit" has always been highly regarded in the Syriac tradition, but his reception in the West has not always been favourable. In recent decades, however, his work has been highly praised, and comprehensive studies by notable scholars such as Robert Murray and Sebastian Brock have led to a deeper appreciation of his symbolic theological method. The increasing awareness of the significance of Syriac language and culture as the *Lingua Franca* in the Middle East between the fourth to seventh centuries CE has developed the view that the greatest writer in the history of the Syriac-speaking church, Ephrem, stands as the pillar of Syriac Christian literature and culture.[8]

The cycle of hymns on the Nativity by St Ephrem provides us with an obvious beginning point for interacting with his work. In the following passage, which has been beautifully set to music by Sir John Tavener in his work "Thunder Entered Her," Ephrem's use of paradox is very much in evidence. He begins by addressing the infant Christ himself, writing about his mother Mary:

> "Your mother is a cause for wonder: The Lord entered into her
> - and became a servant;
>
> he who is the Word entered—and became silent within her;
>
> Thunder entered her—and made no sound;
>
> There entered the Shepherd of all and in her he became the Lamb, bleating as he comes forth. Your mother's womb has reversed the roles: the Establisher of all entered in his richness but came forth poor;
>
> The Exalted One entered her but came forth meek;
>
> The Splendrous One entered her but came forth having put on a lowly hue.

---

7 Sebastian Brock. "The Syriac Orient: A Third 'Lung' for the Church?" 71 (January 1, 2005): 5–20, 8.
8 Sebastian Brock, *The Luminous Eye: The Spiritual World Vision of Saint Ephrem the Syrian*. 1992.

The Mighty One entered, and put on insecurity from her womb;

The Provisioner of all entered—and experienced hunger; he who gives drink to all entered - and experienced thirst: naked and stripped there came forth from her he who clothes all."
(Hymns on the Nativity, XI.6-8).[9]

Evoking similar themes to the Magnificat, St. Ephrem helps us to engage with the mystery of the union of the divinity and humanity of Christ. The Lord becomes a servant. The Mighty and exalted becomes meek and insecure. The rich becomes poor. The provisioner, experienced hunger and thirst. This beautiful hymn emphasizes the paradoxes and mysteries of the Incarnation, where God, in the person of Jesus Christ, took on human form and experienced human limitations and sufferings; and in doing so, reveals God to us. Below are the key attributes and themes highlighted in this poetic reflection:

1. Divine Humility
    a. *Incarnation as Servitude*: The Lord, in his divinity, entered into Mary and became a servant.
        i. "The Lord entered into her - and became a servant."
    b. *Silence of the Word:* The eternal Word of God, who created all things, entered into Mary and became silent.
        i. "he who is the Word entered - and became silent within her."

2. Majesty and Meekness
    a. *Thunder and Silence*: The powerful and majestic God, symbolized by thunder, entered Mary quietly.
        i. "Thunder entered her - and made no sound."
    b. *Shepherd and Lamb*: The Shepherd of all, representing authority and guidance, became the Lamb, symbolizing meekness and sacrifice.
        i. "There entered the Shepherd of all and in her he became the Lamb, bleating as he comes forth."

---

9 The full cycle of Hymns on the Nativity have been translated into English by Kathleen McVey in her Ephrem the Syrian: Hymns (Mahwah: Paulist Press, 1989). The translations used here are taken from *my Bride of Light: Hymns on Mary from the Syriac Churches* (Kottayam: St Ephrem Ecumenical Research Institute, 1994).

3. Reversal of Roles
   a. *Richness to Poverty:* The one who established all things entered in richness but was born into poverty.
      i. "The Establisher of all entered in his richness but came forth poor."
   b. *Exaltation to Meekness*: The exalted and glorious one entered Mary and was born in meekness.
      i. "The Exalted One entered her but came forth meek."
   c. *Splendor to Lowliness*: The splendorous one took on a lowly appearance.
      i. "The Splendrous One entered her but came forth having put on a lowly hue."

4. Divine Vulnerability
   a. *Mighty to Insecure*: The Almighty entered and experienced human vulnerability.
      i. "The Mighty One entered, and put on insecurity from her womb."
   b. *Provisioner to Needy*: The one who provides for all experienced human needs such as hunger and thirst.
      i. "The Provisioner of all entered - and experienced hunger; he who gives drink to all entered - and experienced thirst."
   c. *Clothed to Naked*: The one who clothes all creation entered the world naked and stripped.
      i. "Naked and stripped there came forth from her he who clothes all."

This hymn profoundly illustrates the mystery of the Incarnation, where God, in his infinite greatness, chose to enter into the human experience in the most humble and vulnerable manner. It emphasizes the themes of divine humility, the paradox of majesty and meekness, the reversal of roles, and the profound vulnerability that Jesus embraced by becoming human. This reflection invites us to marvel at the depth of God's love and the mystery of the Incarnation, where the divine became intimately involved in the human condition.[10]

---

10   Space is limited here to discuss which of Christ's attributes are divine attributes, and whether can we easily distinguish between the divine and human attributes? However, worth to refer briefly to is the place of kenosis in Ephrem's theology? The concept of kenosis, which means "self-emptying," is a significant theme in the theology of St. Ephrem the Syrian, particularly in his understanding of the Incarnation. St. Ephrem emphasizes the humility of Christ in the Incarnation. For Ephrem, the act of God becoming man is the ultimate expression of humility and love. Christ's self-emptying is seen as an essential part of his mission to redeem humanity.

IV. WOMEN'S CHOIRS[11] - BANAT QYAMA[12]

St. Ephrem wrote hymns containing profound theology, but women's choirs sang them. What follows is a discussion on the Sons and Daughters of the Covenant who sang St. Ephrem's hymns, and what these teach us about the attributes of God.

The institution of the Sons and Daughters of the Covenant, the *Bnay* and *Bnat Qyama* is one of the best-known characteristics of ancient Syriac Christianity. Apparently originating in the third century CE, the office was characterized by vows of celibacy, voluntary poverty, and service to the local priest or bishop. Members were supposed to live separately with others of the same office, or with other families. The office appears to have been widespread in Syriac speaking territories both east and west by the fourth century. The early fourth century acts of the Edessan Martyrs Shmona and Guria note that Daughters of the Covenant were being specifically targeted, along with priests and deacons, for public tortures and execution during the Diocletianic Persecution, attesting to their public prominence.

The Daughters of the Covenant held a distinctive office in Syriac Christianity for its public ministry of sacred music performed for liturgical purposes in civic churches. Syriac tradition ascribed the establishment of these choices of consecrated virgins to Ephrem the Syrian. Jacob of Srug's homily on St. Ephrem presents these choirs as modeling soteriological as well as eschatological significance for the larger church community.[13]

---

11   According to Jacob of Sarug, Ephrem the Syrian (late 4th c.) established a choir of women to sing his hymns. In this role, they embodied and taught the eschatological and soteriological ideals of the wider religious community. By the medieval period the bnay/bnāt qyāmā had declined in importance. On the one hand, the bnāt qyāmā became assimilated with deaconesses and nuns. On the other hand, bnay qyāmā were eclipsed by both clerics within the ecclesiastic hierarchy and cenobitic monks. Aside from a smattering of literary references, the bnay/bnāt qyāmā had largely disappeared by the tenth century. The geographic extent of the bnay/bnāt qyāmā was much broader than the region marked here, namely the Roman province of Osroene in the fifth century, which was chosen both for the sake of simplicity and due to the importance of Edessa as a cultural and religious center. Syriac Christianity and the institution of the bnay/bnāt qyāmā certainly extended into other provinces of the Roman empire and the Persian empire to the east.

12   The precise social and linguistic origins of the designation are debated. The noun often translated "covenant" (qyāmā) derives from the root qwm ("to stand"), and it has a wide range of meanings, including status, station, oath, and contract. Robert Murray has suggested an origin for the term in baptismal rites, where the catechumen took a proverbial "stand" and rose from the waters (Murray 1974/5). According to another view, the related noun for "resurrection" (qyāmtā) may have played a role in this use of bnay qyāmā (cf. Luke 20:36). Finally, M.R. Macina has argued that the term related to Greek kanon and tentatively proposed that the bnay qyāmā – "members of the [church] institution" – were more integrated into the clerical hierarchy (Macina 1999).

13   Susan Ashbrook Harvey. "Revisiting the Daughters of the Covenant." *Hugoye: Journal of Syriac Studies* 8, no. 1 (February 1, 2011): 125–50. https://doi.org/10.31826/hug-2011-080111, 125.

Late antique Syriac sources mention women's choirs with brief yet vivid references. Jacob of Sarug (d. 521), for example, refers to the women's choirs as '[female] teachers' (*malphanyatha*, in the feminine plural), whose singing declared the 'proclamation' (*karuzutha*, corresponding to the Greek kerygma) in the liturgy. According to Jacob, the 'pure' voices of these 'pious' women sang 'instructive melodies,' with 'soft tones' and 'wonderful tunes.'[14] Biblical and underpinned by God's words and truth, these melodies and tunes were used to defeat the heresies of the earliest centuries. Both Ephrem the Syrian (d. 373) and Jacob of Sarug urged their congregations to pay close heed to the women's choirs, which, Jacob admonished, were nothing less than a gift from God for the church's benefit. The more one heard these choirs, Jacob assured his listeners, the more one would become 'pure, modest, and full of hope and discernment.' In one homily, he extolled the women's choir in a prayer, 'By the sweet voices of the young women who sing Your praise, [O Christ], / You have captured the world.'[15] A reminder for us that it is not sufficient to only know the attributes of God, and have a cognitive experience of these, but to also declare and embody them as we seek to make God known in our context.

Scholars, including Joseph Amar and Kathleen McVey have drawn attention to an important, but little-considered aspect of the work of the female members of this office: that of the liturgical choirs of the daughters of the Covenant. Daughters of the Covenant were charged with the task of singing psalms and various kinds of hymns in certain liturgical celebrations of the civic churches.

This practice contrasted sharply, for example, with the normal pattern of the Greek and Latin civic churches to the west. These areas permitted women's singing in convent choirs. But with the possible exception of Ambrose's cathedral in Milan, women's voices were excluded from choral participation in civic liturgical celebrations.[16] While deaconesses were allowed to visit and instruct female catechumens and women who were ill, the role of civic liturgical singing positioned daughters of the Covenant publicly in the midst of the entire worshiping community.

---

14 Susan Ashbrook Harvey, "Training the Women's Choir: Ascetic Practice and Liturgical Education in Late Antique Syriac Christianity, in Wisdom on the Move: Late Antique Traditions in Multicultural Conversation," *Essays in Honor of Samuel Rubenson,* Edited by, Susan Ashbrook Harvey, Thomas Arentzen, Henrik Rydell Johnsén, Andreas Westergren, Leiden, Boston: Brill, 2020, 204-223, 205
15 Ibid. See Psalm 149:6 the high praises of God are linked with the sword of the Spirit (the Word) and bring judgment on evil.
16 Susan Ashbrook Harvey. "Revisiting the Daughters of the Covenant." 125–50. https://doi.org/10.31826/hug-2011-080111, 128.

Skilled singing was not enough for the task of choir or chanter; one had to know the content one was singing, and to understand it rightly. Proper performance of liturgy required serious biblical and theological training. Often the hymns they performed told stories of biblical women, in terms that spoke to the needs, desires, and obligations of the present congregation. As such, women's choirs and the women's stories they sang featured women's significance for the church's health and flourishing, both liturgically and in the social order.[17]

V. CONTEMPORARY WOMEN OF THE MIDDLE EAST

Perhaps this hymnology space is where women are well situated in the Middle East to make a difference. The following lines will discuss the envisioning of this space. With their singing, Daughters of the Covenant they preserved and taught theology. Singing is an easy way to remember. People carry it with them through the week, so it stays in their hearts and minds. The tunes they sing are deeply contextualized culturally, and so bring people to true worship. Singing is non-threatening, so it works well missiologically, but within a culture, not imposed from outside.

Part of my endeavour is to think theologically about the historically deep, rich and complex ecclesial setting in the Middle East today. One of the questions on which I have been reflecting is how Arab Protestant women might reimagine and reengage in theological reflection. This contribution strengthens my desire to see Arab Protestant women acknowledged in the theological academy and their potential reached and released to contribute theologically and poetically in the church and academy so that the church can benefit from theologically informed poetry. Poetry has many of the same qualities as hymnology. Because of rhythm, meter, rhyme, and parallelism, it is also easy to remember and recite. Poetic styles are also cultural, so not foreign impositions. Theology has a lot of mystery, so metaphor is an important tool to understanding. There are alternate, non-expository ways to study and communicate theology. Women have worked long and well in these ways and could do so again. Women also have a theological role to play in the church.

I envision a significant moment in the Middle East offering a new dynamic context which allows for a new theological engagement with moments of contemporary significance for culture and society in the Middle East, but also to retrieve a

---

17   Susan Ashbrook Harvey, "Training the Women's Choir" 2020, 204-223, 217.

renewal of Christian theological thought within this ecclesial complexity and contemporary religious challenges. I posit this as a real opportunity for women to offer a distinct voice to contemporary church leadership and theological renewal both as receivers, but also as educators. This is an intentional ecumenical undertaking of mutual respect and sharing of scholarly and theological ideas and thought. The contributions of women will help overcome challenges which confront the presence of Christianity in the Middle East. It would undoubtedly strengthen the church in terms of its theological and ecclesial contribution, but it would also be resourced by Arab Christian women who have often been at the margins of this endeavor. There has been a distinct lacuna in Protestant Christianity, which has never sought to update or creatively develop its ecclesial contributions, particularly in relation to the complexities of Eastern Christianity within the Middle East.

I suggest that Protestant Christianity in the Middle East requires a deeper maturing and expansion of its own self-consciousness, towards its own originality and how that allows for it to engage with the wider community of Christianity in the region who are themselves experiencing dynamic change. This includes revival of certain trends within the Eastern tradition, which have been received in the wider Christian tradition, despite a certain type of Protestant reticence which is built within its reformational character. The anticipated Renaissance becomes the modern application of this. That woman again, in a way that is culturally appropriate for this new generation, pick up the mantle of being theologians.

Fairouz, the Syriac Maronite singer beautifully sang about Mary, the mother of Jesus the following words in an original Syriac tune. A great figure in Arabic cultures, her Father is a Syriac Christian, mother is Syriac Christian, one is Maronite the other is Orthodox. Is Fairouz echoing the deep culture of St. Ephrem in her song?

> '[Anā 'l-ummu 'l-ḥazīnatu wa-mā man yu'azzī-hā], '[18]
> 'I am the mournful mother, without any comforters.'

> انأ الألم الحزينة ومن امو يعزيها
> Anā 'l-ummu 'l-ḥazīnatu wa-mā man yu'azzī-hā
> I am the mournful mother, without any comforters

---

18 فيروز - انا الأم الحزينة, 2012, https://www.youtube.com/watch?v=9OzmKcAsutE. Narrow transliteration applied, as classical grammar, showing nominal notional declension as superiors. These, of course, are not usually shown. Note the lines of the song have a line-end rhyming requirement: -īhā. How the song is actually articulated will vary from suggested transliterated text.

فليكن موت ابنك حياة لطالبيها

Fal-yakun maut^u 'bnⁱ-ki ḥayāt^{an} li-ṭālibī-hā

May the death of your Son be life to its seekers [Refrain]

أم يسوع قد بكت فأبكت ناظريها

Umm^u Yasū' qad bakat fa-abkat nāẓirī-hā

The mother of Jesus cried and made onlookers cry

May the death of your Son be life to its seekers

لهفي على أمة قتلت راعيها

Lahf-ī 'alā ummatⁱⁿ qatalat rā'ī-hā

My passion is for a nation that killed its Shepherd

May the death of your Son be life to its seekers

ناح الحمام على تشتت أهليها

Nāḥa al-Hamām 'alā tashattut ahlī-hā

The doves mourned the scattering of its people

May the death of your Son be life to its seekers

عذارى أورشليم تبكي على بنيها

'Adhārā Ūrushalīm tabkī 'alā banī-hā

The virgins of Jerusalem are lamenting their sons

May the death of your Son be life to its seekers

تعالوا إلى مريم أمه نعزيها

Ta'ālū ilā Maryam^a ummⁱ-hi nu'zī-hā

Let's come to Mary, his mother and bring her comfort

May the death of your Son be life to its seekers

This lament, expresses sorrow and grief, reflecting on the sorrow of Mary, the mother of Jesus, during his crucifixion. The repeated refrain emphasizes the hope that Jesus' death brings life to those who seek it. The lament reflects various attributes of God, particularly focusing on the context of Jesus' crucifixion and its impact on his mother, Mary. The following are some attributes of God that can be derived from this lament:

1. *Compassionate:* The lament speaks of Mary's sorrow and the communal grief, indicating God's awareness and empathy towards human suffering.

2. *Life-Giver:* The refrain, "May the death of your Son be life to its seekers," highlights God's role as the giver of life, even through the death of Jesus.

3. *Sacrificial:* The reference to Jesus' death underscores the attribute of God's sacrificial love for humanity.

4. *Just:* The lament's mention of a "nation that killed its Shepherd" reflects God's concern for justice and righteousness.

5. *Merciful:* The lament calls for comfort to Mary, the mother of Jesus, indicating God's mercy and willingness to console those who are mourning.

6. *Provider:* The lament suggests that through Jesus' sacrifice, God provides spiritual nourishment and hope to believers.

7. *Sovereign:* The context of the lament reflects God's sovereignty over life and death, and his ultimate plan for redemption through Jesus' sacrifice.

8. *Comforter:* The call to comfort Mary, Jesus' mother, reflects God's attribute as a source of comfort and solace to the afflicted and grieving.

These attributes collectively highlight the triune God, who through the incarnation, who is deeply involved in human suffering, offering compassion, justice, mercy, and ultimate hope through the sacrificial act of Jesus. Theology is only ever a response to God's self-revelation in these majestic acts of love. We recognize the limitations of such human activity. Theology is a human endeavor, and we must undertake it in humility. When we refer to God's attributes, we honor God and worship him in doing so. Theology can be done in theological arguments in theological paper, or it can be done just as faithfully in songs. Human language points to a mystery that we cannot contain with our language. As T.F Torrance reminds us:

> It is above all through the incarnation, the Word of God become flesh, that God reveals to us something of his own nature as the mighty living God who is who he eternally is and yet who will not be without us whom he has created for fellowship with himself and with whom he freely shares his own divine Life and Light and Love. It is in Jesus Christ, therefore, that we really understand and think aright about God's unchanging constancy, for it is in him, the only-begotten Son of the Father, that we may really know God

in accordance with the inmost nature of his eternal being.[19]

As we reflect on God's triune self-revelation as the God who makes himself known to us through the incarnation by becoming human, dwelling in our midst, and then sending the Spirit who gives life to the church and is at work in the church's process of understanding theology, we can be tempted in the process of seeking to understand God, to create structures that don't always follow the narrative flow of revelation. However, in listening to these hymns, we hear an alternative approach to the often more structured shape of systematic theology. These hymns are no less true theology but expressed in poetry and hymns. While much written-theology seeks to explain doctrine, hymns proclaim it. The song of Mary declares the goodness and justice of God, and while it isn't a theological treatise, it is no less profound. We must consider the way that we see and hear the attributes of God proclaimed in alternative ways, which helps us to enrich our vision of God.

VI. CONCLUSION

Although Christianity in the Middle East is a highly contested and dynamic field of study, it is an indispensable element of understanding Christianity and conveying God's attributes in a global context. Within the Middle Eastern context there is a constant awareness of engaging with other theological traditions that have their own understanding of theology and education. There is an opportunity for women to contribute a distinct [singing] voice and a leading role within Middle Eastern Christian theological education as we seek to understand more about the attributes of God.

As I reflect again on the confidence of the tradition which I am exploring, I am reminded that singing of God's goodness, holiness, justice and mercy in individual song and communal hymn, is no less the "theological task" than that which we might consider the more traditional approach of the systematic theologian: publishing a book.

The Middle East is in dire need of the original singing by the people of the land, the proclamation of God's goodness, justice, and graciousness. We can see through the

---

19 Thomas F. Torrance, *The Christian Doctrine of God, One Being Three Persons* (Edinburgh, Scotland: T&T Clark, 1996), 238.

Magnificat, in St. Ephrem's poem, and in Fairouz' song, how God's attributes are described for us. We share in that description because we share in the image and likeness of God. By taking our lead from Mary in the Magnificat, and the Syriac tradition represented by our exploration of St Ephrem and traditions like that of the public singing of the daughters of the Covenant, Protestant Christians might be able to helpfully re-engage with history to explore alternative frameworks for allowing females theological voices to be heard as we seek to understand who God is.

The Fatherhood of God
A Biblical-Theological Reflection and Analysis

DR. VIJAI SINGH TAGORE
Associate Professor of New Testament,
Presbyterian Theological Seminary
India

The Fatherhood of God

The appropriateness of the term "Father" as a self-disclosure of God in the Bible has been questioned by some feminists,[1] and is also being discussed within the evangelical debate on gender and transgender issues over the last few decades.[2] The major issue concerns the broader question of God's gender and the appropriateness of the masculine expressions in Scripture describing God and his character.[3] As such, the masculine expression of God as "Father" has been brought into question asking whether it is an essential, eternal and immutable attribute or description of God, or an outdated, time and culture-bound analogy or anthropomorphism that needs to be replaced with feminine or gender-neutral terms in place of "Father."

Renowned Feminist theologian, Mary Daly, famously wrote long ago, "If God is male, then the male is God,"[4] describing the term "Father" and the concept of the Fatherhood of God in the Bible carrying notions of an oppressive patriarchy designed to subjugate women. Proposals have been offered to replace the term "Father" with "Mother" or "Parent" for God to rid patriarchal notions of God from Scripture.[5] There have even been efforts to introduce such changes into the official doctrinal statement of some denominations within evangelicalism.[6] Biblical descriptions of God in masculine expressions or images (husband, king, judge, father) have been sought to be explained away, even denied as a result of the influence and outcome of the patriarchal world in which the Old and New

---

1 E.g., Mary Daly, *Beyond God the Father: Toward a Philosophy of Women's Liberation* (Boston: Beacon, 1973); Paul K. Jewett, *God, Creation, and Revelation* (Grand Rapids, MI: Eerdmans, 1991); Eizabeth Johnson, *She Who is* (New York: Crossroad Publishing, 1996).

2 Ronald Pierce and Erin Heim, "Biblical Images of God as Mother and Spiritual Formation" in *Discovering Biblical Equality: Biblical, Theological, Cultural, and Practical Perspectives,* ed. Ronald Pierce and Cynthia Long Westfall, 3rd ed. (Downers Grove, IL: IVP, 2021), 372–92; Amy Peeler, Women and the Gender of God (Grand Rapids, MI: Eerdmans, 2022).

3 See the discussion in John Frame, *Systematic Theology: An Introduction to Chirstian Belief* (New Jersey: P&R Pub., 2013), 107–114. The background or the context of the issue concerns the wider issue of gender equality within Christendom, especially the role of women in church i.e., the ordination of women into church ministry. Some Bible translations now also include gender-neutral language – e.g. NIV (2011), TNIV (Today's New International Version), NRSV (New Revised Standard Bible), REB (Revised English Bible), NLT (New Living Translation), NCV (New Century Version), CEV (Contemporary English Version). Some even hold that the Bible itself affirms transgender ideology (e.g. Mark Sameth, "Is God Transgender" (August 12, 2016). Available at https://www.nytimes.com/2016/08/13/opinion/is-god-transgender.html. Accessed on 31/12/23.

4 Daly, *Beyond God the Father,* 19.

5 E.g., Peeler, *Women and the Gender,* 17; Pierce and Heim, "Biblical Images of God as Mother," 385.

6 E.g. The United Church of Christ's official website, along with the original Statement of Faith, also lists the Robert V. Moss' adaption of the statement and doxology which do not mention "Father" with references to God available at https://www.ucc.org/what-we-believe/worship/statement-of faith/#:~:text=United%20Church%20 of%20Christ%20Statement,ways%20of%20life%20and%20death. Accessed on 30/12/23. A worship service in the 2018 annual conference of the United Methodist Church in Minnesota had removed "Father," replacing it with "Creator" (available at https://www.christianpost.com/news/umc-minnesota-conference-removes-father-from-apostles-creed-for-worship-service.html. Accessed on 30/12/23).

Testaments were written.[7] There are often constant efforts to strip the Scripture of male conceptions of God by redefining the names and descriptions of God, even of Jesus. As such, the Fatherhood of God has been regarded or questioned as an outdated anthropomorphism, resulting from male-dominant Jewish and Greco-Roman description of God promoting misogyny. Amy Peeler's recent book argues that God is not male even though the Bible uses masculine language to describe God (e.g., Father). Rather, "Mother" or "Parent" are legitimate terms to describe the First Person of the Trinity.[8]

A major issue with such approaches is that they arise from an assumption that the traditional view of God as "Father" puts male gender into a superiority position over female. Such an approach confuses the masculine expressions of God as "Father" or "husband" with the sexed male gender. On the contrary, no orthodox or evangelical theologian holds to the view that God is male. God is neither male, nor female but a non-sexual Spirit (John 4:24.).[9]

However, the eternal God chose to reveal himself to humanity using masculine expression of fatherhood, and the image of "Father" in biblical history. "Father" has been the most significant term for God both traditionally and theologically in the evangelical world. Among all the descriptions, names and attributes of God, "Father" has been the most common and the most familiar term used by Christians worldwide to address God in prayers. The Apostles' Creed begins with the description of God as "Father." Apart from 3 John, every NT canonical book mentions God as "Father." The gospels alone have more than 165 references to God as "Father" or to his fatherhood.[10] Not only was "Father" Jesus' favorite term to address God, but he also taught his disciples and believers to pray addressing God as their "Father" (Matt. 6:9). A closer look at the biblical data confirms that beside his relationship with the Son (Jesus) within the economy of salvation, God the Father chose to reveal himself to mankind in creation and in the history of redemption as "Father."

The biblical evidence reveals that the idea of fatherhood comes from an Eternal and Immutable God (Eph. 3:14) in the context of a Trinitarian (Father-Son) and Covenantal relationship. God is not borrowing human analogy of fatherhood,

---

7   E.g. Daly, *Beyond God the Father,* 19.
8   Peeler, *Women and the Gender,* 17–19.
9   Frame, *Systematic,* 107. For a helpful discussion on male and female imageries of God in the Bible and the theological importance of masculine imagery for God, see Frame, Systematic, 105–114.
10   Cf. Robert H. Stein, "Fatherhood of God," *in Evangelical Dictionary of Biblical Theology* (Grand Rapids, MI: Baker, 1996), 247 (cf. 247–48).

rather sharing his eternal immutable character of fatherhood with humanity.[11] God's Fatherhood is prior to and is the basis of creaturely fatherhood (Eph. 3:14). In fact, eternal generation of the Son is the primary grounds for naming God as Father and God's eternal nature determines his self-disclosure as Father. Herman Bavinck puts it well:

> This name "Father," accordingly, is not a metaphor derived from the earth and attributed to God. Exactly the opposite is true: fatherhood on earth is but a distant and vague reflection of the fatherhood of God (Eph. 3:14-15). God is Father in the true and complete sense of the term... He is solely, purely, and totally Father. He is Father alone; he is Father by nature and Father eternally, without beginning or end."[12]

Before God became the Creator, he was the Father in eternity in an eternal loving relationship. Hence, "Father" is a key term for our understanding of God. The biblical description of God's Fatherhood conveys not just the idea that God is our Creator but the very fact that he is our Redeemer.

This paper attempts to defend the notion that "Fatherhood" is an essential, eternal, and immutable characteristic and attribute of God as revealed in the Scripture and is not time or culture-bound. It must not be replaced or denied. It must continue to be held, defended, cherished, and used in Christian tradition both in theology and worship. To substantiate this claim, support will be sought in a biblical-theological analysis and reflection of the Fatherhood of God in the Bible. It will be shown that God's Fatherhood is a central theme in the Bible, particularly in the NT with Jesus' coming and because of his redemptive work. The theme of God's Fatherhood often appears in the context of redemption both in the Old and New Testaments. As such, the paper will provide a biblical-theological study of the Fatherhood of God highlighting its prevalence and importance in God's self-disclosure to humanity and confirming that Fatherhood is an essential theological characteristic within the divinity of God.

The focus of this paper pertains primarily to the Fatherhood of God in relation to his people. As such, the paper will not focus on the current God and Gender

---

11 Kyle Claunch, "Theological Language and the Fatherhood of God: An Exegetical and Dogmatic Account." Available at https://cbmw.org/2023/11/21/theological-language-and-the-fatherhood-of-god-an-exegetical-and dogmatic-account/. Accessed on 30/12/23.
12 Herman Bavinck, *Reformed Dogmatics,* Vol. II: God and Creation (Baker: Grand Rapids, MI, 2004), 307–308.

debate,[13] as well as the Father-Son relationship within the Trinity regarding the nature of the Son's subordination to the Father.[14]

I. THE FATHERHOOD OF GOD IN THE BIBLE

In the Scripture, the term "Father" or the idea of God's Fatherhood is used in different contexts and may refer to various relationships between God the Father and others. "Father" as a description for God in the Bible has a deeper meaning and wider implications that are often overlooked or are not generally realized. Finlayson and Jensen's categorization helps pointing them out by defining the various facets of God's Fatherhood expressed in four different relationships, namely Creational, Theocentric, Generative, and Adoptive.[15]

Creational Fatherhood of God means he is the Father of all by virtue of creation (Acts 17:28). Since God is the Creator and Sustainer of the whole universe (cf. Job 1:6; 2:1; 38:7; Ps. 8:6; Luke 3:38), and the giver of life to all (cf. Num. 16:22; Acts 17:28–29; Heb.12:9), it includes the fundamental relationship of God with all humans.[16] Without this Fatherhood of God, there will be no humanity at all.[17]

Theocentric Fatherhood of God refers to God's relationship with his covenant people, the nation of Israel. Collectively, God calls Israel his son ("first-born son," Exod. 4:22–23) and refers to himself as its "Father." The context of this relationship is Israel's redemption from slavery in Egypt as a chosen people.[18] As such, God calls himself "Father" to Israel not because he was their Creator but because he was their Redeemer and had established an exclusive covenantal relationship with them. Bray points out this covenantal relationship of God with Israel from Isaiah 63:16–17 and 64:8–9 where Israel was able to call God as

---

13   Nancy Pearcey, *The Toxic War on Masculinity: How Christianity Reconciles the Sexes* (Grand Rapids, MI: Baker, 2023).
14   Much has been debated and written on it. See, Kevin Giles, *The Trinity and Subordinationism: The Doctrine of God and the Contemporary Gender Debate* (Downers Grove: IVP, 2002); Bruce A. Ware, *Father, Son, and the Holy Spirit: Roles, Relationships, and Relevance* (Weaton: Crossway, 2005).
15   R. A. Finlayson and P. F. Jensen, "God," in *New Bible Dictionary*, 3rd ed (Hyderabad: Authentic Books, 2000), 419–20.
16   The Aramaic Abba and its Hebrew cognate av, as well as the Greek pater carry the notions of originator, progenitor, one who imparts life. See, Joseph Henry Thayer, *A Greek-English Lexicon of the New Testament: Being Grimm's Wilke's Clavis Novi Testamenti* (New York: Harper & Brothers, 1889), 494.
17   Cf. Frame, *Systematic Theology,* 105.
18   This covenantal context of God's Fatherhood to Israel is also present in other OT texts even without the word "Father" (Deut. 14:1–2; Ps. 103:13; Jer. 31:20). For a detailed study of the connection of the Fatherhood of God to Israel, see Svetlana Knobnya, "God the Father in the Old Testament," *Evangelical Journal of Theology* 20.2 (2011), 139–148; Goran Medved, "The Fatherhood of God in the Old Testament," *Evangelical Journal of Theology* 10.2 (2016), 203–214.

"Father" because he was their Redeemer.[19] Even within the covenant community in OT, there appears to be a restricted sense of God's Fatherhood where he is only the "Father" of the God-fearing among the nation and not of the whole nation (cf. Ps. 103:13; Mal. 3:17).

Generative Fatherhood of God is only applied to the Second Person of the Trinity, the only begotten Son of God. It is unique since it is not applied to any other creature.[20] Christ speaks of this unique and eternal relationship with the Father repeatedly in the gospels (Matt. 7:21; 10:32, 33; Luke 10:22; 22:29; John 2:16; 5:17). God was his Father by eternal generation, whereas believers are God's children through adoption (John 1:12; Rom. 8:15; Gal. 4:5–6; Eph.1:5).[21] Christ clearly made this distinction between his Sonship and the sonship of believers as indicated in John 20:17 ("my Father and your Father") although the two are linked together since the former is the basis of the latter. He is the pre-existent eternal Son, equal with the Father (Matt. 11:27; John 8:58; 10:30, 38; 14:9; 16:28).[22] Thus, God is not the Father of believers in the same sense he is the Father of Jesus the Son. Jesus never addressed God as "our Father" (Matt. 6:9 is not an exception but Jesus teaching his disciples how they [plural] were to pray to God), also confirmed from his use of "your" (singular and plural) and "my" Father but never "our" Father (Matt. 5:16, 45, 48; 6:1, 4, 6; 7:21; 10:32–33). He is the divine and sinless Son of the Father by nature, whereas believers are sinners who have been adopted by the Father in and through the Son.

Adoptive Fatherhood of God refers to the believers' adoption into the family of God as his children (John 1:12, 13; Rom. 8:15; Gal. 4:5–6; Eph. 1:5) as a result of their union with Christ. The context of this relationship is redemption, which is made possible by Christ's redemptive work (Gal. 3:26).[23] Hence, the Adoptive Fatherhood of God is restricted and exclusive to believers because they become

---

19   Gerald Bray, "God as Father." Available at https://www.thegospelcoalition.org/essay/god-as-father/. Accessed on 28/12/23.

20   Cf. Thomas R. Schriener, *New Testament Theology* (Grand Rapids, MI: Baker, 2008), 130, 136. Bray observes that there is no explanation in the New Testament as to why the Father and the Son are related to each other in this way. They are eternally present in the Trinity, but why one of them is the Father and the other is his Son is a mystery (John 1:1–3). See, Bray, "God as Father."

21   Cf. Frame, *Systematic Theology*, 106. Micheal Horton also points out that Christ is the Son "in a qualitatively different sense, by eternal generation. He is God's Son ontologically (i.e., in his essence) and brings us by adoption into that same intimacy that he enjoys with the Father" Michael Horton, *Pilgrim Theology* [Zondervan: Grand Rapids, MI, 2013], 206.

22   Cf. W. J. Cameron, "Father, God as," in *Evangelical Dictionary Theology*, ed. Walter A. Elwell (Grand Rapids, MI: Baker, 1984), 408; also, Frame, *Systematic*, 106.

23   The regenerating and sanctifying work of the Spirit in believers is also to be understood as a result and privilege of this relationship i.e., adoption into God's family as they become partakers of the divine nature with all the privileges that belong to this filial relationship (Rom. 8:17).

God's children through Jesus.

Finlayson and Jensen's categorization of the Fatherhood of God above points out the different facets or aspects of it that highlight the essentiality of this attribute and its pervasiveness in the biblical-theological narrative. Others have also recognized the various aspects of God's Fatherhood in the biblical account. For example, both Frame and Bray notice and distinguish between a Creational Fatherhood of God, where God is the Father of all in a general sense being their Creator, and a Special Fatherhood towards his chosen people by virtue of his covenant with them.[24] Hence, theologically, the Fatherhood of God is the very character of God and serves as the framework for the doctrine of adoption of believers into God's family (Gal. 3:26). It is deeply connected to the redemptive work of Christ and the covenantal relationship of God with His people both in the Old and the New Testaments, as seen below.

II. FATHERHOOD OF GOD IN THE OLD TESTAMENT

In comparison to the NT, the concept of God as "Father" is not widely and explicitly developed in the OT.[25] Although clearly indicated in some places in the OT, the depiction of God as "Father" is rarely spelled out.[26] Bray observes that the passages in "the Old Testament where the language of fatherhood is used of God are relatively few and their meaning is sometimes unclear."[27] The OT refers to God as a "Father" to the nation of Israel (e.g. Deut. 32:6; Isa. 63:16 [twice]; 64:8; Jer. 3:4, 19; 31:9; Mal. 1:6; 2:10) as their protector, provider, caretaker, and redeemer, and of Israelite kings and certain individuals (2 Sam. 7:14; 1 Chron. 17:13; 22:10; 28:6; Ps. 68:5; 89:26) in a metaphorical sense.[28] Other times, the father imagery is used while the term "Father" is not used (Ex. 4:22–23; Deut. 1:31; 8:5; 14:1; Ps. 2:7; 103:13; Prov. 3:11–12; Jer. 3:22; 31:20; Hos. 11:1–4; Mal. 3:17). The idea of God being the "Father" also emerges in the personal names of the Israelites (e.g. 1 Sam. 8:2; 2 Sam. 8:16).[29] A significant point is that the Fatherhood of God to

---

24   Frame, *Systematic Theology,* 105; also, Bray, "God as Father." Also, Gerald Bray, *God has Spoken: A History of Christian Theology* (Wheaton, Ill: Crossway, 2014), 115–128.
25   For a survey of OT and second Temple Judaism on the Fatherhood of God, see Marianne M. Thompson, *The Promise of the Father: Jesus and God in the New Testament* (Louisville: Westminster John Knox, 2000), 35–55; idem, *The God of the Gospel of John* (Grand Rapids, MI: Eerdmans, 2001), 21–34.
26   Cf. Frame observes that "Father" as a title or name for God is infrequent in the OT and is closely associated with Jesus in the NT (Frame, *Systematic Theology,* 102).
27   Bray, *God has Spoken,* 115.
28   Cf. Stein, "Fatherhood of God," 247.
29   Chris Wright, *Knowing God the Father through the Old Testament* (Oxford: Monarch Books, 2007), 24–25.

The Fatherhood of God

Israel in the OT is often linked to its redemption as God's covenant and chosen people (Ex. 4:22–23; Deut. 1:31; 32:6; Isa. 63:16; 64:8).[30] The allusions to God's fatherly care for Israel (Ps. 103:13; Deut. 1:31; 32:6) also indicate God's special relationship with Israel as son based upon his covenantal promises (Ex. 4:22–23; Jer. 31:9). This is an important point since it shows the covenantal and theological nature of the term "Father."

Altogether there are about 25 references to God as "Father" or his Fatherhood OT. In comparison to other descriptions of God (such as Creator, Lord, King, Judge), the Fatherhood of God does not appear to be a key description of God in OT. Hence, it is suggested that although people in the OT were aware of the Fatherhood of God in some sense, "Father" was not a popular term to address God even in Jewish prayers.[31] Bray points out that the only two examples where the Jewish people are known to have called on God as their "Father" are Isaiah 63:16–17 and 64:8–9.[32] Similarly, Jeremias had argued earlier that "Father" seems to be not an available form of address for God in Judaism since for Judaism "God was primarily the Lord...the Creator."[33] Although "Judaism had a great wealth of forms of address to God at its disposal...Nowhere, however in the Old Testament do we find God addressed as 'Father,'" Jeremias concludes.[34] He also refers to the evidence in the Targum, which suggests that "Jew deliberately avoided applying the word abba to God even outside prayers."[35] It is proposed that the Jews avoided such a description of God due to its frequent use in fertility cults of the Ancient Near East with sexual overtones.[36]

Outside of the OT, there a few isolated references to God as "Father" in the intertestamental post-canonical Jewish sources, e.g. Apocrypha (Wis. 2:16; 14:3; Tob. 13:4; Sir. 4:10; 23:1, 4; 51:10); Pseudepigrapha (Jub. 1:24, 28; 19:29; 3 Macc. 5:7; 6:3-4, 8; T. Levi 18:6; T. Judah 24:2); and Dead Sea Scrolls (1 QH 9:35f.).[37] However, they are seen as lacking clarity.[38] Jeremias suggests that they may be due to the Greek influence upon the diaspora Hellenistic Judaism.[39]

---

30   Knobnya has a made a strong case from the OT in favour. See, Knobnya "God the Father in the Old Testament," 139–148.
31   Cf. Joachim Jeremias, *New Testament Theology* (New York: Charles Scribner's Sons, 1971), 65–66.
32   Bray, "God as Father." Idem, *God has Spoken,* 119.
33   Jeremias, *New Testament Theology,* 178–79.
34   Jeremias, *New Testament Theology,* 63.
35   Jeremias, *New Testament Theology,* 65–66.
36   Cf. Stein, "Fatherhood of God," 247 (cf. 247–48); Frame, *Systematic Theology,* 112.
37   Cf. Stein, "Fatherhood of God," 248.
38   Cf. Donald Guthrie and Ralph P. Martin, "God," DPL, 357.
39   Cf. Jeremias, *New Testament Theology,* 63.

The evidence in the OT suggests that although "Father" as a description for God or references to the Fatherhood of God are surprisingly few, the concept was known to the people of God in the OT and was understood in the context of their redemption and God's covenantal relationship with Israel as a chosen nation. Hence, in the OT the idea of Covenantal or Theocentric Fatherhood of God is more prominent than God's Creational or General Fatherhood to all.[40]

It appears that "Father" was not a popular term to address God among the Jews in the OT and during the intertestamental period. It could be because the OT lays a greater emphasis on the distance between God and His people where God seems to be more separate and less intimate due to his holiness. The sacrifices and the priesthood in the OT imply the same. The general emphasis of the OT is upon God's holiness and the reverence that His people are to show toward him being their powerful Creator and High King and Judge.

It can be said that in the OT, as Medved says, "God sees himself and proclaims himself as the Father of Israel. Moreover, his acts toward Israel clearly exhibit his fatherhood."[41] Hence, while the Fatherhood of God in the Old Testament is present, it is taken to a new level in the NT.[42]

III. FATHERHOOD OF GOD IN THE NEW TESTAMENT

The theme of the Fatherhood of God in relation to his people is significantly and most characteristically taught and expanded in the NT by Jesus himself in the gospels and later by Paul in his epistles.[43] As pointed out earlier, almost every NT canonical book mentions God as "Father." It is the third most frequently used term for God in the NT and probably the most theologically significant description of God in the NT. Proportionally, the frequency of references to God's fatherhood in the NT (almost 250 times)[44] is greater than in the OT (15 direct, 9 indirect), which indicates that it becomes a major doctrine in the NT, primarily because of

---

40   Knobnya's proposal that the Father-God motif is prominent in OT and second temple Judaism is probably far too fetched than the evidence suggests but she is right to point out the God's Fatherhood to Israel is closely linked to its redemption and deliverance from Egypt (Knobnya, "God the Father," 139–148).

41   Cf. Medved, "The Fatherhood of God," 213.

42   Cf. Medved, "The Fatherhood of God," 213.

43   Frame observes that Jesus generally does not address God as Lord and as king but as "Father" and he is closely associated with him (Frame, *Systematic Theology,* 102). Also, Schreiner, *New Testament Theology,* 129. For a survey of the same see Thompson, The Promise of the Father, 71–86.

44   Horst Robert Balz and Gerhard Schneider, *Exegetical Dictionary of the New Testament* (Grand Rapids, MI: Eerdmans, 1990–), 53.

Jesus.[45] It almost appears, as Bray says that "when Jesus called God his Father and taught his disciples to do the same he was doing something new."[46] The reaction of the Jews to Jesus' statement in John 5:18 seems to indicate that they were neither comfortable, nor familiar with addressing God as Father.[47]

Undoubtedly, the Fatherhood of God takes a decided turn with Jesus since it was his favorite term for addressing God (almost 65 times in the synoptic Gospels and over 100 times in John's gospel).[48] In fact, Jesus' teaching on God's Fatherhood and his special relationship with God opens a whole new way for his disciples and the believers to connect to God as Father like never before. Jeremias agrees that "for the disciples of Jesus, God is the Father."[49] This is indicated by his use of "your Father" statement in the gospels (Matt. 5:16, 45; 6:1, 4; 10:29; Mark 11:25; Luke 6:36; 12:30, 32; John 20:17).

As such, while the OT view of God as the Creator (Mark 2:27; 10:6; 13:19), Lord, King (Matt. 18:23–25) and Judge (Matt. 10:28) is affirmed and maintained in the NT, it is not the center of NT view of God. Instead, the Fatherhood of God dominates the description of God both in the gospels and the epistles.

IV. FATHERHOOD OF GOD IN THE GOSPELS

The term "Father" is constantly used by Jesus to address God, particularly in the gospels of John and Matthew (among the synoptics).[50] Although it is unevenly distributed in the gospels (4 times in Mark, 44 in Matthew, 15 in Luke, and 109 in John),[51] Jesus repeatedly calls God as "my Father"[52] (e.g., Matt. 7:21; 10:32, 33; Luke 10:22; 22:29; John 2:16; 5:17) or "the Father" (Matt. 11:27; 24:36; Mark

---

45   Cf. Stein, "Fatherhood of God," 247; also, Frame, *Systematic Theology*, 106; Medved, "The Fatherhood of God," 203–214.

46   Bray, *God has Spoken*, 120.

47   See Jeremias, *New Testament Theology*, 63–66.

48   Frame points out that "Father" is the name most closely associated with Jesus (Frame, *Systematic Theology*, 102). When Jesus wanted to explain what God was like, he teaches about the Father's enduring love for his lost sons even though each of them in their own way had hardened themselves towards him (Luke 15:11–32). When Jesus himself faced his most agonizing moments, he turned to his heavenly Father in Gethsemane and cried out, "Abba, Father" (Mark 14:36). On the cross, he calls out to God as "Father" (Luke 22:46; 23:34).

49   Cf. Jeremias, *New Testament Theology*, 180.

50   The gospel of John has the most detailed description of Jesus addressing God as "Father" and his teaching on God's Fatherhood to the disciples. See Medved, "The Fatherhood of God," 212.

51   Cf. L. W. Hurtado, "God," in *Dictionary of Jesus and the Gospels*, 271. Some count 107 occurrences in John's gospel depending upon the textual variants (cf. Cameron, "Father," 408).

52   The phrase appears almost 19 times in the synoptics (majority in Matthew) and almost 26 times in John's gospel alone indicating a distinctive and unique relationship of Jesus with the Father (see Schriener, *New Testament Theology*, 130.

13:32; Luke 10:22; John 1:14) or "your Father"[53] (Matt. 5:16; 10:20; Mark 11:25; Luke 6:36; John 20:17), particularly in the gospels of John and Matthew (among the synoptics).[54] Being Jesus' favorite term to address God, particularly in prayer, he also teaches and encourages his disciples to do the same by relating to God as their Father (e.g., Matt. 6:9). Hence, Jesus' teaching on the fatherhood of God portrays his own intimacy with God that he opened to believers to enjoy and have access to as part of His mission (John 14:7). Hurtado puts it well that Jesus "became the pioneer and catalyst for a special filial relationship to God to be enjoyed by his disciples."[55] With Jesus' coming, the idea of the Fatherhood of God emerges into greater depth and emphasis with a view of God portraying the most intimate relationship believers have with God i.e., parent children).[56]

Significantly, Jesus sees the Fatherhood of God as a privilege enjoyed by His disciples and later believers only, and not by everyone in general (cf. John 8:19, 38, 41–42, 44) because this relationship is only made possible through the redemptive work of Christ.[57] While in line with the OT, Jesus acknowledges that all people are God's children by creation and are objects of his providential kindness (Matt. 5:45), he also sees them as fallen and sinful and are now objects of his wrath requiring rebirth and reconciliation with God (John 3:3; 8:42; 14:6). Jesus' response to the Jewish opposition in John 8:37–59 confirms the same. He challenges the Jewish assumption that God was their Father in the covenantal sense (v. 41) because they were Abraham's children (v. 53). To their surprise, Jesus calls them the children of the devil, and not of God (v. 44) because they had rejected the Son of God. According to Jesus, only those who accept his Sonship and put their trust in his redemptive work may truly call God "Father."[58] Hence, the idea of Adoptive Fatherhood is central to Jesus' teaching on Fatherhood.

---

53 More than 20 times, Jesus describes God as "Your Father" to his disciples and followers in the gospels, indicating that he assumed them to be familiar with the image of God as "Father." Hence, he was not introducing an entirely new concept of God but an uncommonly used concept from OT to address God. However, it is surprising that Jesus never appeals to OT passages to refer to God's fatherhood or teach about him as "Father." It appears that although familiar to OT saints, "Father" appears to be an exclusively Christian address to God introduced by Jesus to his disciples and believers, and later continually used by NT writers and NT church.
54 The Fatherhood of God is central in John's gospel and is emphasized more in John than in the Synoptics. Also, John's focus is more on describing God as the "Father" of Jesus than of believers. Hence, the phrase "my Father" appears more in John alone than in the synoptics together. See Schreiner, *New Testament Theology*, 136.
55 Hurtado, "God," 276.
56 See Donald Guthrie and Ralph P. Martin, "God," in *Dictionary of Paul and His Letters*, 357
57 See Guthrie and Martin, "God," 357; Schreiner, *New Testament Theology*, 130. The same restrictiveness of God's Fatherhood is also seen in OT with the nation Israel where God expresses a special relationship only with the chosen ones within the covenant community (see Medved, "The Fatherhood of God," 203–214).
58 Cf. Jeremias, *New Testament Theology*, 180–81.

V. FATHERHOOD OF GOD IN THE PAULINE CORPUS

The Fatherhood of God is also clearly seen in Paul's letters. His theology of God is dominated by it. The opening salutations in Paul's letters describe God repeatedly as Father of believers through Christ (Rom. 1:7; 1 Cor. 1:3; 2 Cor. 1:2; Gal. 1:3; Eph. 1:2; Phil. 1:2; Col. 1:2; 1 Thess. 1:3; 2 Thess. 1:1, 2; Phil. 3). Paul has more than forty references describing God as "Father" or referring to his "Fatherhood" in blessings (Rom. 1:7; 1 Cor. 1:3), doxologies (Rom. 15:6), thanksgiving (2 Cor. 1:3), exhortations (Eph. 5:20), and creeds (Eph. 4:6).

Paul too points out the Generative Fatherhood of God in relation to Jesus (Rom. 15:6; 1 Cor. 15:24; 2 Cor. 1:3; 11:31; Eph. 1:3; Col. 1:2), Adoptive Fatherhood of God in relation to believers in Christ (Rom. 1:7; 8:15; 1 Cor. 8:6; 1 Cor. 6:18; Gal. 1:1, 3, 4; 4:6; Eph. 1:2; 2:18; 3:14; 5:20; Phil. 4:20; Col. 1:12; 1 Thess. 3:11, 13; 2 Thess. 2:16), and Creational Fatherhood of God in relation to all creation (1 Cor. 8:6; Eph. 4:6).[59] However, it is the Adoptive Fatherhood of God to believers that takes a pivotal place in Pauline theology since it is made available through Christ's redemptive work, which is the center of Paul's Christology. Hence, Paul also calls God, "Father of our Lord Jesus Christ" (Rom. 15:6 ; 2 Cor. 1:3; 11:31) since it is through the work of Christ that God invites believers to call him "Abba, Father" (Rom. 8:15; Gal. 4:6). And it is through Christ that believers have become God's children (Rom. 8:14; cf. Gal. 4:5). Thayer's lexicon notes that "this conception, common in the New Testament epistles, shines forth with especial brightness in Romans 8:15 and Galatians 4:6."[60]

In Paul's view the Fatherhood of God is not derived from human fatherhood but is the basis of it (cf. Eph. 3:14–15). It shows that God's Fatherhood is to be understood as "inherent in the nature of God," and not a result of a human analogy.[61]

VI. ABBA, FATHER

The use of the Aramaic term Abba (translated as the Greek Pater in other occurrences) both by Jesus (Mark 14:36)[62] and later by Paul (Rom. 8:15; Gal. 4:6)

---

59 Cf. Guthrie and Martin, "God," 357

60 Thayer, *Greek-English Lexicon,* 495.

61 Guthrie and Martin, "God," 357.

62 Mark is unique among the gospels in recording Jesus' use of abba used elsewhere in the NT only by Paul (Rom. 8:15; Gal. 4:6). It could be because Mark's gospel, like Paul's letters, is addressing Greek-speaking (i.e., gentile) community who was already familiar with this expression (see, Hurtado, "God," 273).

further confirms the Adoptive Fatherhood of God, central in the Pauline letters.[63] It is an intimate term that was thought to be used often by young children carrying the notion of the English "daddy."[64] However, it has been pointed out that both Abba and its Greek equivalent, Pater were also used by both older children and adults to address their father.[65] Jesus' use of this term to address God is unique and rare since it finds no parallels either in OT or in Jewish literature as an address to God.[66] Mark retains the Aramaic Abba (Mark 14:36) indicating that it was Jesus' distinctive way of addressing God that he wants his readers to remember.[67] The context of the use of this term is Jesus' agonizing prayer in view of the impending suffering on the cross that awaited him. Jesus calls out to his beloved father in the poignant moment, addressing him Abba, which shows Jesus' intimate relationship with the Father.[68] It was also the way the disciples were taught by Jesus to address God in prayer (Luke 11:2).

Jeremias points out that "He spoke to God like a child to its father, simply, inwardly, confidently. Jesus' use of abba in addressing God reveals the heart of his relationship with God."[69]

Distinct from any Jewish antecedent and following Jesus (Mark 14:36), Paul also introduces Abba to his predominantly Gentile congregations (Rom. 8:15; Gal. 4:6). Although Greek-speaking, Paul wants the Gentile Christians to address God using the Aramaic term Abba because it was taught by Jesus himself.[70] Hence, Paul cites it in its Semitic formulation to keep the original sense intended by Jesus in Mark 14:36 where it serves as a unique expression of Jesus' relationship to the Father. Significantly, in both places (Rom. 8:15; Gal. 4:6), Paul introduces it in the context of the believers' adoption into God's family where the Spirit enables believers to recognise and acclaim God as their "Abba! Father!" Hence, the term

---

63   The use of abba by Paul in the context of prayer (Rom. 8:15; Gal. 4:6) indicates that Christians were already addressing God as "Father" in prayer (probably in corporate worship settings) even before the time of Paul's letters (50–60 AD). See Hurtado, "God," 275.

64   Cf. Guthrie and Martin, "God," 358; Frame, *Systematic Theology*, 106.

65   Cf. Stein, "Fatherhood of God," 247; also, G. Kittle, Ἀββᾶ, TDNT 1 (1964), 5–6. Hence, to strictly equate Abba with the term "daddy" may be misleading and since it runs the risk of irreverence in addressing God (see, J. Barr, "Abba Isn't Daddy," JTS 39 [1988], 28–47; also, Jeremias, *New Testament Theology*, 66–67; T. E. McComiskey, "God, Names of," *Evangelical Dictionary of Theology*, 466).

66   See Jeremias, *New Testament Theology*, 63–65.

67   Cf. Morna D. Hooker, *A Commentary on the Gospel According to St. Mark* (London: A & C Black, 1991), 348.

68   Cf. Schriener, *New Testament Theology*, 129. The term conveys a sense of intimacy and familiarity missing in both OT and Judaism in general, introducing a completely new way to view God distinct from any formal approach that the Jews were familiar with.

69   Joachim Jeremias, 'Abba,' in The Prayers of Jesus, *SBT II* 6 (London: SCM Press, 1967), 62.

70   Stein, "Fatherhood of God," 247-48.

in Paul's usage serves as a mark or proof of believers' adoption as "sons of God" (Rom. 8:14; Gal. 4:5).[71] In fact, it implies that the doctrine of adoption assumes the Fatherhood of God as an unchangeable and eternal reality since believes' adoption as God's children is an unchangeable and eternal reality.

V. CONCLUSION

The above discussion shows that the description of God as "Father" and his Fatherhood, are present both in the Old and New Testaments. The references to the Fatherhood of God in the OT are linked with the idea of redemption expressing God's covenantal relationship with Israel as his chosen people. People in the OT were aware of God as "Father" being their Creator and Redeemer but did not generally address God as "Father" in their prayers, nor did they experience the level of intimacy with God based on this relationship as do the NT believers.

It is important to note that while there is both continuity and progression of the Fatherhood of God in the NT from the OT, it is taken to a new level in the NT with the coming of Jesus and his teaching on it. Jesus inaugurates a new depth to the relationship between God the Father and believers as his adopted children that was not experienced or emphasized earlier in Judaism. The basis of this renewed relationship was the redemptive work of Christ, which is a key theme in NT theology. Paul relates the Fatherhood of God with his adoption of believers in and through Christ (Rom. 8:14–16; Gal. 3:26) Hence, the Fatherhood of God is at the forefront of NT Theology since it is closely associated with the doctrine of adoption in the NT. This is beautifully expressed by J.I. Packer:

> You sum up the whole of New Testament religion if you describe it as the knowledge of God as one's Holy Father. If you want to judge how well a person understands Christianity, find out how much he makes of the thought of being God's child, and having God as his Father. If this is not the thought that prompts and controls his worship and prayers and his whole outlook on life, it means that he does not understand Christianity very well at all. For everything that Christ taught, everything that makes the New Testament new, and better than the Old, everything that is distinctively Christian as opposed to merely Jewish,

---

71   See Guthrie and Martin, "God," 358; Medved, "The Fatherhood of God," 212.

> is summed up in the knowledge of the Fatherhood of God. 'Father' is the Christian name for God. Our understanding of Christianity cannot be better than our grasp of adoption.[72]

The pervasiveness of the "Fatherhood of God" in the Scripture points to its essential immutable character specifically in its relationship to the theme of redemption in the Old and the New Testaments which is theological in nature. Being of theological nature in essence, it is neither cultural, nor time-bound. Therefore, it is imperative to emphasize its necessity both in theology and worship. To reject or avoid or modify the biblical description and designation for God as "Father" would be to lose sight of the fact that Jesus chose it to address God and taught his disciples to do the same. Replacing "Father" with "Mother" or "Parent" or anything else also loses sight, as Stein accurately points out, of the continuity and fraternity "with those who have called God "Father" over the centuries. These include the disciples of Jesus; the earliest congregations; the earliest church councils ('I believe in God the Father Almighty, Maker of heaven and earth'); and Christian churches all over the globe who over the centuries have prayed together, "Our Father who art in heaven, Hallowed by thy name."[73]

The Christian understanding of God as "Father" is unique among world religions. In fact, the idea of a divine Fatherhood in other religious traditions is either totally absent or entirely distinct from the Christian idea of God's Fatherhood. The Romans had Jupiter as father Jove but lacked clarity in what it meant.[74] The Platonists in the NT times thought of the divine Father as a hidden deity dwelling above the heavens and without any direct contact with the material world.[75] The Gnostics in the early church had a similar idea of a hidden Father. In Buddhism, there are no gods, or if there are, there is no way we can know them. Hinduism has thousands of gods (brahman for creation; shiva for destruction; Ganesh for learning) and behind them one impersonal force, but no idea of God as Father. Islam has 99 names for God but not Father. Judaism had some idea of God as Father but not commonly used in prayers. It is only in Christianity, with Jesus' coming, "Father" becomes the most important and common address for God in the NT and throughout church history. And that is because of one person, Jesus. Hence, for Christians today, "Father" is Christo-centric because they can pray to

---

72   J. I. Packer, *Knowing God* (IVP: Westmont, Ill, 1993), 17, 201–202.
73   Stein, "Fatherhood of God," 248.
74   Bray, *God has Spoken,* 120.
75   Bray, *God has Spoken,* 122 (cf. Plato, Timaeus, 28c–34b; 41a–44e).

God and relate to him as "Father," not because he is primary their Creator but because he is their Redeemer in and through Christ. Jesus reveals the Father to us (John 14:9–11).

Since the context of the Fatherhood of God in Scripture is covenantal and theological, it does not cease with changing times and cultures. "Father" is his eternal nature. Colin Smothers echoes the words of Herman Bavinck as a great reminder asserting, "Let it be clear: we do not name God. He names himself, and he has named himself Father."[76]

---

76 Colin Smothers, "Editorial: The Toxic War on Fatherhood," in *Eikon: A Journal for Biblical Anthropology*, vol 5.2 (2023). Available at https://cbmw.org/2023/11/21/editorial-the-toxic-war-on-fatherhood. Accessed on 31/12/23 (cf. Bavinck, *Reformed Dogmatics II: God and Creation,* ed. John Bolt, trans. John Vriend (Grand Rapids, MI: Baker, 2004), 98–99.

The Attribute of God's Fatherly Love

an African Theological and Leadership Perspective

DR. WOLE ADEGBILE

Senior Lecturer and Director of Quality Assurance,
Africa College of Theology
Nigeria/Rwanda

Fatherhood is a metaphor for leadership, taken from the Bible and African culture. The study presents God as the perfect model of father-leader, stressing that he loves the Israelites as a parent loves their child and, therefore, intends for them to experience well-being. God's intention for the Israelites' well-being as the Father of the nation led to his appointment of Israelites' kings as his sons. He desires that the kings should lead his people with much care he has for them. A king must be a representation of God, the Father-Leader.

Based on the premise that African traditional societies are not without the revelation of God and his attributes,[1] this study, therefore, explores the traces of father-leadership in African culture. It argues that the Bible and African culture teach that leadership is a divine responsibility and must be about people's well-being. As such, the paper intends to draw leadership application from God's fatherly love that aims at well-being, a similar attribute typified in African traditional leadership (ATL).

Although God's attribute of fatherly love is demonstrated in both the Old and New Testaments, our focus is on God's relationship to the nation of Israel as a father. Also, as a representation of ATL, we shall focus on Rwandan and Yoruba traditional political leadership. This study does not seek to equate God's attributes with human practices but rides on the grounds of general revelation to explain how African people exhibit the will of God in their leadership system, vague and imperfect as it might be. Through this, the paper evokes an African theological and leadership identity.

I. THE HISTORICAL THEOLOGY OF GOD'S FATHERHOOD AND LOVE

In the earlier Christian theological discussion, starting with Origen, God's fatherhood was primarily seen in the context of the Trinity.[2] In the Reformation, John Calvin argued that God is only a Father to the redeemed. In the late nineteenth century, in response to Calvin's theology that limited God's fatherhood to the elect, Adam Clarke, Francis Greenwood Peabody, and Walter Rauschenbush

---

1 Pius Oyeniran Abioje, "Divine Revelation in African Religion among the Yoruba and in Christianity," *Legon Journal of the Humanities* 18 (2007): 73.
2 John Behr, "'One God Father Almighty,'" *Modern Theology* 34, no. 3 (2018): 320–26, https://doi.org/10.1111/moth.12419; David Tasker, "The Fatherhood of God," in *Hermeneutics, Intertextuality and the Contemporary Meaning of Scripture*, ed. R. Cole and P. Petersen (Hindmarsh, Australia: ATF Press, 2014), 275.

developed a "social gospel" that affirmed the brotherhood of all human beings and God as Father of them all.[3]

Randolf Foster hints that "The older theologians distinguished the attributes of God...from properties which are technically the distinguishing characteristics of the several persons of the Trinity. There are certain acts or relations peculiar to the Father, others to the Son, others to the Spirit."[4] As Paul indicates in the trinitarian text, 2 Cor. 15:13, the prominent attribute of the Father is love. Drawing an application from the teaching of the Trinity and emphasizing the perichoresis, Jurgen Moltmann advocates that "The trinitarian concept of God the Father doesn't justify any patriarchalism or dominance of the father in society, but only communal love."[5]

In a general sense, creation expresses God's fatherly love for all humanity. As Foster rightly says, in creation, we see "the measure of the Father's love, and it shall appear forever and ever that creation is a simple expression of love."[6] Whether concerning the Israelites or the entire human race, God's fatherhood often refers to his love. Randolph Foster summarises it well by saying, "It is a father waiting at the gate for the returning prodigal."[7]

II. THE UNIQUENESS OF GOD'S FATHERHOOD

The concept of divine fatherhood is not limited to the Jewish/Christian religions and cultures. In a discussion of divine fatherhood, it is essential to note that "In many religions, particularly the Mediterranean ones, the supreme god was called 'Father of the universe,' whether it was Zeus, the father of all, or Jupiter, the father of the gods."[8]

In his book *Ancient Near Eastern Literature and the Hebrew Scriptures about the Fatherhood of God* and his article "The Fatherhood of God," David Tasker explores the concept of divine fatherhood across various ancient cultures. According to Tasker, the Sumerians viewed their gods, such as An and Utu, as paternal figures with authority and responsibility. One of the Sumerian songs portrays Utu as a

---

3   Tasker, "The Fatherhood of God," 276.
4   Randolph Sinks Foster, *God: Nature and Attributes* (New York: Eaton & Mains, 1897), 75.
5   Jürgen Moltmann, "God the Father in the Life of the Holy Trinity," *International Journal of Orthodox Theology* 1, no. 1 (2010): 38–48.
6   Foster, *God*, 251.
7   Foster, 263.
8   Moltmann, "God the Father in the Life of the Holy Trinity," 39.

father (and a mother) whose benevolent act is praised.[9]

A similar idea occurs in Ugarit. In one Ugaritic epic, "El as father-god is moved with pity for his earthly son Kirta, and orders circumstances so that Kirta sires a number of children, including Aghat."[10] In the ANE, Resheph was "a widely worshipped deity."[11] Also, in Emar (a Syrian city), one of the most common names given to people is Abi-Rashap, which means "Resheph is my father."[12] This hints at God's fatherhood in the Syrian religion and people's devotion to him in their willingness to be identified as his children. In Babylon, there is evidence that people pray to the god Marduk, referring to him as "father" and asking him to watch over them, give them a favor, and prosper them.[13]

One notable thing about the ANE concept of divine fatherhood is that it is hardly about a human-god relation. For example, Tasker notes, "The Egyptian gods are called 'father' in the context of the generation of other gods, the world, and everything in it. They are also called 'father' in relation to the pharaohs, and in relation to assisting souls in the afterlife into the presence of Ra. It is in the context of creation and resurrection that their fatherhood is made evident."[14]

The preceding discussion indicates that divine fatherhood is not limited to the Israelite's territory. The people of Israel themselves might be aware of this. Nevertheless, this does not make them equate their God with the gods of the neighboring nations. Despite their awareness of the fact that peoples around them identify themselves as "children" to their gods and that they attribute divine benevolence to the father nature of their gods, the people of Israel sing:

> Who among the gods
>   is like you, Lord?...
> You stretch out your right hand,
>   and the earth swallows your enemies.
> In your unfailing love you will lead
>   the people you have redeemed (Exod. 15:11 – 13).[15]

---

9   David Tasker, *Ancient Near Eastern Literature and the Hebrew Scriptures about the Fatherhood of God* (New York: Peter Lang, 2004), 26.
10   Tasker, 60.
11   Maciej M. Münnich, *The God Resheph in the Ancient Near East* (Mohr Siebeck, 2013), 1.
12   Münnich, 190.
13   Takayoshi Oshima, *Babylonian Prayers to Marduk* (Tubingen: Mohr Siebeck, 2011), 21.
14   Tasker, "The Fatherhood of God."
15   All the scriptural passages in this study are taken from the New International Version.

If the above song may relate to the concept of divine fatherhood and people's well-being, underneath would be an implied assertion that there is no Father like Yahweh, the Father figure who redeemed his people as no other gods did. Although there is an indication of fatherhood self-proclamation and attribution to the ANE gods and that benevolent acts are attributed to them, the people of Israel see the person and fatherhood of God as something incomparable.

One quality that marks out the inferiority of the ANE gods compared to the God of Israel is their aloofness. For example, as was earlier noted in this study, the fatherhood of the Egyptian gods does not depict or entail intimacy. Tasker further notes that when discussing god-human relations in Egypt, "the masses did not really count for much" before the gods of the land.[16]

Moses might be aware of the aloofness of the gods of the neighboring communities when he rhetorically asked: "What other nation is so great as to have their gods near them the way the LORD our God is near us whenever we pray to him?" (Deut. 4:7). In contrast to the father-gods of the nations around, God's fatherhood to Israel demonstrates a personal, covenantal relationship whereby God is present among his people, combining His divine authority with intimacy to result in the well-being of the people.

III. ISRAEL AND THE FATHERLY LOVE OF GOD

In the Book of Exodus, God's fatherhood to the Israelites was affirmed in the call of Moses (Exod. 3:21 – 23). In Walter Kaiser's words,

> Moses' first act as the newly appointed spokesman for the living God was categorically to command Pharaoh, "Israel is my first-born son: ... Let my son go" (Exod. 4:22 - 23). Yahweh was now to be seen as a "Father" by what He did: He brought Israel into being as a nation: He fostered the nation and led it. This is what fatherhood was all about.[17]

---

16 Tasker.

17 Walter C. Kaiser, *Toward an Old Testament Theology* (Zondervan, 1991), 101.namely the inability of the discipline to restate and reapply the authority of the Bible, Walter Kaiser here offers a solution to the unresolved issues of definition and methodology in Old Testament theology. A proper understanding of biblical theology, explains the author, 'shows us an inner center of plan to which each biblical writer consciously and deliberately contributed; however, this inner biblical unity, which biblical theologians traditionally have been loathe to adopt for fear of gratuitously imposing a grid of their own devising over the text, is a center that is inductively supplied and confirmed by the text of Scripture itself. That center is the promise of God.' In Part I of his book, Dr. Kaiser discusses the inherent difficulty in determining the true nature, method, scope, and motivation for Old

It is important to note that God's initial introduction of Himself as the Father of Israel is within the context of deliverance: "Let my son go." On this note, Svetlana Knobnya concludes, "The idea of God the Father is developed with reference to his redeeming activity in the deliverance of Israel from Egypt when he elected and lifted Israel to the status of 'son' (Ex 4:22)."[18]

In Deuteronomy, the theme of God's fatherhood is also evident. Moses reminds Israelites of God's fatherhood when he says: "And in the wilderness. There you saw how the Lord your God carried you, as a father carries his son, all the way you went until you reached this place" (Deut. 1:31). Since this verse is taken within the context of Moses' narration of the Israelites' journey and how the people rebelled, Moses' expression here affirms God's ability to take them through the rest of the journey. However, the critical point to note for this study is how Moses reminded them of God's fatherly care for them as his sons.

Also, Deuteronomy portrays God as a Father intending to teach discipline to his "son." In the book, Moses rehearses the Law of God to the people and encourages them to obey Yahweh. He reminds them of the wilderness experiences so they might fear Yahweh and obey his instructions. For Moses, the Israelites' wilderness experience is God's way of dealing with them as their Father: "Know then in your heart that as a man disciplines his son, so the Lord your God disciplines you" (Deut. 8:5).

Likewise, in Deuteronomy, Moses' narration of Israel's deliverance from Egypt and preservation in the wilderness underscores God's love for his people. Moses' message to the people was direct: "Because [God] loved your ancestors and chose their descendants after them, he brought you out of Egypt by his presence and his great strength" (Deut. 4:37).

Although William Moran, in his article "The Ancient Near Eastern Background of the Love of God in Deuteronomy," is skeptical about the Father-son love of God for Israel, however, he did not deny the centrality of love in the book. He notes that the book contains the theme of "Yahweh's love for Israel and the imperative necessity of Israel's love for Yahweh in return."[19] Reading Deuteronomy in light

---

Testament theology. In Part II, he applies his solutions clearly and methodically by chronologically discussing the Old Testament eras from the Prepatriarchical.

18   Svetlana Knobnya, "God the Father in the Old Testament," *European Journal of Theology* 20, no. 2 (2011): 146.

19   William L. Moran, "The Ancient Near Eastern Background of the Love of God in Deuteronomy," *The Catholic Biblical Quarterly* 25, no. 1 (1963): 77.

of Exodus 4:11 indicates that God's love for Israel is that of a father to his son. As Kaiser notes, "All Israel's freedom was owed to the loyal love of God (*hesed*—Exod 15:13) Yahweh had for His people."[20] Yahweh's deliverance of his people is grounded in the expression, "Israel is my firstborn son."

Isaiah is another biblical book that reflects the fatherly love of God for Israel. Chapters 40 – 55 discuss the Israelites' exile and deliverance. Chapter 43 stresses the love of God, as it reads, "I will say to the north, 'Give them up!' and to the south, 'Do not hold them back.' Bring my sons from afar and my daughters from the ends of the earth" (Isa. 43:6). As in Exodus, Isaiah links God's fatherly love to his deliverance of the Israelites. Isaiah explicitly connects the idea of God 'our Father' with 'our Redeemer'", especially in chapter 63, verse 16.[21] In verses 15b and 16a, Isaiah highlights God's compassion.[22] God's compassion is shown repeatedly in the life of the Israelites as evident in the book of Judges. Conleth Kearns talks about God's compassion rooted in his fatherly love when he concludes:

> In one sense the Old Testament is nothing else but the story of God's fatherhood in communicating his own divine life to man, thus making him his son, and man's response or failure to respond: the Prodigal Father open-handed with his benefactions, and the Prodigal Son squandering his birthright.[23]

Although Israel would not stop wandering away from God's compassionate, fatherly love, "God deals with the situation as a father, gently but firmly, guiding his errant children, not as a conquering king wiping out all opposition."[24]

Like Exodus, Deuteronomy, and Isaiah, the books of Jeremiah, Hosea, and Malachi remarkably reflect the attributes of God's fatherly love for Israel. Knobnya summarizes these attributes in Jeremiah and Hosea as follows:

---

20 Kaiser, *Toward an Old Testament Theology*, 104.namely the inability of the discipline to restate and reapply the authority of the Bible, Walter Kaiser here offers a solution to the unresolved issues of definition and methodology in Old Testament theology. A proper understanding of biblical theology, explains the author, 'shows us an inner center of plan to which each biblical writer consciously and deliberately contributed; however, this inner biblical unity, which biblical theologians traditionally have been loathe to adopt for fear of gratuitously imposing a grid of their own devising over the text, is a center that is inductively supplied and confirmed by the text of Scripture itself. That center is the promise of God.' In Part I of his book, Dr. Kaiser discusses the inherent difficulty in determining the true nature, method, scope, and motivation for Old Testament theology. In Part II, he applies his solutions clearly and methodically by chronologically discussing the Old Testament eras from the Prepatriarchical (Prolegomena to the Promise

21 Knobnya, "God the Father in the Old Testament," 144.

22 Goran Medved, "The Fatherhood of God in the Old Testament," *Kairos : Evangelical Journal of Theology* 10, no. 2 (December 5, 2016): 207.

23 Conleth Kearns, "The Fatherhood of God," *The Furrow* 10, no. 3 (1959): 155.

24 Tasker, "The Fatherhood of God," 289.

Jeremiah recalls the time when God delivered Israel out of Egypt, when he cared for them (31:1-6). Jeremiah implies that the appeal for mercy to God the Father reflects Israel's tradition and their history that constantly illustrates God's election and the redemption of Israel out of Egypt (Jer 31). Hosea also remembers the exodus: when God brought Israel out of Egypt he treated it like a child (11:1). Hosea uses the beautiful metaphor of a 'father' treating his 'child' with love to represent the relationship of God and Israel (11:1-3).

Malachi also portrays God's special love for Israel (1:2 – 3). It proceeds to point out Israel's failure to honor God, who is their father. "The whole book talks about Israel breaking covenant with God by their wrongdoing."[25] Chapter 3, verse 2 expresses the threat of judgment, and Jeremiah (e.g., 3:4 – 5), Hosea (e.g., 11:5 – 6), and Malachi all have these themes in common.

Considering God's combination of love and justice in dealing with his people, Tasker is therefore correct when he writes, "[God] not only deals with oppressors of His people, but with their rebellion against divine order as well. He declares that He will punish His sons if they forsake His law and judgment, statutes and commandments."[26] God's discipline of his people is also a demonstration of His favor. This is because "[Justice] is that form of love which respects rights."[27]

Finally, as we discuss the OT fatherhood of God, it is important to note how this title is used not only concerning the nation of Israel but also to David and his descendants (2 Sam 7:14; 1 Chr 17:13; 22:10; 28:6; Ps 2; 89:26-27; Prov 3:11-12). The use of this title suggests that God set the kings of Israel apart as his representatives, thereby seeking his well-being mission for his people. [28] As such, God desires that his people be led the way he has always led them as a Father. As we have earlier indicated, God's fatherhood to the people of Israel led to his care for them, and his desire for leaders to lead them in the way of well-being is all about his love for his people. In the entire story of Israel, God, in his relationship with them, did what a father does: He led them and loved them, love that is demonstrated in his benevolent acts.

---

25 Medved, "The Fatherhood of God in the Old Testament," 211.
26 Tasker, "The Fatherhood of God," 289.
27 Foster, *God*, 265.
28 Knobnya, "God the Father in the Old Testament," 142.

IV. AFRICAN DEMONSTRATION OF FATHERLY LOVE IN LEADERSHIP

Examining the ATL, it is observed that a similar concept of fatherhood modeled and instructed by God is demonstrated. Meanwhile, we must emphasize that "Human fatherhood, however provident and tender, is only a shadow of the loving fatherhood God exercises towards every one of his human creatures."[29] In this section, we shall highlight the father-leader concept in the ATL, discuss the role of a king in relation to God, and explore three different areas where the king, as a father-leader, ensures the well-being of the people.

1. *The existence of father-leader concept*

In the Rwandan culture, the king (*umwami*) was...known as *Sebantu* (the father of all the people and clans). As the "father," "he was the ultimate proprietor of all lands and cattle in the hands of the larger family of the nation."[30] Also, the father-leader concept is implied in the belief that everybody belongs to the king and the king belongs to everyone – whether Tutsi, Hutu, or Twa.[31]

Similarly, in Yoruba culture, the idea of a king's fatherhood is evident in the common saying *Oba ni bàbá* (the king is the father). Generally, the metaphoric use of fatherhood for leadership is reflected in traditional leadership titles such as *baálé* (head of a clan) and *baálẹ̀* (village head), which respectively mean "father of who owns the house" and "father who owns the land."[32]

2. *Kings as God's agents for people's well-being*

The Rwandan political system is theocratic. *Imana*, the creator God, chooses the king who will shepherd his people.[33] Frank Rusagara says, "The Rwandese of long ago conceived the notion of *Imana* as a special being – a creator and a perfect benevolent being. [He] governed through the king."[34] This is why it is believed

---

29   Kearns, 158.
30   Frank K. Rusagara, *Resilience of a Nation: A History of the Military in Rwanda* (Kigali: Fountain Publishers Rwanda, 2009), 35.
31   Rusagara, 32.
32   Wole Adegbile, *Development as Peace: A Contextual Political Theology of Development from Yoruba Culture* (Carlisle: Langham Monographs, 2023), 170.
33   Gamaliel Mbonimana, "The Kingdom of Rwanda from the Beginning to 1900," in *History of Rwanda: From the Begining to the End of the Twentieth Century* (Kigali: National Unity and Reconciliation Commission (NURC), 2016), 38; Rusagara, *Resilience of a Nation*, 31.
34   Rusagara, *Resilience of a Nation*, 33.

that "the king participated in the realization of the divine right to rule while at the same time remaining a man among men."[35] This implies that "God did not physically distance himself from humans."[36] The Rwandan traditional people pride themselves on God's closeness to them as a people and thereby hold that *"Imana yilirwa ahandi igataha i Rwanda"* (God may spend the day elsewhere but he always comes back to Rwanda).[37]

In the Yoruba view of God, Olodumare is known for his creation role and mighty power.[38] Nevertheless, the saying *"adáni mágbàgbé"* (He who created but never forgets the created one) relates God's creation with care. He created and ensured the well-being of his works.

In the Rwanda culture, the government of the king was, above all, spiritual,[39] and "The essence of the monarch was that the king was God," as it is traditionally believed that *"Umwami si imuntu"* (the king is not human).[40] The *Ubwiru* was constituted to preserve the kingship's sacredness. According to Gamaliel Mbonimana, "*Ubwiru* was perhaps the most important institution among all the other subsidiary institutions of the kingdom. It was an esoteric institution which is essentially political in nature; its major role was to preserve, adapt, present and glorify the monarchy as a "sacred" institution."[41] As a leader of his people, a Rwanda king serves as a link between them and the spiritual universe. For people to tap into *Imana*'s benevolence, "offerings should be made to appease him.... The

---

35   Mbonimana, "The Kingdom of Rwanda from the Beginning to 1900," 99.
36   Mbonimana, 99.
37   Rusagara, *Resilience of a Nation*, 31.
38   John A. I. Bewaji, "Olodumare: God In Yoruba Belief And The Theistic Problem of Evil," *African Studies Quarterly* 2, no. 1 (May 25, 1998): 7–12.Idowu, Mbiti, Parinder, Ray, Tempels, and others, have shown that Africans are not so intellectually impoverished as to be lacking in a sophisticated conception of the Supreme Being. Such a Being is recognized and given a premier position or status in their religions. These scholars have also identified some of the attributes of the Supreme Being within the indigenous African religions that they have studied. Some of these attributes have been very similar to those projected in the Christian religious understandings of the Supreme Being–omnipotence, omnipresence, omniscience, benevolence, divinity, creator, etc. Their works have provided starting points for further research and discussion, but most students of religions have been wont to ignore this aspect of their worthy contribution to scholarship, and have rather taken their works as definitive and beyond question. Even when contrary views are aired, the pioneering works of these first African theologians, religious scholars, and anthropologists are often cited as authorities to uphold a point of view that was fast losing credibility. The African, particularly the Yoruba, about whom Idowu, Mbiti and others have written, unarguably, possess a conception of Supreme Deity. In fact, this Supreme Being has many superlative attributes, but the possession of these qualities does not lead to the type of impasse or contradiction that arises within theistic Christian religion; namely, the irreconcilability of the existence of God and evil in the universe. Staying strictly within Yoruba religion, these writers present;Olodumare; as Christian God, Muslim Allah, and Esu; as Satan or Devil. That this interpretation is wrong and misleading in the consequences it produces is argued here."*African Studies Quarterly*" issue 1.
39   Jan Vansina, *Antecedents to Modern Rwanda: The Nyiginya Kingdom* (Oxford: James Currey, 2005), 38.
40   Mbonimana, "The Kingdom of Rwanda from the Beginning to 1900," 99.
41   Mbonimana, 101.

king is considered a national priest" in this regard.[42]

In the Yoruba culture, all the kings have their line of succession traced back to Oduduwa, who descended from Olodumare. More so, the most critical role of a Yoruba king is to undertake "the spiritual search of the society's well-being," which implies regular consultation with the divinity.[43]

3. *The role of a king in ensuring well-being*

A Rwandan king is the "guarantor of personal wealth, health and justice,"[44] who ensures all is well in all spheres of life. This belief is evident in the proverb, "*[Umwami] uyu akamirwa n'Imana, natwe akadukamira amata akadukwira* (the king who is present drinks milk which is milked by *Imana* and, in turn, the king milks it for us, hence the milk becomes abundant...).[45]

Just like the Rwandan people, the Yoruba believe that the king, the father to his people, exists for nothing other than to ensure people's well-being. The story below illustrates this belief:

> Once upon a time, there was a woman, Ìyá *Alàkàrà*, who sells àkàrà (bean cake) for her daily business. Tortoise (ìjàpá) employed the service of a giant rat (òkété) in digging an underground hole from his house to Ìyá *Alàkàrà's* business joint. He dressed himself in masquerade regalia and used the underground hole to access the joint. On getting there, he changed his voice like that of a masquerade and scared Ìyá *Alàkàrà*, who took to her heels and left her àkàrà behind. Tortoise packed and ate all the àkàrà. He did this repeatedly.

The first time this incident happened, Ìyá *Alàkàrà* brought it to the notice of her husband who attempted to do something about the predicament. He did not succeed; therefore, he took the matter to the village head (*Baálè*), who in turn reported the matter to a chief in the king's court, who finally reported the matter to the king. This is when the king reported the matter to the ancestor, the Ifa oracle.

Then, the ancestors instructed them to make use of àrònì (a handicapped man with

---

42 Mbonimana, 152.
43 Adegbile, *Development as Peace*, 109.
44 Rusagara, *Resilience of a Nation*, 35.
45 Mbonimana, "The Kingdom of Rwanda from the Beginning to 1900," 152.

one hand and one leg) to fight the battle against the mischievous "masquerade." The àrònì set a net trap for the Tortoise-turned-masquerade and was captured, and killed. And thus, the predicament came to an end.[46]

This story suggests that the king (or a leader) is responsible for finding solutions to anything that hinders the people's well-being. In the ATL, leadership is about responsibilities and ensuring that people are in a state of well-being. Like the God of Israel, who ensures provision, security, and justice of the people and desires that his chosen leaders follow the same model, we shall explore how the ATL ensures well-being in these three areas: security, prosperity, and justice.

4. *Security*

From the olden days in Rwanda, military activities have been an essential aspect of the government. In fact, "Rwanda's traditional society was organized around the military, which defined each individual and his or her place in the society."[47] Military conquest was one of the essential pillars of Rwanda's political philosophy.[48] Although the Rwandan military played an economic role, particularly in cattle gathering,[49] it mainly aimed at securing the land and its people. It is noted that the Rwandan military was so strong "during its heyday [that] no slave trader could tread its soil."[50] The necessity of the military to the reign of a king is found in the fact that, upon his enthronement, every new king must "create new battalion from his age group/generation.[51] Also, kings, such as Ndori, had causes to prove their legitimacy through military conquest.[52]

In earlier Yoruba history, kings were known for their military prowess. Oduduwa, the people's historical progeny, became the leader of the race because of his military conquest. His son Oranmiyan was said to have been on an aborted military

---

46 Adegbile, *Development as Peace*, 83–84.
47 Rusagara, *Resilience of a Nation*, xii.
48 Mbonimana, "The Kingdom of Rwanda from the Beginning to 1900," 98.
49 Rusagara, *Resilience of a Nation*, 51.
50 Rusagara, xii.
51 A. Ndahiro and J. Rwagatare, *Rwanda: Rebuilding of a Nation* (Kigali: Fountain Publishers, 2015), 7.From its recent past as a nearfailed state to its present as a beacon of hope and successful innovations. Rwanda's rise from the ashes detailed in this book is the culmination of a visionary and laborious process of rebuilding a nation from the brink of collapse. It is also a story of reconciling a people that had been taught to see each other as enemies.Twenty years ago, the world wrote off Rwanda after the worst genocide in recent times left over one million of its people dead and another three million in refugee camps in neighbouring countries. The country was broken in every way possible - socially, culturally, economically and politically. Today, Rwanda has been rebuilt and has become a respectable country, receiving many international accolades for its extraordinary leadership and achievements.
52 Vansina, *Antecedents to Modern Rwanda*, 55.

expedition when he founded the Oyo Kingdom. Subsequent kings ensured the safety of the land by constituting an aristocratic military group headed by the ààrẹ ọ̀nà kakàǹfò (the warlord), supervised by the king.

5. *Prosperity*

For Traditional Rwandans, kingship "guaranteed prosperity by its very existence and by the execution of rituals destined to ensure the fertility of the land, fecundity of cattle, and that of his objects."[53] *Gicurasi* and *umuganura,* the rituals of the first fruits, "reemphasized the essential role of the king in maintaining the prosperity of his subjects."[54] Like kingship expectations in the Rwandan culture, Yoruba measures the success of a leader by the amount of well-being the society enjoys in his time. This is evident in the proverb, "Ọba tó jẹ t'ílùú r'ójú, a kò ní gbàgbé rẹ̀" (We will forever remember the king whose reign brings much prosperity).

As a personal act, Rwandan kings are in the habit of sharing royal dues with the less privileged. The royal dues "included cows, harvested food grains, and other items paid as tribute. Many of these goods were partly redistributed to the poor in the name of the king."[55]

6. *Justice*

Both in Rwandan and Yoruba cultures, the well-being of society also entails that no one suffers oppression from another member of the society. It also ensures that disputes are settled following an established system. In traditional Rwandan society, one means by which justice is served is through *Gacaca*, which is made up of the village's traditional councils. *Gacaca* concept "derived its impetus and legitimacy from *ubumwe bw' Abanyarwanda* (Rwandan unity), a system which is spearheaded at the national level by the *umwami* (king) himself.[56] A Rwandan king is known to be the national custodian of justice and occasionally moves around the nation to make himself available to people and serve justice when required.[57]

In the Yoruba society, the justice system is so entrenched in the kingship role that he is directly involved in the national law-making. Tunde Onadeko says, "The

---

53   Vansina, 38.
54   Vansina, 38.
55   Mbonimana, "The Kingdom of Rwanda from the Beginning to 1900," 100.
56   Rusagara, *Resilience of a Nation*, 35.
57   Rusagara, 36.

Oba and his chiefs and Ogboni promulgated the laws."[58] More so, a political leader in Yorubaland is also saddled with a judge's responsibility.[59]

ATL cannot be deemed a direct replica of God's demonstration of fatherly love to the Israelites. However, African political leadership, described in the discussion, reminds us of God's fatherly leadership, characterized by love that seeks people's well-being. For example, in Israel's case, he kept them secure by defending them against the army of Pharaoh, and he was thereby declared to be "a warrior" (Exod. 15:3). He fed them miraculously in the wilderness. He gave them the Law and saw to it that they were punished when they erred. He instituted sacred leadership that would ensure the well-being of his people.

In its similarity, ATL still falls short in comparison to God's love as a father because God is incomparable in his attributes (Exod. 15:11). More so, there exist the aspects of African traditional politics that fall short of what God instructed his chosen people – "You shall have no other gods before me" (Exod. 20:3). For examples, references are made to ritual making in this study. Such rituals are done in the names of other gods. Further studies will reveal the involvement of Rwangome and Sango worship alongside the Supreme Being in Rwandan and Yoruba politics, respectively, an act God is displeased with.

V. CONCLUSION

God declares Himself the Father of the nation of Israel and demonstrates this through his love, which ensures their well-being. This study has shown that ATL seeks to follow God's example as it imbibes the notion of father-leadership that exists for nothing other than society's well-being. As God himself perfectly models it, leadership is a sacred responsibility for Africans and must ensure people's well-being. This is a critical area of African beliefs and practices that reflects the mind of God for his people. The father-leadership concept in African traditional society affirms that the people have God's mind through general revelation, but with the twist that other gods are involved aside from Yahweh.

---

58   Tunde Onadeko, "Yoruba Traditional Adjudicatory Systems," *African Study Monographs* 29, no. 1 (March 2008): 20, https://doi.org/10.14989/66225.
59   Onadeko, 22–26.

A Biblical Theology of the Wisdom of God

TSEDEY ALEMAYEHU GEBREHIWOT
Lecturer in Biblical Studies/Old Testament
Ministry Program Manager, Samaritan's Purse
Ethiopia

Wisdom plays a significant role in the Scriptures, particularly in the Old Testament. The wise individuals or sages mentioned in the Old Testament were indeed important figures in Israel's national life. They held a prominent place in society and often provided counsel and advice to the people.

Jeremiah 18:18 mentions three important figures: the priests, the prophets and the wise person or sage. These three groups had distinct roles but all contributed to the guidance and well-being of the community. The priests were responsible to teach the law, for the religious rituals and maintaining the connection between the people and God. The prophets served as messengers of God, proclaimed the Word and often providing guidance and warnings to the people on God's behalf. The wise person or sage, on the other hand, offered practical wisdom and advice, most likely as the professional adviser (2 Samuel 16:23). Examples of such are Joseph in Egypt and Daniel in Babylon.

The study of the Old Testament as a whole has marginalized wisdom. While it is true that certain aspects of the Old Testament, such as narrative texts and the prophecies, often receive more attention, wisdom also holds a significant place within the Scriptures. This paper argues that wisdom, or the wisdom of God, is one of the outstanding themes of the Scripture.

Definition of Wisdom

According to Donald K. Berry, the concept of the Hebrew term *hokma*, translated wisdom, "embodies all the ethical and social abilities that distinguish the wise person from the fool or the unrighteous—skill, discretion, education, morality and faith."[1] The Scriptures link wisdom to skill or ability such as "to perform manual labor like spinning (Exodus 35:25), to discern good and evil (Job 28:28), to solve riddles (Prov. 1:6) or, generally, to know how to live well."[2] The term also denotes the ownership of a specific skill, like that of a goldsmith (Jeremiah 10:19), stonemason (1 Chronicles 22:15), or shipbuilder (Ezekiel 27:89). Bezalel and his companions were chosen to create the tent and the ark because they possessed the essential technical and artistic abilities required for the task. (Exodus 31:1-11; 35:30-36). This means that "in the Hebrew Bible wisdom refers to predominantly

---

1 Donald K. Berry, *An Introduction to Wisdom and Poetry of the Old Testament* (Nashville, TN: Broadman & Holman Publishers, 1999), 5.
2 Ibid.

practical activities. Action and thinking are inseparable. To possess wisdom is to excel at pragmatic activity rather than to participate in sustained reflection."[3]

An Aristotelian understanding of *hokma* is "If unused, knowledge remains unrecognized."[4] A person will be considered foolish if they know what is right but fail to act on it. Conversely, anyone who can perform a task skillfully will be regarded as "wise" in their area of expertise. Wisdom encompasses all aspects of human action and existence, addressing the entirety of human behavior while specifically focusing on practical matters related to our lives. *Hokma* "designates both the exercise of reason and the reception of the divine will."[5]

I. WISDOM AS AN ATTRIBUTE OF GOD

A biblical theology of wisdom must begin with the One Wise God, for God is the source of all true wisdom. The wisdom referred to in the Scriptures derives its significance solely from its connection to the one true God and Creator of the universe. Therefore, wisdom is depicted in Scripture as one of the essential attributes of God. (Isaiah 31:2; Job 12:13; Rom 16:27).

God is frequently depicted as having boundless wisdom and knowledge, with wisdom being inherent to his nature. The Bible contains many verses that highlight the deep connection between God and wisdom. For example, Daniel stated that wisdom and might belongs to God (2:20), Isaiah said God is wonderful in counsel and excellent in wisdom (28:29) and Paul in the New Testament declares that God is the "only wise God" (16:27). God is seen as the ultimate source of wisdom, embodying perfect knowledge, understanding, and discernment. The wisdom of God is understood to include not just intellectual insight, but also moral and spiritual perception. This divine wisdom is what enables God to govern the world and guide his creations.

Wisdom of God is also portrayed in the Bible as both the creature of God and the tool by which God created the whole creatures. According to the book of Proverbs, God established wisdom before the creation of all things (Proverbs 3:19-20). Furthermore, the Scriptures teaches that God grants wisdom to those who seek it humbly and sincerely. James 1:5 states, "If any of you lacks wisdom,

---

3 Ibid.
4 Ibid.
5 Ibid., 22.

you should ask God, who gives generously to all without finding fault, and it will be given to you." This implies that wisdom is not exclusive to God alone but can also be attained by individuals through their connection with Him.

One perfect example in receiving and possesses God's wisdom is king Solomon in the Old Testament. When Solomon inherited the throne from his father David, the first thing he did was pray and ask God to grant him his wisdom. And God gave him wisdom in abundance. The foundational aspect of biblical wisdom is understanding God—not in an abstract or theoretical manner, but through the tangible act of dedicating your life to Him.

1. *Wisdom Outside Wisdom Literature*

Recently, wisdom literature has emerged as a distinct discipline within the development of Old Testament theology. According to Richard "This emergence has not occurred without its own problems, including the definition of wisdom, the relationship of wisdom literature to the rest of the Old Testament and the relationship of Israel's wisdom literature to that of the Ancient Near Easter" (Richard, 14). Old Testament scholars have wrestled with understanding how wisdom literature relates to the rest of the Old Testament. However, there is a consensus that wisdom material is composed in both poetry and prose and is present throughout the Old Testament. The wisdom theology, language, and metaphors which is the main focus of wisdom study can be found especially in places like Deuteronomy, 1 and 2 Kings, many of the Psalms, the Song of Songs, and the prophets like Isaiah and Jeremiah.[6] Thus wisdom themes, vocabulary, and concerns are not limited to the basic wisdom canon of Job, Provers, and Ecclesiastes.[7]

2. *Wisdom in the Torah*

In the first five books of the Bible, themes of wisdom are primarily highlighted in the story of Joseph (Genesis 37-50) and in the teachings of Deuteronomy. After being sold into slavery by his brothers, Joseph took on the roles of counselor and judge in the land. His wisdom was unique and seen as a direct gift from God (Genesis 41:38-39). Joseph's journey to Egypt, along with his talent for

---

6   Richard P. Belcher, *Finding Favor in the Sight of God: A Theology of Wisdom Literature* (Downers Grove, Illinois: IVP Academic, 2018), 18.
7   Berry, *An Introduction to Wisdom and Poetry of the Old Testament*, 15.

interpreting dreams and his role in saving the nation from famine, underscores the theme of divine intervention throughout his life. He himself acknowledges this intervention, recognizing that God is the true source of wisdom and guidance. He had the "spirit of God" (Genesis 41:38) and introduces himself to his estranged brothers as someone who fears God (Genesis 42:18). The focus on the "fear of God" in the Book of Proverbs is a defining characteristic of Israel's wisdom tradition. The term "fear of the LORD" encompasses far more than simply acknowledging wisdom as a divine gift; it signifies that the origins of this wisdom extend beyond human influence.[8]

In the book of Deuteronomy, wisdom literature and prophetic language intertwine, especially regarding the connection between prosperity and obedience. The Shema (6:4-5) emphasizes that blessings or curses are contingent upon how one responds to the laws it entails. The continuum of blessing and curse encompasses both wisdom and Torah. What sets the wise apart from the foolish is their capacity to make choices that result in blessings. In much of the wisdom literature, there exists a subtle distinction between wisdom as the foundation for righteous living and wisdom itself being equated with righteous living. Deuteronomy connects the observance of the Torah with wisdom, intertwining obedience with insight: "You must observe them diligently, for this will demonstrate your wisdom and discernment to the nations. When they hear all these statutes, they will exclaim, 'Surely this great nation is a wise and discerning people!'" (Deut. 4:6).[9]

3. *Wisdom in Historical Books*

The linkage between wisdom and obedience in the subsequent books after Deuteronomy and Joshua provides an example of reviewing Israel's history in terms of punishment or reward based on obedience. In Joshua 23:14-16, Joshua addresses the Israelites near the end of his life, reviewing their history and reminding them of the importance of obedience to God's commands. He emphasized the consequences that come from either obeying or disobeying God's instructions. The absence of the word wisdom does not remove this passage from consideration. The focus on divine blessings and curses extends beyond wisdom literature, appearing often in historical texts as well. Notably, in the historical accounts, there is a reference to Solomon's wisdom in relation to God's invitation

---

8   Berry, *An Introduction to Wisdom and Poetry of the Old Testament*, 15.
9   Ibid.

to make a single request (1 Kings 3:5–14; 2 Chronicles 1:7–12). According to Berry "his wisdom included at least three aspects: (1) skill to rule with distinction, (2) skill to perform as a judge in deciding right and wrong, and (3) precocious depth and breadth of intelligence, particularly associated with the natural order."[10]

The first few chapters of 1 Kings, also, praises Solomon for his renowned wisdom. Solomon is depicted as a king who possessed exceptional wisdom and discernment, bestowed upon him by God. The account of Solomon's wisdom is primarily found in 1 Kings 3:5-28. According to the narrative, when Solomon became king after his father David, he had a dream in which God appeared to him and offered to grant him anything he desired, Solomon humbly asked for wisdom and understanding to govern the people of Israel. God was pleased with his request and granted him not only wisdom but also riches and honor surpassing any other king before him.

Solomon's wisdom became renounced through the region, attracting visitors from far and wide who sought his counsel. One of the most well-known stories demonstrating Solomon's wisdom is the account of the two women who came before him, both claiming to be the mother of the same baby. Solomon's famous decision to divide the baby in two and give each woman a portion revealed the true mother's love and led to the restoration of the child to her.

Solomon's wisdom extended beyond matters of judgment and governance. He was known for his vast knowledge and understanding of various subjects, including biology, botany and poetry. The biblical account attributes the compilation of many proverbs and songs to Solomon. The wisdom bestowed upon Solomon transcended the political and social concerns required for his royal responsibilities. In this context, wisdom encompasses far more than just the skills needed to complete specific tasks; it is Solomon's overall intellectual prowess that truly marked him as "wise."

4. *Wisdom in Prophetic Books*

Berry states that, "the use of wisdom languages and forms in the prophetic literature indicates merely that prophets drew from existing wisdom material for their oracle."[11] Thus they borrowed wisdom forms and themes but do not conceive wisdom according to any special pattern. Of all the prophets, Isaiah seems most

---

10 Berry, *An Introduction to Wisdom and Poetry of the Old Testament*, 16.
11 Berry, *An Introduction to Wisdom and Poetry of the Old Testament*, 17.

acutely aware of wisdom traditions (19:11-15; 28:23-29, and 40:13-14). On the other hand, Ezekiel, rather than referring directly to wisdom, employs wisdom forms to convey the prophetic message (16:44 and 18:2). Other wisdoms forms such as rhetorical questions similar to those occurring in Proverbs 6:27-28 and units resembling the depiction of God in Job 38-41 are present in the Book of Amos. Habakkuk deals with the theodicy question at length, whereby theodicy explains apparent injustice in a world controlled by God.[12]

5. *Wisdom in Psalms*

While Psalms, for example, are primarily a collection of poetic prayers and songs, many Psalms contain wisdom elements. They explore themes of trust in God, the righteous verses the wicked, and the rewards of living according to God's wisdom. Psalms contains numerous verses that highlight the importance of living in accordance with God's commandments and seeking wisdom through the study and observation of his law (Psalm 19 and 119). Like Deuteronomy, "Psalms makes use of wisdom themes to support a retributive theology."[13] Retributive theology suggests that there is a direct correlation between one's actions and the corresponding rewards and punishments from God. It emphasizes the idea that the righteous will be blessed, and the wicked will be punished. Some Psalms do reflect this theme by expressing the psalmist's belief in God's justice and the expectation that the wicked will face consequences for their actions.

For example, Psalm 37 contrasts the fate of the wicked with that of the righteous, affirming that God will ultimately bring judgment upon the wicked and reward the righteous. Similarly, Psalm 73 explores the apparent prosperity of the wicked and the Psalmist's struggle to understand why they seem to go unpunished. It raises the theodicy issue, a view of divine compensation settling issue, similar to the challenges of Job and Ecclesiastes. While it is true that the Psalms occasionally associate wisdom with the divine blessings upon the righteous and the curses upon the wicked, it is important to note that wisdom in the Psalms serves a broader range of functions and themes. Wisdom is note solely employed to reinforce retributive theology but is also used to convey the important of seeking God, living in alignment with his ways, and experiencing his guidance and deliverance (Psalms 25:4-5; 139:6).

---

12 Ibid.
13 Berry, *An Introduction to Wisdom and Poetry of the Old Testament*, 17.

6. *Wisdom in the New Testament*

In early Christianity wisdom literature serves as the basic instruction in religious practice. According to William Horbury book titled "Old Testament interpretation in the Writings of the Church Fathers," a large number of Greek translations of wisdom books confirm this. The presence of wisdom literature in the New Testament highlights the early church's significant reliance on biblical wisdom. References to wisdom frequently emerge in the teachings of Jesus. The Sermon on the Mountain is an example of wisdom literature in which the wise authority figure sits in the middle of his disciples and instructs them. Paul's writings suggest a deeper reliance on wisdom than may be evident at first glance.

The most pronounced example of direct dependence can be found in the Epistle of James. This book primarily aligns with the genre of Wisdom Literature, evident in both its structure and thematic content. We can observe a sequence of concise, self-contained units that unfold in rapid succession, reminiscent of the style found in wisdom literature, particularly in the Book of Proverbs. We often encounter the remarkable ability to express truth through memorable and concise sayings: "be doers of the word, and not hearers only" (1:22); "draw near to God and he will draw near to you" (4:8). With respect to the subject at hand, practical Christian morality aligns closely with the principles found in wisdom literature.

A prevalent technique in biblical wisdom literature is to use nature extensively as a source of similes and analogies for understanding human behavior. The Epistle of James often employs the technique of: "If we put bits into the mouths of horses that they may obey us, we guide their whole bodies. Look at the ships also; though they are so great and are driven by strong winds, they are guided by a very small rudder wherever the will of the pilot directs. So the tongue is a little member and boasts of great things. How great a forest is set ablaze by a small fire! And the tongue is a fire." (3:3-6). One of the remarkable strengths of wisdom literature lies in its capacity to resonate with the everyday realities of human life.

II. WISDOM LITERATURE

Biblical Wisdom Literature includes books such as Job, Proverbs, and Ecclesiastes, plus wisdom passages from other books in the Hebrew Canon.[14] The three

---

14   Ellington, 31.

foundational wisdom texts in the Bible embody the characteristics of wisdom as described earlier. According to Berry, "They each describe as wisdom: (1) the ability to live well, (2) vocational or practical skill, and (3) ultimate concepts."[15] The deuterocanonical books of Sirach and the Wisdom of Solomon reflect various elements of Hebrew wisdom literature. They offer valuable comparisons that highlight the shift from Hebrew Old Testament wisdom to the New Testament perspective on wisdom. While these books are not wisdom in themselves, they are influenced by or connected to wisdom across all Scriptural literature.

The Wisdom Literature in the Old Testament addresses themes distinct from those found in the other parts of the Old Testament. In contrast to the other books of the Old Testament, which frequently focus on themes such as covenant, the temple, the nation of Israel, the Exodus, Davidic kingship, and worship, the wisdom writings uniquely concentrate on insights regarding the natural world, human behavior, and practical knowledge. Wisdom literature explores into the details of life, the essence of human nature, moral principles, and the quest for insight.[16]

Wisdom literature tends to offer practical advice and guidance for living a righteous and fulfilling life. It draws upon general observations and insights that can be gleaned from observing the world and human behavior. As a result, wisdom is not dependent on or limited to the special revelation given to Israel. It provides insights that are accessible and applicable to anyone, regardless of their religious background or belief system.[17]

The wisdom writings often employ poetic language, metaphor, and vivid imagery to convey their messages. They explore profound questions about the nature of existence, the meaning of life, the problems of suffering, and the pursuit of knowledge and understanding. The wisdom books also contain reflection on the fleeting nature of life, the importance of humility, the consequences of folly, and the pursuit of wisdom as a valuable virtue.

Wisdom literature consists of those biblical documents preoccupied with human response to God and the world. They focus on man's reflection on God and his response rather than on God's search for man.

While biblical wisdom literature may have its own distinct style and purpose,

---

15   Berry, *An Introduction to Wisdom and Poetry of the Old Testament*, 11.
16   Ellington, 19.
17   Ibid.

it is interconnected with the rest of the Old Testament. It provides additional insights into God's character, human nature, and practical application of faith. By studying wisdom literature alongside other genres and readers can gain a more comprehensive understanding of the Old Testament's teachings and the biblical worldview. Let us now consider the testimony wisdom literature.

1. *Wisdom in Job*

Job is never identified as wise and his struggle is not introduced as a struggle for wisdom. But his identification as a righteous and pious person (1:1; 42:7) links him to wise conduct so often praised or commended by a vast array of biblical proverbs.[18] In the major poetic section of the book, Job struggles with God's silence regarding the suffering of the righteous, as interpreted within his own religious beliefs. As a voice of wisdom, Job articulates the frustration felt by those who remain steadfast in their devotion to God yet face hardships that rival or exceed those endured by the wicked. The question, "Is God unjust?" does not particularly resonate with wisdom; however, Job's quest for understanding and his urgent need for answers certainly align with the realm of wisdom.[19]

The story of Job exemplifies the definition of wisdom as "the exercise of mind as a religious pursuit." It illustrates the human quest for understanding profound questions, even though Job himself does not receive a clear "answer."[20] Wisdom typically focuses on how humans respond to God rather than on God's actions. Even though the prologue and epilogue include more direct involvement of God in the struggle for understanding, it is God's revelation of Himself in chapters 38-42 that brought Job to the point of understanding. For Job, "wisdom comes not so much through human device or natural revelation as through an act of God (special revelation)."[21] In certain ways, God's powerful speeches at the conclusion of Job's trials offer him a sense of satisfaction. These divine messages, much like the prologue, highlight God's actions rather than human endeavors. True wisdom encompasses both the human quest for religious understanding and God's intervention, which offers clarity and silences grievances. While Job uniquely emphasizes this aspect of wisdom, the themes of God's sovereignty and the recognition of his wisdom reflected in creation are present throughout all wisdom literature.[22]

---

18 Berry, *An Introduction to Wisdom and Poetry of the Old Testament*, 11.
19 Berry, *An Introduction to Wisdom and Poetry of the Old Testament*, 11-12.
20 Berry, 12.
21 Berry, 12.
22 Berry, 12.

2. *Wisdom in Proverbs*

According to Bartholomew, "scholars sometimes label the book of Proverbs as 'early,' or 'traditional' wisdom. The dating of Proverbs is actually very complicated, but the idea of 'traditional' wisdom is true in that Proverbs is the foundation for wisdom in the Old Testament." (64). Wisdom can be categorized into four in Proverbs: (1) wisdom is grounded in the "fear of LORD [Yahweh]:" (2) wisdom is concerned with discerning the order that the LORD has built into the creation; (3) wisdom focuses on discerning God's ways in particular circumstances, and (4) wisdom is grounded in tradition. These categories stand at the heart of Proverbs and thus of Israel's view of wisdom as a whole.[23]

The first seven chapters of the book set forth the purpose of the book in four infinitives: "to know wisdom and instruction;" "to understand words of insight;" "to receive instruction in wised dealing, in righteousness, justice, and equity;" and "to give prudence to the simple, knowledge and discretion to the youth." Thus the very purpose of the book is to know wisdom and instruction. Wisdom can be summarized as the ability to understand how life works in order to respond appropriately. It allows someone to develop skillfulness in living a wise life by being able to navigate life in order to achieve success. Understanding the character of different kinds of people is necessary in order to know how to respond to them.

Wisdom in Proverbs also includes understanding the way the world that God has created works because God has built wisdom into his creation (Proverbs 3:19). Certain actions or attitudes may lead to certain results. These results are not amoral but reflect God's justice because the divine order of the world derives from the righteous character of Yahweh. The better one understands the way the world works the better decisions a person will be able to make in seeking the path of wisdom.

Coupled with wisdom is the word "instruction." This word could be translated "discipline," as it refers to a chastening lesson that shapes character and corrects moral faults. It has a wide variety of uses. Positively, it is used to encourage correct behavior (Proverbs 15:5; 19:20). Negatively, it is used to reprove wrong behavior and can even be used of corporal punishment (Proverbs 13:24; 22:15; 23:13). The knowledge that comes from wisdom and instructions is not theoretical knowledge that is learned through a variety of experiences of life. This aspect of wisdom is

---

23   C.G. Bartholomew, Ryan P. O'Dowd, *Old Testament Wisdom Literature* (Downer's Grove, IL: InterVarsity Press, 2011), 65.

highlighted in the phrase "to receive instruction in wise dealing." The instruction of discipline shapes people's character to help them grasp the implications of a situation in order to make beneficial decisions. The right decisions lead to righteousness, justice and equity.

3. *Themes in Proverbs*

Proverbs presents significant themes that are predominantly found in the wisdom literature. These themes often appear in pairs, such as diligence versus laziness and wisdom versus folly. Common themes associated with wisdom often include the notion of the persistent wife, the importance of moderation, and the willingness to accept criticism. Proverbs demonstrates a strong focus on the subject of speech, a recurring motif in the Hebrew Bible. It underscores the importance of controlling personal communication so profoundly that it introduces a distinctive variation of this theme.[24]

According to Berry, the "doctrine of the two ways" and "retribution for good and evil" are the two recurring themes constitute the most distinctive feature of Proverbs and provide much of its character as a unique book. "The doctrine of the two ways is a part of the doctrine of retribution, providing a form in which to express the universally applicable doctrine of retribution. The choice of a "one or the other" mode of conduct is the premise for nearly all the ethical content of the book."[25]

The fear of the Lord is prominently showcased as a key theme throughout Proverbs, particularly within the Israelite context. The editors highlighted its significance by positioning it as the first statement immediately following the introduction in 1:2-6. This phrase serves an important theological function. The vast majority of Proverbs do not independently show direct theological connections and might be seen as part of the international wisdom literature common to Egypt, Mesopotamia, and Canaan. Israel's sages sought a way to showcase wisdom as a distinctive trait of the Hebrews. By defining knowledge as the "fear of Yahweh," they established a unique theological framework. A correct interpretation of the term "fear of God" reveals how the editors of Proverbs perceive the compilation as sacred literature.[26]

The phrase appears more frequently in Proverbs than in any other part of the

---

24 Berry, *An Introduction to Wisdom and Poetry of the Old Testament*, 121-2.
25 Ibid., 122.
26 Berry, *An Introduction to Wisdom and Poetry of the Old Testament*, 124.

Hebrew Bible. To better understand the meaning of the fear of the Lord, we can examine its most common antonym: "The fool says in his heart, 'There is no God'" (Psalm 14:1). The fool's hesitation to "do the right thing" reveals a deep-seated unbelief within their consciousness. Acting foolishly entails a rejection of one's own religious instincts, and this relationship works in the opposite direction as well. The assertion that "The fear of the LORD is the beginning of wisdom" ties ethical behavior directly to religious belief and commitment. This aligns with the Aristotelian concept of knowledge, encapsulated in the idea that "to know the good is to do the good."[27]

The Proverbs are meant to guide rather than command, fostering a tone that promotes contemplation over mere compliance. This results in a more reflective and less authoritarian atmosphere within the text. Readers who align with the insights of the sages recognize a deeper truth that transcends conventional morality and logic, engaging with the teachings through understanding.

Central to Proverbs is the idea of choice. The reader can take one of two ways and is constantly being asked to choose between the two. One way leads to life, and the other to death. "The upright will live in the land, and the blameless will remain in it; but the wicked will be cut off from the land, and the faithful will be torn from it" (2:21–22). The notion that our choices set the direction of our lives echoes Moses' summation of the terms of the Torah. After laying out the conditions of the covenant, he called the people to respond with a decision: "This day I call heaven and earth as witnesses against you that I have set before you, life and death, blessings and curses. Now choose life, so that you and your children may live" (Deuteronomy 30:19). Proverbs consistently presents the idea of two ways, that of the wise and that of the fool. This is the central theme from which the others derive. The focus is on the direction we choose and its ensuing destination.[28]

4. *Wisdom in Ecclesiastes*

The wisdom of Ecclesiastes is characterized by the identification of its author as Solomon (1:1), the wise king (2:12). The nature of the inquiry—an exploration of all human activities—aligns with themes of wisdom and underscores its deep focus on human behavior and its often ironic turns. The frequent emphasis on the speaker's wisdom and the pursuit of understanding provide compelling evidence

---

27 Ibid., 125.
28 Ellington, 53.

of the text's connection to wisdom literature. This includes the use of vocabulary typical of wisdom traditions, as well as the intrinsic aim of "discovering the truth."

A casual reading of Ecclesiastes reveals many proverbs and proverbial expressions, suggesting that the text is aimed at an audience well-acquainted with proverbial teachings. Additionally, many of the book's messages align closely with the viewpoints presented in the Book of Proverbs. These includes: "(1) the embracing of opposing truths, (2) leaving outcomes to God, (3) the feat of God, (4) the limitation of human thinking, and (5) the doctrine of "retribution." The counsel offered to the king and his subjects is a recurring theme in Ecclesiastes and is also highlighted in Proverbs. Ecclesiastes' focus on the ironies of human life and behavior is echoed in Proverbs. The persistent notion that the speaker undertook a journey in search of wisdom reflects Ecclesiastes' most direct connection to wisdom literature.[29]

Like the Book of Job, Ecclesiastes questions the fairness of life's retribution. Such inquiries are as integral to the pursuit of wisdom as the strong endorsement of the strict view of retribution found in Proverbs. The text illustrates two contrasting approaches to life, which do not clearly relate to other Hebrew wisdom literature. While other wisdom books generally affirm the meaningfulness of life, the author of Ecclesiastes adopts a different viewpoint. The assertion that life is ultimately empty seems to conflict with the book's counsel to fear God and enjoy life. However, the themes present less of a challenge than the apparent contradictions. Wisdom can sometimes convey opposing truths, yet it does so with acknowledgment of the complexities and offers consistent guidance throughout.[30]

In summary while Job and Ecclesiastes deal specifically with how to live when life appears to have turned upside down, Proverbs presents the ABC's of wisdom when life is generally going right.

III. WISDOM IN THE DEUTEROCANON

The Septuagint, which is the Greek translation of the Old Testament, contains two extra books of wisdom: Sirach and The Wisdom of Solomon. Sirach effectively mirrors the poetic structures found in Proverbs, while also upholding the traditional teachings that advocate for prosperity for the righteous and adversity for the wicked.

---

29 Berry, *An Introduction to Wisdom and Poetry of the Old Testament*, 157.
30 Berry, 157.

1. *Wisdom in Sirach*

The deuterocanonical book entitled the Wisdom of Jesus Son of Sirach (or Ecclesiasticus) provides a snapshot of Jewish wisdom around 180 B.C.E. Since the entire book was conceived as a book of wisdom, it yields information regarding continuity and discontinuity with the wisdom tradition associated with Solomon. No other book offers such a useful comparison to Proverbs, Job and Ecclesiastes. Ben Sirach employed citations from Proverbs to support encouragement to faithful worship and living in accordance with the teaching of the Pentateuch. He apparently intended to protect the Jewish community from assimilation into Hellenism.[31]

To some degree, Sirach equates the practice of traditional Jewish piety with wisdom. His wisdom narrows the scope of wisdom to the nation Israel for the first time, effectively eliminating its international character.[32]

Sirach emphasizes the Torah as an ultimate goal in itself. The religious teachings within Sirach exhibit a pronounced authoritarian tone. Unlike Proverbs, which conveys wisdom through a more anonymous voice, Sirach features Jesus son of Sirach as a distinct speaker. This text adopts a unique perspective on wisdom, linking it more intimately with the faith and culture of Judaism. The son of Sirach perceived wisdom as an essential quality that allowed Israel to maintain its identity. The references to Israel's history, especially in chapters 44-50 of Sirach, which are unprecedented in wisdom literature, reinforce this viewpoint. This perspective connects wisdom with the specific expressions of Israel's faith. In contrast, earlier wisdom literature related wisdom to sound decision-making applicable to various historical contexts. While faith in Yahweh was one of those crucial decisions, wisdom encompassed activities in a broader range of areas. By identifying wisdom with the Torah, Sirach positions religious identity as a fundamental aspect of wisdom.[33]

2. *Wisdom is Wisdom of Solomon*

The Wisdom of Solomon marks a significant shift from the earliest traditions of Israelite wisdom. The opening verse and sections 6:1–11 seem directed towards rulers, yet it is evident that Wisdom aims to reach a broader audience.

---

31   Ellington, 133-134.
32   Coert Rylaarsdam, *Revelation in Jewish Wisdom Literature* (Chicago, IL: University of Chicago Press, 1946), 27.
33   Berry, *An Introduction to Wisdom and Poetry of the Old Testament*, 18.

This work emphasizes God's (Yahweh's) sovereignty in stark contrast to Greek rationalism. At times, the Wisdom of Solomon equates wisdom with God's personal transcendence, illustrated through his involvement in (1) creation, (2) the history of Israel, and (3) the ultimate end of the world. The text serves as a medium for conveying a deeper theological message to the faithful community, one that offers hope and encouragement anchored in the nature of God. In this context, wisdom becomes a vital tool for defending faith in Israel's God rather than merely providing guidance for everyday life, as seen in the three books of the Hebrew canon.[34]

IV. WISDOM THEMES

Israel's wisdom teachers were first and foremost students of the universe. They studied Yahweh's creation to determine order and commend human conduct which would sustain that order socially and cosmologically. They were not philosophers, since their interest was in the world as it existed and not in speculations on origins or cosmic significance. They assumed rather than questioned the world's origin as God's creation (Job 28).[35]

1. *The Fear of the Lord and Wisdom*

The Fear of the Lord is one of the basic themes of biblical wisdom especially wisdom literature. One overarching concern in wisdom literature is the close association of "the fear of the LORD" with wisdom. Five passages from wisdom literature intimately related the two: Proverbs 1:7; 9:10; 15:33; Psalm 111:10; and Job 28:28.

The Hebrews viewed religious devotion as an aspect of wisdom, but they did not equate the two. Much of Hebrew wisdom remains pertinent regardless of whether it is applied in a religious context. The phrase "the fear of the LORD is the beginning of wisdom" can be interpreted in at least three ways. First, it can be understood as a positive assertion: "a person who reveres God inherently possesses a crucial element of wisdom." Those who acknowledge their obligation to God hold a distinct advantage over those who seek wisdom without making this acknowledgment, giving them a considerable head start.[36]

---

34   Ibid., 18.
35   Berry, *An Introduction to Wisdom and Poetry of the Old Testament*, 19.
36   Ibid., 20.

Furthermore, the phrase likely speaks to the listener's way of life. A person who lives with honesty, integrity, and reverence demonstrates a true fear of the LORD. This connection effectively associates the fear of the LORD with wisdom. Living in this manner not only reflects a deep respect for God but also indicates the capacity to make sound decisions. This discernment is an essential element of wisdom.[37]

Third, the phrase serves as a reminder that the realm of wisdom is enveloped in mystery, much like the name and nature of Yahweh. The name Yahweh evokes a sense of mystery and transcendence. If wisdom is rooted in the fear of Yahweh (translated as "LORD"), it suggests that wisdom exists in a realm that is partially beyond human grasp. While humans can possess and apply wisdom, its true origins belong to the creator.[38]

The recent interpretation of the phrase "the fear of the LORD is the beginning of wisdom" presents an intriguing perspective on wisdom. However, it's important to note that "fear of the LORD" typically pertains to how humans respond to God, rather than describing God's inherent nature. This fear encompasses devout living more than it highlights God's unique attributes. Therefore, the first two interpretations seem reasonable: they suggest that piety is integral to wisdom and characterize the religious individual as inherently wise. The final explanation, however, remains questionable.[39]

The fear of the Lord primarily encompasses a heartfelt response characterized by humility, love, and trust in God, leading an individual to willingly align their life with God's ways. It signifies a God-centered approach to living that includes deep reverence for Him. Recognized as the foundation of knowledge, the fear of the Lord serves as the essential guiding principle of one's life; without it, true wisdom—defined by God—remains out of reach. While the term appears less frequently in the New Testament than in the Old Testament (notably in Acts 9:31; Philippians 2:12; Colossians 3:22; Revelation 19:5), it remains linked to those who embrace God's paths of repentance and faith.

2. *Prosperity and Suffering*

Concerns about prosperity and suffering stand out as a central theme in the

---

37 Ibid., 20.
38 Bartholomew, *Old Testament Wisdom Literature,* 70.
39 Ibid., 71.

pursuit of wisdom. The book of Proverbs presents a theology of retribution that seemingly addresses nearly all inquiries regarding human experiences. It suggests that the wicked face suffering, while the righteous enjoy prosperity. The Wisdom of Solomon and Sirach present similar perspectives, but two wisdom literature texts notably challenge the traditional notion of retribution: Job and, to a slightly lesser extent, Ecclesiastes. These texts argue that personal experiences contradict the widely held belief in fair retribution. In Job, his three friends articulate the conventional understanding that his suffering is a manifestation of God's disapproval of his actions. Job consistently upheld his innocence throughout the entire ordeal: "If I have walked with falsehood, and my foot has hurried to deceit— let me be weighed in a just balance, and let God know my integrity!" (31:5 – 6).[40]

Ecclesiastes presents a straightforward claim: "There are righteous people who perish in their righteousness, and there are wicked people who prolong their life in their evil doing" (7:15). The challenges in Job and Ecclesiastes reveal a key contrast within wisdom literature, emphasizing the distinction among these texts. This divergence is crucial when examining the overall collection of wisdom writings. A major obstacle in achieving a unified understanding of Hebrew wisdom lies in reconciling the positive perspective of Proverbs with the skepticism found in Job and Ecclesiastes. The wisdom found in Proverbs emphasizes the expectation of God's rewards and punishments. In contrast, the books of Job and Ecclesiastes introduce the idea that good and evil can occur without clear reasons. While they challenge traditional beliefs, the sages of Israel still refrain from delving into the origins of evil. Job's inquiry, "Shall we receive good from God, and shall we not receive the evil?" (2:10) emphasizes that all aspects of human fortune are ultimately determined by God. All experiences, both good and evil, were seen as under the purview of God, with every event being viewed as either an act of divine will or a decision not to intervene. Consequently, Hebrew theology highlighted the supremacy and autonomy of God while downplaying human capacity to influence or fully grasp the divine intentions.[41]

V. CREATION AND ORDER

God's initial act in the narrative of Biblical history is creation. In his infinite wisdom, He intricately designed all living beings. The universe and all it

---

40   Berry, *An Introduction to Wisdom and Poetry of the Old Testament,* 21.
41   Bartholomew, *Old Testament Wisdom Literature,* 181.

encompasses came into existence through his profound understanding (Jeremiah 10:12; 51:15; Psalm 104:24; Proverbs 3:19). In Proverbs 8, wisdom is depicted as a woman who stands alongside God at the very dawn of creation. This portrayal emphasizes that wisdom existed before anything else came into being. She is described as the craftsman at God's side, born as the first act of creation, prior to the formation of the oceans or the shaping of dry land. The authors of Proverbs take care to clarify that wisdom is not a co-equal with God; instead, she refers to herself as the initial work of the Lord and joyfully witnesses God's creative acts (8:22-31). It is important to note that Lady Wisdom does not claim equality with God or suggest she is a goddess like those worshiped by neighboring cultures. Instead, she is portrayed as the foremost of God's creations, granted a unique role to perceive and comprehend the importance of all that God accomplishes.[42]

The entire system of creation on Earth, in the universe, across galaxies, and throughout the cosmos profoundly reflects the wisdom of God. This divine wisdom is magnificent and exceeds human comprehension. The mysteries of creation reveal God's extraordinary intellect and understanding. He crafted his master plan with wisdom, knowledge, and perfect goodness, imbued with love. The wisdom of God is pure and inherently good, and all of his works are executed with perfect wisdom.

The wisdom found in the Old Testament presents a view of life that is fundamentally shaped by God's order. There is a deep-seated conviction that God is the creator of the world, having imbued it with purpose and structure. The initial chapters of Genesis recount the divine act of creation, detailing how God formed the universe, the earth, and all living beings. The narrative emphasizes that everything was created with deliberate intention and design, highlighting that human beings were made in God's own image.[43]

The Old Testament conveys the notion that God's authority permeates every facet of life. It offers direction on moral and ethical conduct, social justice, worship practices, interpersonal relationships, and many other domains. The laws and commandments presented to the Israelites, particularly in books such as Exodus, Leviticus, and Deuteronomy, are viewed as divine guidelines for aligning one's life with God's order. Furthermore, the wisdom literature within the Old

---

42　Ellington, 57.

43　Scott Ellington, *Wisdom Literature: An Independent-Study Textbook* (Springfield, MO: Global University, 2008), 103.

Testament underscores the significance of living wisely and in alignment with God's principles to attain blessings and steer clear of adverse outcomes.

The Old Testament wisdom literature reflects a shared awareness of the order in creation that was prevalent in the Ancient Near East. However, it stands out due to its belief in a singular divine source responsible for that order, setting it apart from other cultural understandings.

VI. CHRIST: THE WISDOM OF GOD

No examination of Old Testament wisdom is complete without exploring its fulfilment and embodiment in Jesus Christ. Jesus used the style and form of the wisdom teacher. For instance, He utilized proverbs in his teaching, such as, "All who draw the sword will die by the sword" (Matthew 26:52). John touches on elements of Hellenistic thought and Hebrew wisdom in his portrayal of Jesus as the Logos of God. Alyce McKenzie draws a number of connections between the "I am" sayings of Jesus in John's Gospel ("I am the light of the world"; "I am the true vine," and so on) and Israel's wisdom tradition (2002, 204–207). For example, she indicates that Jesus' statements, "I am the bread of life . . . I am the living bread that came down from heaven. If anyone eats of this bread, he will live forever" (John 6:35, 51) are reminiscent of the feast offered by Lady Wisdom in Proverbs 9:5–6: "Come, eat my food and drink the wine I have mixed. Leave your simple ways and you will live; walk in the way of understanding." Interestingly, both meals promise life to those who partake of them.

Paul offers an extended discussion contrasting human and divine wisdom in 1 Corinthians 1:18–2:16. Extending the claims of Proverbs 8:22 Paul equates Christ with wisdom (1 Cor. 1:24).

Colossians 1:15 – 20 is a key text in discussing the person of Jesus and his relationship to wisdom. Paul identifies Christ as the one "in who are hidden all the treasures of wisdom and knowledge." In this text we do so recognize that Paul's doctrinal exposition flows out of his prayers:

> "Asking God to fill you with the knowledge of his will and through all spiritual wisdom and understanding...that you may live a life worthy of the LORD and may please him in every way: bearing fruit in every good work, growing in the knowledge of God (Colossian 1:9 – 10).

At the height of the prayer, Paul then says of the Son:

> He is the image of the invisible God, the firstborn of all creation. For by him all things were created, in heaven and on earth, visible and invisible, whether thrones or dominions or rulers or authorities—all things were created through him and for him. And he is before all things, and in him all things hold together. And he is the head of the body, the church. He is the beginning, the firstborn from the dead, that in everything he might be preeminent. For in him all the fullness of God was please to dwell, and through him to reconcile to himself all things, whether on earth or in heaven, making peace by the blood of his cross" (Col 1:15 – 20).

In this passage Paul is able to use wisdom to orient our epistemology (knowing and believing), ethics (behaving), redemption (salvation and transformation) and sense of communing (human flourishing) in a prayer for wisdom.

Bauckham points out that this text has been used in Christian theology for three major purposes: (1) in seeking to establish the pre-existence of the Christ as Creator, (2) in developing a theology of the Son's dominion in overcoming both cosmic and worldly power, and (3) in renewing a theology of creation, especially in response to the recent ecological crises.[44] While these are all fruitful lines of study, Bauckham suggest that it is better to say that the text moves from one extraordinary central reality in a thousand related direction all at once: It is God's wisdom that orders creation for its well-being, God's wisdom that ordains good ways of human living in the world, and God's wisdom that, beyond the disruption of creation's good and evil, purposes the ultimate wellbeing, the shalom, the peace of the whole creation. Where is this wisdom to be found?[45] Wisdom is found in the whole creation, and it is found in the crucified and risen Jesus and somehow these two are the same wisdom.

---

44   Richard Bauckham, *Where is Wisdom to be found?: Colossians 1:15-20* (CMC Press, 2003), 20.
45   Bauckham, 20.

Why Historical Theology Matters
The Trinity and the Dangers of Biblicism

DR. MICHAEL S. HORTON
Founder and Editor-in-Chief, Sola Media
Professor of Systematic Theology and Apologetics,
Westminster Seminary California
USA

A t least for many evangelical theologians and pastors, 2016 will be remembered for one of the most contentious debates over the Trinity ever in evangelical circles. I am not interested in going into the weeds on the debate, particularly the more acrimonious exchanges, but it does point up the importance not only of being creedal and confessional but of understanding the debates in which they were forged.

The good news is that after a few or more centuries of functional unitarianism in academic theology and frequent neglect in evangelical circles, the Trinity is one of the most popular topics in both audiences today. The downside is that the versions of Trinitarian theology that receive the most attention often reflect the agendas of the author more than the actual positions that have formed the ecumenical consensus of orthodox Christianity.

The fourth century was the richest post-apostolic era in terms of providing the foundations and formulations that we often take for granted. How are the Father, Son, and Holy Spirit one in essence (*homoousios*) and yet distinct persons? There are several ways of coming to a wrong answer and the church became well aware of all of them by the late fourth century. The Nicene consensus, forged through controversy and finally adopted at the Council of Constantinople in 381, yielded a simple formula that said what had to be affirmed and denied (over against the various heresies) yet expressed humble restraint before majestic mystery. There are two processions in the Godhead: The Son proceeds from the unbegotten Father as the only-begotten and the Spirit proceeds by spiration (being breathed). This single act of double-procession is eternal—there is no point when the Son or the Spirit was not God. It is perfect, admitting no degrees of sharing in the divine essence. And it is necessary. While the missions in the economy (history) of creation and redemption are contingent (resulting from a free decision), the double procession is essential to the life of the Triune God.

Thus, God is God without creation, but he cannot be God without the eternal procession of the Son and the Spirit from the Father. The external works of the Trinity in our world reveal the Godhead, but must not be confused with the immanent life of the Trinity in these eternal processions. God doesn't depend on the world for his existence and identity. But to understand the results—especially as we confess in the Nicene-Constantinopolitan Creed, we have to engage the context of controversy, revision, over-reactions, more revision, and so on, that produced this consensus. When we do, we discover that we are often re-inventing the wheel and it's not always round. Many of the dead-ends of the fourth century are repeated in contemporary projects and debates.

The Nicene Creed remains the touchstone of the orthodox Christian faith. As an ecclesiastical summary of Scripture, it is fallible, but as a summary of Scripture, the statement is binding upon all Christians as a subordinate authority to Scripture. The debates that led to this remarkable consensus seemed likely to pull the church apart into different factions. At the risk of over-simplification, they turned on the following views, which are admittedly assigned to various figures by us rather than labels that they would necessarily have accepted.

Many (like the early Origen) taught an ontological subordination, where the Son and the Spirit were seen as different in rank, authority, and essential Godhood from the Father. Arianism went further, placing the Son on the "creature" side of the Creator-creature ledger. Though the first and most glorious creature, the Son is qualitatively different from the Father—not of the same essence. Others argued that "Father," "Son," and "Spirit" are just different names or masks for one person—like personas on the stage in a one-person play. Hence, they were called modalists (or Sabellians after the Roman presbyter who taught this view). In reaction against this rejection of the plurality of persons, others veered toward tritheism: namely, that the Father, the Son and the Spirit are different persons in exactly the same sense as human persons; consequently, there are three gods.

Among the important conclusions of these church fathers is the distinction between the eternal processions (also called the immanent Trinity) and the historical missions (the economic Trinity). While the Triune God reveals himself truly in history, we do not know what God is in himself or how the processions of the Son and the Spirit from the Father actually work. But if we confuse the processions and the missions, we open the door to heresies like Arianism, where Jesus' statement about his inferiority to the Father, for example in John 14:6, is taken to refer to his eternal status.

Navigating between the Scylla of one heresy and the Charybdis of another, the ancient pastors we justly revere not only arrived at a simple but grand statement of the faith. In the process, they showed us their work, as it were, wrestling with opponents and sometimes each other in letters, treatises and biblical commentaries that are with us today. Especially for teachers, exploring the history of the developments leading to Nicea is not just for fun. It is essential if we are to get beyond merely repeating their words, much less thinking that we can come up with a better formula. We need to try to understand the deeper contexts and arguments that led them to conclusions that all Christians confess more than 1,600 years later.

In his magisterial work Lewis Ayres, Nicea and Its Legacy observes that while "Trinitarian theology" has become a cottage industry, many theologians have engaged the legacy of Nicea "at a fairly shallow level, frequently relying on assumptions about Nicene theology that are historically indefensible." What is remarkable is that Ayres addresses this criticism not to the general public or the media but to "modern Christian theologians."[1] There is plenty of evidence of such "historically indefensible" interpretations across a broad spectrum ranging from conservative to liberal, especially in recent years. Often, the theologian comes to the subject with an already-settled set of convictions about the way things should look in the world today and then proceeds to develop a Trinitarian theology to ground it.

For example, Jürgen Moltmann is famous for developing a social model of the Trinity that eliminates the unity of essence in favor of a unity of purpose and will. Then he offers this model as a way of justifying a political, economic and cultural program of democratic socialism. Moltmann commends his model over against the oppressive hierarchies (and especially patriarchies) that orthodox formulations supposedly assumed and extended. However, virtually no specialist in patristic studies recognizes the fourth century in Moltmann's version of the story. As conservative Protestants, we are alert to the penchant for "theologies of correlation" (i.e., systems in which the ideals of modernity function as central dogmas). We know when liberals are projecting their own secular assumptions as if they were talking about God, when they're really talking about humanity. But it is more difficult to detect it when conservative agendas are in play.

Noted conservative theologians Wayne Grudem and Bruce Ware have led the charge for what they call "the eternal functional subordination of the Son" (EFS). According to these writers, the subordination of the Son to the Father is the basis for that of wives to their husbands. In fact, Grudem sees the relations of the Father, the Son and the Spirit along the lines of father, wife and child in a family.[2] Whereas Moltmann and others appeal to a Social Trinitarian model to defend a more egalitarian ideal, Grudem and Ware seem to adopt certain of its features with a more "subordinationist" interpretation for a complementarian (male headship)

---

1 Lewis Ayres, *Nicea and Its Legacy* (Oxford: Oxford University Press, 2004), 1.
2 Wayne Grudem, *Systematic Theology* (Grand Rapids: Zondervan, 1995), 257.

perspective. Bruce Ware pleads, "May God help us to see that Trinitarian roles and relationships are meant to be reflected in marriage as both husbands and wives manifest what is true eternally in the very triune nature of God."[3] Although Ware is obviously not a Social Trinitarian, the phrase "society of Persons" nudges in that direction, along with the tendency to turn distinct roles in every work into distinct works of the Father that he often delegates to the other persons.[4]

Unlike Moltmann, the author clearly and unequivocally affirms the equality of the persons on the basis of their unity of essence. Nevertheless, as I will argue, this affirmation is at least qualified if not abrogated by many of his formulations. In any case, conservative and liberal Protestants—in quite different ways—sometimes use their "return to the Bible" as a justification for dissenting from classic formulations while insufficiently engaging or in some cases even misunderstanding those historical arguments.

According to Ware, "The Father possesses the place of supreme authority... This hierarchical structure of authority exists in the eternal Godhead" despite their being identical with respect to essence.[5] Each person "possesses fully the identically same divine nature."[6] In fact, the Son and the Spirit "possess fully the attribute of omnipotence by possessing fully the undivided nature."[7] This is a major point where clarification is needed, however. How can consubstantiality be maintained if the Father alone is:

- "supreme among the Persons of the Godhead" (46);

- "...is the one who reigns over all" (48);

- "...stands above the Son" (49);

- "...gets top billing, as it were...as the highest in authority and the one deserving of ultimate praise" (51) with "...the place of highest honor" (55);

- "...the one who is on top" (58) and "...retains the position for which highest honor and glory is owed" (66; cf. 67: "...the Father who rightly deserves ultimate honor and glory")?

---

3   Bruce Ware, *Father, Son, & Holy Spirit: Relationships, Roles, & Relevance* (Crossway, 2005), 147.

4   Ware, 21.

5   Ware, 21.

6   Ware, 42.

7   Ware, 45.

The Son "is worshiped with the Father," but is he worshiped equally with the Father? From Ephesians 3:14-19, Ware concludes:

> Paul begins his prayer bowing his knees neither to the Son nor to the Spirit but to the Father, 'from whom every family in heaven and on earth is named.' The Father, then, is the sovereign Ruler over heaven and earth, controlling even the very names that every creature is given. From this position of sovereign supremacy, it is the Father who has the authority to grant this prayer's fulfillment, and so ultimately all glory and thanksgiving must go to him.[8]

We do have to be careful here. Paul does indeed begin with the Father, as indeed all prayer is directed to the Father, in the name of the Son, through the power of the Spirit. This does indeed indicate differing roles in the economy. But does it entail different ranks, particularly eternal ranks of superior and inferior, justifying the conclusion that the Father alone "is the sovereign Ruler of heaven and earth" and that "ultimately all glory and thanksgiving must go to him"?

There is an "Arian" way of reading the passages according to which the Son being granted by the Father authority over heaven and earth, "the name above every name," and the right to have life in himself is seen as grounding his inferiority. Then there is the orthodox way of reading the same passages, according to which being "from the Father" means being exactly what the Father is, "Light from Light," except that the Son is not the Father. In On the Trinity Augustine was especially keen in his anti-Arian interpretation of these passages. "Light from Light" means that there can be no rank, diminution or subordination. The order (from Light, i.e., the Father) does not cancel the substance (Light from Light) (De trin. IV.27). Luigi Gioia's work, *The Theological Epistemology of Augustine's De Trinitate* offers a terrific exposition of this point. To be begotten is to be inferior, according to the "Arian" logic, while for the orthodox it is to be of the same essence as the begetter. "In this Trinity none is before nor after another; none is greater or less than another," according to the Athanasian Creed. I am not at all suggesting that Ware, Grudem or others are Arians! However, there is a way of reading the relevant passages as highlighting unity and a way of reading that highlights the Son's difference from the Father. On that score, it seems to me that some of Ware's interpretations favor the latter exegetical bias.

---

8   Ware, 125.

If Ware answers that ultimate sovereignty and therefore praise belongs to the Father merely because of different roles, then the question arises as to whether sovereignty (omnipotence) and aseity are proper attributes of the essence. If so, then at least some of his expressions seem at odds with this orthodox conviction that "the Son is fully God."[9] In any case, simply repeating fidelity to essential unity and subordination only in roles will not allay suspicions of ontological subordinationism. The most practical test that pro-Nicenes put to their critics was whether they could affirm equal praise to the Son and the Spirit ("who with the Father and the Son is worshipped and glorified," the Council of Constantinople added). If they are not equally deserving of equal worship, then they are not equally divine.

Ware is correct to remind us of the distinctness of the persons, over against an implicit modalism or tendency to confuse them. At the same time, I wonder at certain points whether Ware is over-correcting. For example, while it is wholly salutary to say that each person contributes uniquely to every external work of the Godhead, expressions such as "distinct tasks and activities"[10] appear to threaten the important maxim that the external works of the Trinity are undivided. The emphasis on the Father's authority threatens to divide the work of the Godhead. "It is not as though the Father is unable to work unilaterally, but rather, he chooses to involve the Son and the Spirit."[11] In fact, there are several places where the works of the Father is distinguished from those of the Son and the Spirit and unhelpful expressions (e.g., that the Father often [!] works through them, though he could do it himself). "Yet though the Father is supreme, he does much of his work through the Son and the Spirit."[12]

As the earlier expressions raise the question about the consubstantiality of the Son and the Spirit with the Father in terms of omnipotence, this statement seems to call into question their shared aseity with the Father. Although they are persons from the Father, what they are from the Father is exactly what the Father is with respect to these attributes. It is both true and important to affirm that each person contributes differently, but it is impossible that the Father could operate apart from the Son and the Spirit any more than he could exist apart from them. Ware even goes so far as to add, "In many ways, what we see here of the

---

9   Ware, 70.
10 Ware, 20.
11 Ware, 57.
12 Ware, 59, emphasis added.

Father choosing not to work unilaterally but to accomplish his work through the Son, or through the Spirit, extends into his relationship to us."[13] Here is another example, it seems to me, of the blurring of the line between immanent and economic trinities (which ultimately threatens the Creator-creature distinction). While it is salutary to observe that God freely chooses to work through creatures even though he could work unilaterally, it is dangerous to say that this is just as true of the Father in relation to the Son and the Spirit. "Marvel at how the Father delegates his work to others."[14] The unity of the persons in every work hardly accommodates this picture of a boss delegating his work to others. According to Scripture, interpreted by classical formulations, everything done by the Father, in the Son, through the Spirit is God's work—that is, the work of the three persons in unison. "When others participate," Ware adds, "it becomes 'our work' even if all was designed and 'empowered' by one person. And this principle is most astonishing when seen as carried out by none other than God the Father—the one who can do anything he wants, by himself and without any assistance, but who instead determines to do so much of his work through another."[15]

Ware reminds us that the intent is practical ("The lessons here are manifold"): to encourage men in authority to allow others to join them in their tasks. "While those in authority need to be more like the Father,...those under authority need to be more like the Son..."[16] But to emphasize (repeatedly) that it is properly the Father's work and he allows the Son and the Spirit to help him though he could do it himself calls into question the essential unity that Ware clearly affirms elsewhere. "It is as if the Father says, 'Shine the spotlight on my Son, and praise and honor his name.' How many of us in positions of authority have a heart to put the spotlight on our subordinates and say, for example, 'Look at the work of our youth minister!'"[17] But the Father is not merely manifesting his magnanimity, choosing to spotlight his Son. He is calling everyone everywhere to honor the Son just as they honor him because he is equally God. He deserves the same worship as the Father because he is not a subordinate person of the Godhead. The subordination extends to the third person according to Ware: "Jesus has authority over the Spirit..."[18] "As a man, Jesus submitted fully to the Spirit, even though in

---

13   Ware, 57.
14   Ware, 64, emphasis added.
15   Ware, 64, emphasis added.
16   Ware, 67.
17   Ware, 65, emphasis added.
18   Ware, 87, emphasis original.

terms of rank, within the Trinity, Jesus has authority over the Spirit."[19] Introducing the idea of rank in the Godhead is to move in an Arian or at least ontological-subordinationist direction. And it is due in large part to Ware's collapsing of the immanent Trinity (i.e., eternal processions) into the economic Trinity (historical missions). "By this, the Son is shown to be under the Father but over the Spirit," he adds, since "the Spirit is the 'Spirit of Jesus' (Acts 16:7)."[20] However, orthodox theology has always taught that such identification of the Spirit with the incarnate Son pertains to their work in the economy of grace, not to the eternal processions and status of the persons. It is difficult to reconcile such language as Ware's with the confession that the persons are of the same essence. Indeed, Ware states that in Christ's submission to the Spirit, the Spirit "recognizes that, even here, he is third."[21] And yet again, the lesson for us is of paramount concern: "Can marriages be like this?" And churches? "What a beautiful case study in humility the Spirit is"—namely, of one who is content "to accept the behind-the scenes place...all for the glory of another."[22] If one might question the practical application to husbands or pastors, it is surely a controversial claim to make concerning the persons of the Trinity. Ware rightly points up the Spirit's focus on Christ. However, in my view the way in which he argues this point is by downgrading the Spirit's significance in the history of revelation. If the Father is "on the top," supreme, sovereign, and worthy of ultimate worship and the Son is eternally inferior at least in rank or role, the Spirit occupies "what might be called 'the background position' in the Trinity." "The Holy Spirit embraces eternally the backstage position in relation to the Father and the Son."[23] "Finally, in the age to come, the Spirit will take the backseat to the Son and the Father."[24] Ware bases this on Revelation 5, where worship is given to the Father and the Lamb.[25] "And while the Spirit is represented in this passage [Rev 5:9] in a veiled and subtle way, it is the Son and the one on the throne, his Father, who receive primacy in worship."[26]

What then does this mean for the confession that the Spirit is also "the Lord" and "with the Father and the Son is worshiped and glorified"? Further, the author concludes that "all worship of the Son, in and of itself, is penultimate...The ultimate object of our honor, glory, praise, and worship is the Father of our Lord

---

19 Ware, 91, emphasis original.
20 Ware, 97.
21 Ware, 129.
22 Ware, 130.
23 Ware, 104.
24 Ware, 125.
25 Ware, 125-127.
26 Ware, 127.

Jesus Christ, who himself alone is over all."[27] But if the Son and the Spirit are God in the fullest sense, then there is no rank. They are worshiped and glorified not only with the Father, but with the Father equally.

The Son and the Spirit proceed from the Father. The Father is the "origin" of the persons, orthodox theology teaches. Nevertheless, this has never meant that the Son and the Spirit have less authority—or anything else that belongs to the one essence they all share—than the Father.

As I mentioned above, "Light from Light" means that precisely because the Son and the Spirit proceed from the Father, they are "Light" in exactly the same sense as the Father. Ware even quotes Augustine on this very point, although it goes against his entire argument: "Not because one is greater and the other less, but because one is the Father and the other the Son; one is the begetter, the other begotten...For he was not sent in virtue of some disparity of power or substance or anything in him that was not equal to the Father, but in virtue of the Son being from the Father, not the Father being from the Son."[28] It is striking that Ware italicizes the very phrases that I would appeal to against his conclusion at this point. Has he not argued repeatedly that the Father is greater in some sense, solely deserving of ultimate worship and glory? Has he not asserted that the Son was in fact "sent in virtue of some disparity of power" or something "in him that was not equal to the Father"? He might put this "something" down to different roles rather than ontological inferiority, but the predicates to which he refers belong to the essence. This seems to me to be the key point of confusion in Ware's argument.

"For as the Father has life in himself, so he has granted the Son to have life in himself," Jesus says in Jn 5:26. To read this in an "Arian" way is to conclude that the Father is properly "God" because he possesses life intrinsically, essentially, eternally and necessarily and then freely decides to grant this to the Son as a creature. To read it in an orthodox way is to conclude that the Son is as properly "God" as the Father because he receives from the Father eternally all of the attributes of the Father himself, including aseity (i.e., self-existence). There is a more fundamental problem. In a footnote Ware writes, "The conceptions of both the 'eternal begetting of the Son' and 'eternal procession of the Spirit' seem to me highly speculative and not grounded in biblical teaching. Both the Son as only-begotten and the Spirit as proceeding from the Father (and the Son) refer, in my judgment, to the historical

---

27 Ware, 154.
28 Ware, 80, emphasis original.

realities of the incarnation and Pentecost, respectively."[29]

This notion of "incarnational sonship" assumes that "Son of God" is a title that accrues to the second person at his incarnation. While the three persons existed eternally, according to this view, the Father became "father" and the Son a "son" with Jesus' conception. I do not use the term lightly: this is a heretical concept. It was held by J. Oliver Buswell, Walter Martin and others, while John MacArthur recanted this position in 2000. The assimilation of the immanent Trinity to the economy here reaches its apex. Yet the orthodox formulations of taxis presuppose these eternal processions; there is no taxis apart from them.

While Ware in the recent debate has rejected claims that he and others are developing a Trinitarian model to undergird a complementarian perspective, his repeated applications suggest otherwise. He is eager to draw very specific applications from his model, such as that a woman "should not teach a mixed male-female adult Sunday school class..."[30] At the same time, he states that "men must realize that their position as heads of homes in no way indicates their supposed superiority over their wives, in particular, or over women, in general."[31] But is not precisely this superiority of the Father over the Son and of the Son over the Spirit what he has been defending?

Similarly, John Frame affirms "the eternal subordination of the Son and the Spirit" to the Father.[32] He introduces confusion on these important questions, gliding over the surface of the ecumenical formulations as if they were too confusing in comparison with his own interpretation of the Bible. He says, "Person is simply a label for the ways in which Father, Son, and Spirit are alike, in distinction from the Godhead as a whole'"[33] Actually, "person" is not a label, but a reality (albeit analogically revealed) and it highlights especially how the persons are distinct from each other (I am not sure what he means by "...from the Godhead as a whole"). He continues, "Some theologians have maintained that in a sense the whole triune God is one person...Cornelius Van Til says: 'We do assert that God, that is, the whole Godhead, is one person.'"[34] Mistakenly identifying "personal" as a divine attribute, Frame deduces, "And if God is personal, and God is one, then

---

29   Ware, 162n.3.
30   Ware, 149.
31   Ware, 143.
32   John Frame, *Systematic Theology*, (Philipsburg, NJ: P&R, 2013), 502.
33   Frame, 484.
34   Frame, 484, citing C. Van Til, *An Introduction to Systematic Theology* (Nutley, NJ: Presbyterian and Reformed, 1974), 229.

surely in a sense he is one person. Indeed, through most of the OT, except for some Trinitarian adumbrations, God acts as a single person: planning, creating, governing, speaking, redeeming, judging."[35]

After affirming that each divine person bears unique personal attributes (as well as sharing equally in the essence), Frame reasons that "since each person exhausts the divine nature, the personal properties are predicates of the divine nature, attributes of God."[36] In Frame's account, divine simplicity "embraces distinctness, rather than cancelling it out. That God is a Father, a Son, and a Spirit indicates real complexity in God's nature, a nature that encompasses real distinctions."[37] This confusion of essence and persons is not a different account of simplicity, but a rejection of the concept. By definition, simplicity excludes complexity. In a single stroke, Frame has eliminated simplicity from the divine attributes and a genuine plurality of persons. He seems to throw up his hands when articulating the historical positions: "words fail us" when we speak of divine begetting, since it cannot be "anything closely analogous to human begetting,"[38] although he says three pages later that "the eternal Son is analogous to human sons in some way."

The impression is given that the tradition is hopelessly confusing. "Can Scripture help us to formulate a clearer concept of eternal generation?"[39] Here is the biblicism: Words like "begetting," which the church has found clearly taught in Scripture, fail us. But we can move beyond this impasse apparently by turning to Scripture, the very source of course to which orthodox churches have always turned.

More to the point, Frame says that the church has distinguished economic from ontological subordination (affirming the former while denying the latter). So far so good. But then he suggests a third category: short of ontological, but beyond economic. "That might be called eternal subordination of role," which he asserts "has been discussed for many centuries." He says that "it is right to describe this difference of role as eternal...Subordination, in the sense of serving others in love, is clearly a divine attribute."[40] Now he is talking about the essence rather than the persons. Subordination cannot be a divine attribute—first, because essences do not rule or serve, persons do, and second, because it makes no sense to speak of subordination as an attribute of the essence shared equally by the persons if they

---

35 Frame, *Systematic Theology*, 488.
36 Frame, 488.
37 Frame, 489.
38 Frame, 492.
39 Frame, 492.
40 Frame, 501.

are not in fact equal. They Father would have "subordination" as an attribute every bit as much as the Son and the Spirit. Frame goes further still: "It may be that this eternal hierarchy of role accounts for some of the language in Scripture about the Father being 'greater' than the Son (John 14:28), about the Son's being able to do nothing of himself (John 5:19), and so on."[41] I am not suggesting that Frame is an Arian, but he is interpreting those very passages in precisely the way that the Arians did (and do). Orthodox faith has interpreted these passages as pertaining to the economy: specifically, to Jesus' humiliation. The Nicene fathers saw any form of eternal subordination within the life of the Godhead as at least Semi-Arian. Furthermore, if this subordination of role is eternal, then it is necessary, negating Frame's earlier affirmation of voluntary submission—unless, of course, he believes that God is temporal and mutable.

TAKE-AWAY

I have said no repeatedly that I do not regard the authors I have cited as Arians. Rather, I suggest humbly that they are confused. That is entirely understandable. We are dealing here with the greatest of all divine mysteries and we must have more reflection at our disposal than our own. This is the danger of "biblicism": that is, marginalizing the history of doctrine in favor of explicit biblical statements, when at least among orthodox Christians the history of doctrine is the history of biblical exegesis. There is no Bible verse for the distinction between processions and missions, for example, and yet it is an essential biblical truth.

Church historian Robert Godfrey often says, "We always want to reinvent the wheel...and it's never round." Biblicism keeps us from taking seriously the objections and the solutions that remain relatively unchanged since the fourth century. We can even return to the creeds with a "biblicistic" method, quoting a line here or there to justify our orthodoxy. But confession is not only of the letter, but of the spirit—the intention of the creed, which can only be understood properly by knowing something about the context and the process leading up to it. In addition to Ayres' work, Rowan Williams' Arius: History and Tradition, Khaled Anatolios', Retrieving Nicaea, Gilles Emery's The Trinity and Fred Sanders' recently released The Triune God are superb places to start for this background.

---

41   Frame, 502.

We must always return to Scripture, the only judge in doctrinal controversies. Nothing may be added or subtracted from this canon as the magisterial authority for faith and practice. Yet biblicism is not biblical.

First, at the end of the day, biblicism merely substitutes my reading of the Bible for our reading of the Bible. In other words, in the name of basing everything on Scripture rather than on merely human wisdom, biblicism imagines that one may take a short-cut, circumventing centuries of complicated debates, and arrive at the immediately obvious meaning of Scripture.

Second, biblicism actually reduces the scope of biblical teaching to what is said explicitly in so many words. The Westminster Confession well-expresses the classic rule: "The whole counsel of God concerning all things necessary for His own glory, man's salvation, faith and life, is either expressly set down in Scripture, or by good and necessary consequence may be deduced from Scripture..." (1.6). Notice the high bar for such deductions: they must be not only good but necessary consequences of scriptural teaching. All parties in the current controversy can agree that Scripture teaches the doctrine of the Trinity at least in its basic rule: "one in essence, three in person." Despite the fact that the word "trinity" cannot be found in any concordance, Scripture clearly and explicitly teaches that God is one and that the Father is God, the Son is God and the Holy Spirit is God. The dogma of the Trinity is a good and necessary inference from a host of biblical passages. But this was not realized by each theologian or believer anew who came to the biblical text. Very serious objections from teachers and pastors who were just as concerned to be faithful to Scripture forced the church to wrestle with what it means when it baptizes people in the name of the Father, the Son and the Holy Spirit.

Speaking of baptism, we are reminded that the doctrine of the Trinity emerged especially out of debates provoked by the fact that good Jewish monotheists were being baptized in the name of the Father and the Son and the Holy Spirit. They were praying to the Father, in the Son, by the Spirit, praising the persons equally, and having the threefold name placed on them in the benediction.

In his wonderful book, *The Deep Things of God,* Fred Sanders makes a terrific argument that evangelicals have a clearer belief in the Trinity through their hymnody and prayers than one might suspect by examining sermons and popular books. This underscores the importance of practices in which God's Word richly shapes us.

The fourth-century church father Gregory of Nyssa wrote that none of the persons executes any work apart from the others, "but every operation which extends from God to the Creation...has its origin from the Father, and proceeds through the Son, and is perfected in the Holy Spirit."[42] The Genevan reformer John Calvin frequently repeats these Cappadocian formulas, as when he expresses it in his own words: "To the Father is attributed the beginning of action, the fountain and source of all things; to the Son, wisdom, counsel, and arrangement in action, while the energy and efficacy of action is assigned to the Spirit."[43] This has no small impact on his entire theology. These are great and important rules for us to bear in mind. But it is in the pulpit, at the font, and in the pew where the rubber meets the road. We do not formulate our doctrine of the Trinity on the basis of what we think about ideal or even biblical patterns of human life. But our doctrine of the Trinity will inform and shape our worship, lives and witness. Even where a heresy like modalism is not tolerated formally, one discerns an imprecision in prayers and sometimes even in teaching that inculcate a confusion of the divine persons. If we tend informally to collapse them into one person, we are especially susceptible to collapsing the Holy Spirit into "God." Even in doctrinally orthodox circles, one hears prayers that are more confusing, as if the persons of the Trinity were interchangeable—perhaps even the same person.

At least it seems that the person being addressed shifts back and forth without any specification. Sometimes the Father is thanked for dying for our sins or for indwelling us. Very frequently, prayers conclude with, "In your name, Amen." In whose name? Scripture teaches to pray to the Father in the name of Christ. After all, it is not the Father or the Spirit, but the Son who is our mediator.

One praise chorus leads us to sing as if we were Arians, "You alone are Father / and You alone are good. / You alone are Savior / and You alone are God."[44] It is important to remind ourselves that sound Trinitarian teaching has been not only defined formally in the ecumenical creeds; it is (present tense) confessed by us in the context of public worship. We are baptized into the name of the Father, the Son, and the Holy Spirit. We pray to the Father, in the Son, by the indwelling power of the Holy Spirit. Traditional liturgies inculcate sound Trinitarian prayers. There are obvious examples, such as praise: "Glory be to the Father, and

---

42   Gregory of Nyssa, "On 'Not Three Gods': An Answer to Ablabius" (NPNF2 5:334).
43   Calvin, *Institutes of the Christian Religion*, trans. Lewis Ford Battles; ed., John T. McNeill (Philadelphia: Westminster John Knox, 1960), 1.13.18.
44   David Crowder Band, "You Alone," The Lime CD (Six Step Records, 2004).

to the Son, and to the Holy Spirit." It is not only a creedal rule that the Holy Spirit is to be "worshipped and glorified" together with the Father and the Son; these liturgies lead us to actually invoke the Father, in the Son, by the Spirit.

Luke reminds us that the early Christians "devoted themselves to the apostles' teaching and the fellowship, to the breaking of bread and the prayers" (Acts 2:42). Anyone reared in the synagogue would have known what "the prayers" meant. Like a trellis, the formal prayers (said and sung) were a way of not only directing public worship, but of shaping informal worship in the family and alone. Basil of Caesarea, who revised the liturgy to more intentionally inculcate a full trinitarianism, called pastors "to keep the Spirit undivided from the Father and the Son, preserving, both in confession of faith and in the doxology, the doctrine taught them at their baptism."[45]

The merits of a given liturgy today, however formal or informal, are not measured by their antiquity, but by the extent to which they share that ancient and ecumenical vision of Trinity shaped and Trinity-directed experience. The Holy Spirit works through his Word and insofar as our liturgies convey that Word, they convey nothing less than Christ with all of his benefits. Learning not only from our forebears' successes but also from their failures helps us in our day to direct our hearts—and those of our fellow believers—to sing, "Glory be to the Father, and to the Son, and to the Holy Spirit. As it was in the beginning, is now, and ever shall be, world without end. Amen."

---

45   Basil, *On the Holy Spirit* 10.26 (*NPNF2* 8:17). Emphasis added.

Trinitarian Heresies
What is Lost?

REV. DR. JUSTIN S. HOLCOMB
Bishop of the Episcopal Diocese of Central Florida
Senior Fellow with Theo Global
Professor, Reformed Theological Seminary
USA

The Trinity is not merely one doctrine among others. This article of faith structures all the faith and practice of Christianity: our theology, liturgies, hymns, and lives. "In the doctrine of the Trinity," wrote Herman Bavinck, "beats the heart of the whole revelation of God for the redemption of humanity." As the Father, the Son, and the Spirit, "our God is above us, before us, and within us."

This paper will explore what is lost when various heresies deny the doctrine of the Trinity. We will explore two trinitarian heresies: Sabellianism and Arianism. The purpose for exploring these heresies is historical. Dolezal writes: "The first major challenge to the doctrine of the Trinity modalistic Monarchianism or Sabellianism. The second was Arian subordination. Tritheism seems not to have been a significant threat during the early centuries of the church. In fact, if one surveys the beliefs of both the orthodox fathers and the early heretics, one of the things they all seem to agree on is that God must be one being. The singular unity of being (or substance) was non-negotiable. The challenge lay in characterizing this divine oneness in a way that did justice to the full range of biblical data. The Sabellians feared that saying there are three distinct person who are God would undermine the monarchy of the Godhead, transforming it into an oligarchy and thus implying more than one principle of being back of creation. The Arians also were concerned to safeguard the singularity of God's being or substance. They reasoned that as the begottenness of the Son seems to indicate some beginning of the Son, and since it belongs to the divine substance not to begin to exist, it must be that the Son is of a different and inferior substance to the Father. Indeed, the Son must be the highest creature who began to exist at some point."[1]

I. THE DOCTRINE OF THE TRINITY

By the doctrine of the Trinity, I mean the teaching of the Council of Nicaea, the Nicene Constantinople Creed, and the Athanasian Creed. The Nicene-Constantinople Creed states clearly that there is one God who exists in three persons. The Council of Nicaea was a watershed for the Christian church—shortly after Emperor Constantine legalized Christianity in 313, he convened the first ecumenical, fully representative, universally recognized council of the Christian church. There, the bishops discussed one of the most important questions that

---

1   James Dolezal, *All That Is In God,* 108-109.

Christianity would ever have to face—what was the status of Jesus in relation to God? Everyone there agreed that Jesus was a divine being, but the Arians could not reconcile the idea that he was the same being as God the Father.

After a long and heated debate, the council decided that the evidence from the Bible and tradition lent itself much better to the belief that Jesus was God rather than a lesser being. They phrased this belief as follows: "[We believe] in one Lord Jesus Christ, the Son of God, begotten of the Father [the only-begotten; that is, of the essence of the Father, God of God], Light of Light, very God of very God, begotten, not made, being of one substance with the Father; by whom all things were made [both in heaven and on earth]; who for us men, and for our salvation, came down and was incarnate and was made man; he suffered, and the third day he rose again, ascended into heaven; from thence he shall come to judge the quick and the dead." Later, at the Council of Constantinople in 381, the bishops added a section to include the Holy Spirit as God as well: "[We believe] in the Holy Ghost, the Lord and Giver of life, who proceeds from the Father,[2] who with the Father and the Son together is worshiped and glorified, who spoke by the prophets."[3]

Although the Trinity had been a standard doctrine long before Nicaea, these two councils provided Christians with the language that they needed to discuss the Trinity and the authority to use the Trinity as a basis for evaluating orthodoxy. The Athanasian Creed puts it this way:

1. We worship one God in trinity and the trinity in unity,

2. neither blending their person nor dividing their essence.

3. For the person of the Father is a distinct person, the person of the Son is another, and that of the Holy Spirit still another.

4. But the divinity of the Father, Son, and Holy Spirit is one, their glory equal, their majesty coeternal.

5. What quality the Father has, the Son has, and the Holy Spirit has.

The key is that God is one in essence and three in persons. Gregory of Nazianzus captures the need for both well: "No sooner do I conceive of the One than I am

---

2   Later, Western theologians added "and the Son," while Eastern theologians kept the original text. This contributed to the split between Eastern and Western Christianity later.

3   Philip Schaff, *Creeds of Christendom*, vol. 1, section 8, http://www.ccel.org/ccel /schaff/creeds1.iv.iii.html.

illumined by the Splendor of the Three; no sooner do I distinguish Them than I am carried back to the One."[4]

II. WHAT IS HERESY?

Traditionally, a heretic is someone who has compromised an essential doctrine and lost sight of who God really is, usually by oversimplification. Literally, heresy means "choice"—that is, a choice to deviate from traditional teaching in favor of one's own insights.

As Christianity grew and spread, it increasingly came into contact with competing belief systems such as paganism, Greek philosophy, Gnosticism, and others. Inevitably, teachers arose who attempted to solve the intellectual difficulties of Christian faith and make it more compatible with other philosophical systems.

It should be made clear that most of the heretics were usually asking legitimate and important questions. They were not heretics because they asked the questions. It is the answers that they gave that are wrong. They went too far by trying to make the Christian faith more compatible with ideas that they already found appealing, especially those of pagan Greek philosophy. Others struggled with Jesus' claims to be both sent from God and one with God. The reactions of the religious leaders in the New Testament to Jesus' claims underline the difficulty of this revelation and point to later struggles about Jesus' identity.

III. HERESY AND THE EARLY CHURCH

Following the apostles, the early church maintained that heresy means directly denying the central orthodox beliefs of the church. Early church creedal statements codified orthodoxy into a widely accepted form. Even before important Christian beliefs such as the canon of Scripture (list of books in the Bible) and the Trinity had been carefully articulated, the mainstream of Christian believers and leaders had a sense of the essential truths that had been handed down from the apostles and the prophets and passed along to each generation of Christians through Scripture, sermons, and baptismal creeds. Before the developments at Nicaea and Chalcedon regarding the proper beliefs about the Trinity and the dual natures of Christ, the early church possessed what is known as the "rule of faith." To quote

---

4   Gregory of Nazianzus, Oration 40: The Oration on Holy Baptism, ch. 41, in NPNF2, 7:375.

Demarest again, "The early church defended itself against heretical teaching by appealing to 'the rule of faith' or 'the rule of truth', which were brief summaries of essential Christian truths...The fluid 'rule of faith' gave way to more precise instruments for refuting heresies and defining faith, namely, creedal formulations such as the Apostles' Creed, the Nicene Creed, the Definition of Chalcedon and the Athanasian Creed."[5]

The New Testament speaks frequently about false teaching and doctrine. For the early church, heresy was merely teaching that stood in contrast to the right belief received from the prophets and the apostles in the Scriptures and put into written formulas in the rule of faith and the creeds. The early church formed an accepted and received statement of what is true and essential to the Christian faith. The rule of faith gave birth to more precise statements of the essentials of the faith, such as the Apostles' Creed and the Nicene Creed.[6] These widely accepted formulations of the essential "right doctrine" (orthodoxy) handed down from the apostles were crucial for combating heresy.

It is important to note, however, that the early church did not consider every potential wrong belief to be heretical. Rather, only those beliefs that contradicted the essential elements of the faith were to be labeled heresy, not disagreements on nonessential doctrines.

IV. WHY LEARN ABOUT HERESIES?

Core Christian doctrines such as the Trinity, the nature of Christ, and which books should be included in Scripture were developed through the early church's struggles with heresy. When teachers began to lead movements that were blatantly opposed to the apostolic tradition, the church was forced to articulate the essential elements of the faith.

The history of heretics, heresies, and the orthodox leaders who responded to them can be disheartening. Why learn about arguments over what sometimes seems like theological minutiae? There are two major reasons. The first is that while there is certainly ambiguity in the Bible, the Creator of the world has decided to reveal himself to us and even to live with us. It is important to honor

---

5 Bruce Demarest, "Heresy," *New Dictionary of Theology* (Downers Grove, IL: InterVarsity Academic, 1988), 292.
6 Ibid.

that revelation. When we find this revelation distasteful and try to reshape God according to our preferences, we are beginning to drift away from God as he really is. Imagine a friend who ignores the parts of you that he or she doesn't like. Is that a deep relationship? Ambiguity or not, uncomfortable or not, it is vital that we are obedient to what we can know about God.

The second reason is related to the first. When we have a flawed image of God, we no longer relate to him in the same way. Think of the way that you might have related to your parents when you were growing up. Even if you didn't necessarily understand the reasons behind boundaries they set for you in childhood, they look a lot different when you are confident in your parents' love than when you fear or resent your parents. It is surprising how much our beliefs about God impact our daily lives, which is partly what makes theology such a rewarding discipline.

It cannot be repeated enough that those who forget history are doomed to repeat it. Moreover, as C. S. Lewis warns, if we remain ignorant of the errors and triumphs of our his- tory, we run the risk of what he calls "chronological snobbery," the arrogant assumption that the values and beliefs of our own time have surpassed all that came before. Lewis writes, "We need intimate knowledge of the past. Not that the past has any magic about it, but because we cannot study the future, and yet need something to set against the present, to remind us that the basic assumptions have been quite different in different periods and that much which seems certain to the uneducated is merely temporary fashion. A man who has lived in many places is not likely to be deceived by the local errors of his native village; the scholar has lived in many times and is therefore in some degree immune from the great cataract of nonsense that pours from the press and the microphone of his own age."[7]

V. SABELLIANISM

Sabellius argued that God is like one actor and who wore three hats. He was a third-century presbyter in Rome and argued that the Father, Son, and the Spirit are simply "masks" or modes in which the one person of God is experienced by believers. Although Sabellius was excommunicated by the bishop of Rome in AD 220, Sabellianism or modalism has remained a recurring challenge in church

---

7   C. S. Lewis, "Learning in War-Time," in *The Weight of Glory: And Other Addresses* (New York: HarperCollins, 1949/2001), 58–59.

history. For example, modalistic anti-trinitarianism taught by Michael Servetus (16th century), Emanuel Swedenborg (18th century), Friedrich Schleiermacher (18th-19th centuries), and One Pentecostalism. The dominance of the one over the many, unity over plurality, is the common factor in all these departures from Trinitarian faith.[8]

1. *Historical Background*

During the second and third centuries, Christianity was struggling to reconcile the idea of a single God, as stated in no uncertain terms in the Old Testament: "I am the Lord, and there is no other; apart from me there is no God" (Isa. 45:5)—with the three divine names that appear at the end of the gospel of Matthew—"Therefore go and make disciples of all nations, baptizing them in the name of the Father and of the Son and of the Holy Spirit" (Matt. 28:19). What was to be done about the apparent discrepancy? If there was no God besides the God of Israel, who were the Son and the Holy Spirit? Were they new gods who had just been revealed? Was one or both somewhere in between, a demigod? Some theologians, like Marcion, took the confusion as proof positive that the whole Old Testament had to be rejected, while others concluded that all three names were just three different ways that God wanted people to think of him. The most famous advocate of the latter position was a third-century theologian and priest named Sabellius. Little is known about Sabellius, who was excommunicated sometime around AD 220, but the teaching attached to his name, known as Sabellian-ism or Sabellian Modalism, became a well-known heresy.

2. *Heretical Teaching*

During the second and third centuries, Christianity was struggling to reconcile the idea of a single God, as stated in no uncertain terms in the Old Testament—"I am the Lord, and there is no other; apart from me there is no God" (Isa. 45:5)—with the three divine names that appear at the end of the gospel of Matthew—"Therefore go and make disciples of all nations, baptizing them in the name of the Father and of the Son and of the Holy Spirit" (Matt. 28:19). What was to be done about the apparent discrepancy? If there was no God besides the God of Israel, who were the Son and the Holy Spirit? Were they new gods who had just been revealed? Was one or both somewhere in between, a demigod?

---

8   Michael Horton, *The Christian Faith*, p. 280.

Some theologians concluded that all three names were just three different ways that God wanted people to think of him. The most famous advocate of the latter position was a third-century theologian and priest named Sabellius.

Sabellianism is the most intellectually well-developed form of Modalism, a heresy that claims that the Father, Son, and Holy Spirit are simply different modes, or forms, of God rather than distinct persons. Modalism is itself a variety of an older heresy called Monarchianism, which stresses the "one rule" of God. The universe is so orderly, the Monarchians believed, that it must be the product of one supreme ruler, which means a single being. Trinitarianism seemed to complicate the idea of that single being. Monarchianism emerged as a response to the polytheism around the early Christians, affirming that there is no being equal to God and that he is the ruler over everything.[9]

While early versions of Modalism stood out as simplistic and easily dismissible, Sabellius gave the teaching a facelift, making it much more advanced and defensible. In Sabellianism, Father, Son, and Holy Spirit are just three different hats or masks that God wears, as the situation demands. Therefore, while it was proper to speak of God the Father and God the Son, it would be incorrect to refer to them as interacting with one another or having separate experiences.

According to Hippolytus, an early opponent of Sabellius, Sabellianism divided up the three roles into the actions of the one God at different times in history. In other words, Father, Son, and Spirit are merely adjectives describing how the one divine being acts and is perceived by believers. Sabellius used the analogy of the sun to explain his position on the life of the Godhead. In the same way that the sun, a concrete object, gives off both light and heat, so also the single divine being radiates in history in different fashions. In the Old Testament we see the divine being acting as Father, then again in redemption in a different form as the Son in the Gospels, and finally in the lives of believers as the Holy Spirit in the present age.

Sabellius's idea raises some important questions. First, if God takes one role at a time, who was crucified? Did God actually die? And second, to whom was Jesus speaking when he referred to God the Father? The answers to these two questions made Sabellius famous. As to who died on the cross, he adopted a position that his enemies dubbed "Patripassianism" or "the suffering of the Father."[10] Sabellius

---

9   Henry Chadwick, *The Early Church,* rev. ed. (New York: Penguin, 1993), 86.
10   Ibid., 87.

was consistent with his theory of the different roles: when Scripture said that Jesus was crucified, it was referring to the same person who had made a covenant with Israel in the Old Testament as well as the one who lived with believers in the New. To buttress this point, Sabellius quoted several passages from the Old Testament, such as Isaiah 63:8–9 lxx): "He became to them deliverance out of all their affliction: not an ambassador, nor a messenger, but himself saved them, because he loved them and spared them: He himself redeemed them."[11] It seemed pretty obvious to Sabellius that the prophecy should be taken literally—the God of Israel came down and died to deliver his people, albeit in a new role.[12] He was adamant that it was all of God rather than part of God that suffered, since the point he had taken issue with in the first place was the division of God.

As for whom Jesus was addressing, Sabellius was again consistent in his theory. He proposed that Jesus was demonstrating how to pray for our benefit rather than holding an actual conversation with God. Sabellius used Jesus' words to Philip at the Last Supper as a prooftext: "Don't you know me, Philip, even after I have been among you such a long time? Anyone who has seen me has seen the Father. How can you say, 'Show us the Father'?" (John 14:9). This passage should have priority over the prayer, Sabellius believed, because Jesus was clearly identifying what the nature of God is. The idea that Jesus was praying as a demonstration was also related to Sabellius's interpretation of "the Word" in John 1; while acknowledging that John 1 seems to hint at the divinity of the Word (traditionally seen as Christ by the orthodox), Sabellius maintained that the Word was to be understood in the simplest sense, as a sound that God had made, rather than turning the Word into a person.[13]

Sabellius's writings do not survive—the previously quoted passages are taken from quotations preserved by his opponents—and it is difficult to pin down his theology in its best form. It is also unclear what led him to develop his theory. However, from what we can glean from the reactions of his opponents, he had several legitimate concerns. Naturally, he wanted to defend the oneness of God. At this time, several groups had split from Christianity that proclaimed two or more gods—Marcion, for instance, or the Gnostics. Many of these groups had thrown out Christianity's Jewish heritage. By prioritizing oneness, Modalists were

---

11   This particular reading is found only in the Septuagint, which was the standard Christian Old Testament at the time.
12   Jaroslav Pelikan, *The Christian Tradition: A History of the Development of Doctrine,* vol. 1, The Emergence of the Catholic Tradition (100–600) (Chicago: Univ. of Chicago Press, 1971), 177.
13   Tertullian, *Against Praxeas* I:7, http://www.newadvent.org/fathers/0317.htm.

voting for continuity with Judaism and in particular with Jewish monotheism. The fact that God the Father and God the Son (as the Trinitarians put it) each had their own testament only invited division. Marcion had published a list of differences between what he saw as the personalities of the God of the Old Testament and the God of the New, and declared his allegiance to the God of the New. But what if both books were actually devoted to the same God in different roles? The discrepancies would be resolved. Furthermore, Sabellians defended the full divinity of Christ against what they saw as a worrying tendency to demote him to a demigod.[14] Earlier theologians such as Hippolytus had made claims that Christ and God the Father were two persons; Sabellians must have considered the division too sharp, and they charged Hippolytus and others like him with ditheism (worshipping two gods).[15]

Some of Sabellius's concerns were pastoral. Sabellius thought that the idea of assigning persons to the three names was overly complicated in a way that God himself would not be. Perhaps the Trinity was a distinction that specialized theologians could make, but for the uneducated laypeople who made up the bulk of the church, a God who is both three and one would be impossible to worship without drifting into polytheism.[16] So in addition to trying to maintain Jewish monotheism, Sabellius thought that his theory of "simple Unity" was a way to take Christianity out of the hands of academics and put it back where it belonged.

Sabellianism persisted in the outer regions of the Roman Empire for some time (especially in Libya, Sabellius's homeland), and was condemned at most church councils. Although its theology was influential, largely because it was so easy to grasp, Sabellianism lacked clout as a movement and never made much headway into the church proper. The closest it came to doing so was when Sabellius managed to gain favor with Pope Callistus, a rival of Sabellius's arch enemy Hippolytus, but Callistus soon excommunicated Sabellius and ended his career in the public eye.[17]

---

14 In fact, Origen, one of the main Trinitarian theologians in the orthodox party, developed a model of the Trinity that placed Jesus as a "secondary god," which hinted at a demigod even though Origen understood this to refer to Jesus' position within the Trinity. The model was later refined, and Origen was temporarily excommunicated long after his death. See J. N. D. Kelly, *Early Christian Doctrines,* rev. ed. (New York: Harper Collins, 1978), 128.
15 Kelly, *Early Christian Doctrines,* 123.
16 This is quoted by Tertullian, who never really addresses the issue. However, the introduction of creeds helped alleviate the problem—the content of the faith was condensed into a form that common people could memorize and recite every time they went to worship. Tertullian, *Against Praxeas* I:3, http://www.newadvent.org/fathers/0317.htm.
17 Kelly, *Early Christian Doctrines,* 124.

However, Sabellianism was indirectly credited with creating a much bigger theological crisis in the following centuries. Arianism, which drew sharp distinctions between Father, Son, and Holy Spirit, was in many ways the opposite of the Sabellian heresy. It was rumored that Arius, who had formerly been a Christian monk, developed overly strong views on the distinctions among the Godhead after hearing what he considered to be a Sabellian sermon in Egypt. Indeed, Arianism represented most of the criticisms that Sabellius leveled against the Trinitarians, including the division of God into multiple beings.

3. *Orthodox Response*

In theology, it is much easier to tell when an idea is wrong than it is to articulate precisely the right answer. The church had been adamant that Modalism did not adequately account for the way God had revealed himself in Scripture, but as of yet few theologians had advanced a solution that was adequate. The challenge of Sabellianism and its brief influence in high places motivated the first substantial Trinitarian theologies and generated the terms that we use today. The orthodox party was represented by three major figures: Hippolytus, a failed candidate for pope, Tertullian, a North African lawyer and convert to Christianity, and Origen, a brilliant but eccentric philosopher from Egypt. Together, these figures hammered out the basics of Trinitarian theology that later figures, such as Athanasius, improved upon.

The Sabellians maintained that any Scripture passage that suggests that God is more than one must be interpreted metaphorically. But Tertullian argued that a metaphorical interpretation twisted the terms "Father" and "Son," which were given to humans to convey something real about God. "In order to be a husband, I must have a wife," Tertullian said. "I can never myself be my own wife. In like manner, in order to be a father, I have a son, for I never can be a son to myself; and in order to be a son, I have a father, it being impossible for me ever to be my own father."[18] Furthermore, he showed that Christ showed his deity to the apostles not only by assuming the attributes of the God of Israel (such as when he says, "I am," in John 8:58) but also by calling on God the Father as a separate witness. Quoting John 8:18, Tertullian writes, "'I am one who am bearing witness of myself; and the Father (is another) who has sent me, and bears witness of me.' Now, if he were one—being at once both the Son and the Father— he certainly

---

18   Tertullian, *Against Praxeas* I:10, http://www.newadvent.org/fathers/0317.htm.

would not have quoted the sanction of the law, which requires not the testimony of one, but of two."[19] The fact that Christ did not know when the end of the world would take place, the fact that he was forsaken by God on the cross, and the fact that he constantly pointed his listeners to the Father as well as himself all rendered Sabellius's theory difficult to maintain.

However, it remained for the orthodox party to explain precisely what Christ is in relation to the Father, and this was the real achievement of the controversy. They agreed that there are not two gods, as Marcion and some of the Gnostics said. Tertullian therefore developed terms that emphasized the unity of God as well as his distinctions. He proposed that we speak of the Godhead as "one substance (*substantia*) consisting in three persons (*persona*)," which was rendered in Greek as *ousia* (essence or being) and hypostases (concrete things).[20] That way, God can be understood properly as one being, a single agent, but it can also be acknowledged that God is also three persons who interact with one another and work together. It is from Tertullian that we get the important Christian word "Trinity," although the idea of the Trinity had been around long before and is taught in the Bible.

Tertullian and Origen also set forth explanations of how a Trinity might be possible without creating demigods. They proposed that Christ eternally proceeds from the Father, rather than being born at a single moment in time. (The Sabellians had accused the orthodox of embracing the Valentinian heresy, which said that God created a number of lesser gods, or *aeons*).

Although "begotten" suggests a one-time, completed action in the past, Tertullian pointed out that God is said to beget Wisdom in Proverbs 8:22—a personified, speaking Wisdom—but was there a time when God was without or will be without Wisdom?[21] Surely not. God does not have to create his own insight—it simply flows out of him. Similarly, it is possible to "beget" the Son of God without meaning that God created a separate god.[22] Christ came from, was dependent on, and was inextricably linked to the Father: "I confess that I call God and His Word—the Father and His Son—two. For the root and the tree are distinctly two things, but correlatively joined; the fountain and the river are also two forms, but indivisible; so likewise, the sun and the ray are two forms, but

---

19   Tertullian, Against Praxeas I:22, http://www.newadvent.org/fathers/0317.htm.
20   Both sets of terms have made their way into Christian language in the West, and so both are included here.
21   The Old Testament and some of the deuterocanonical books feature a personified Wisdom that the early church fathers often associated with Christ.
22   Athanasius later used the same argument against the Arians.

coherent ones. Everything which proceeds from something else must needs be second to that from which it proceeds, without being on that account separated. Where, however, there is a second, there must be two; and where there is a third, there must be three. Now the Spirit indeed is third from God and the Son; just as the fruit of the tree is third from the root."[23]

However, even if this is so, why not speak of a divine Triad? Should we refer to God as the three persons of the Trinity, as "them" instead of "him"? Tertullian argued that when Jesus said, "I and my Father are one," he was emphasizing the idea of substance, or divine essence, that allows us to refer to God as a single being. The phrase meant more than the mere unity of purpose that two separate beings would have, even if it also meant less than the complete identification of the Father with the Son that Sabellius had suggested. Instead, Christ was saying that he and the Father are one being, and that the idea that God is a single being came first: to talk to Christ, for example, is to talk to all the members of the Trinity.[24] The later Athanasian Creed puts it this way:

a. [W]e worship one God in Trinity, and Trinity in Unity;

b. Neither confounding the persons nor dividing the substance.

c. For there is one person of the Father, another of the Son, and another of the Holy Spirit. ;

d. But the Godhead of the Father, of the Son, and of the Holy Spirit is all one, the glory equal, the majesty coeternal.

e. Such as the Father is, such is the Son, and such is the Holy Spirit.

Since God is one, it is possible to distinguish the members of the Trinity, but that distinction does not affect worshiping God as a whole. Jesus' glory is also the Father's glory, and so forth. Many of the ideas listed above appeared in Tertullian's work during this controversy.

Relevance

Sabellianism is one of the heresies in the church that sticks around. Anyone who has sat in a Sunday school class and heard that God is like water because he can

---

23 Tertullian, *Against Praxeas* I:8, http://www.newadvent.org/fathers/0317.htm.
24 Tertullian, *Against Praxeas* I:22, http://www.newadvent.org/fathers/0317.htm.

take three forms (liquid, steam, and ice) has been exposed to a contemporary variation of Modalism. God is not one person who can change into three different forms but a being who is essence (unity) and three persons (plurality).

Although it generally has a low profile compared to Arianism, Modalism has also gained some momentum. It is seen today in the oneness Pentecostalism movement, which denies the Trinity. However, Modalism gains ground less because it is strongly advocated than because of apathy. Sabellianism is attractive in its simplicity, and Sabellius's pastoral challenge—that the Trinity is the province of specialized theologians—strikes a chord in modern culture. Compared with the idea that God is merely one, the orthodox answer might seem overly complex and philosophical, or an unnecessary later addition to the authentic Christian faith. After all, the Bible does not spell out the Trinity—though it is clearly taught from passages from all over Scripture.[25]

Perhaps one of the best reasons for complex Trinitarianism comes from C. S. Lewis, who once wrote, "Good philosophy must exist, if for no other reason, because bad philosophy needs to be answered."[26] In some respects, this describes the Sabellian controversy; orthodox philosophy needed to be developed to answer the Sabellian philosophy. But Trinitarian theology is much more than a merely human philosophy. It takes seriously the idea that God has revealed himself in Scripture and wants to be known, and that he has revealed himself in a certain way. The question at the beginning—only one God, or three?—is unavoidable when reading the Bible, and the consequence of leaving the question unanswered is to let it be badly answered.

Sabellianism was one such bad answer. In the Sabellian scheme, God is no longer love, because he no longer has anyone whom he has loved eternally. The intimate relationship between God the Father and Jesus in John 17 becomes a weird sort of schizophrenia. Finally, since God takes on several different roles as he pleases (such as Son and Father), it is questionable whether we have ever encountered God as he really is rather than what he does. The orthodox party—laboriously, with many starts and stops in the first few centuries—worked out the answer that is best in accord with Scripture.

---

25   David S. Yeago, "The New Testament and the Nicene Dogma: A Contribution to the Recovery of Theological Exegesis," in *The Theological Interpretation of Scripture: Classic and Contemporary Readings,* ed. Stephen E. Fowl (Oxford: Blackwell, 1997), 88.
26   C. S. Lewis, *The Weight of Glory and Other Addresses,* rev. ed. (New York: Harper Collins, 1980), 58.

What's more, Modalism undercuts the atoning work of Jesus Christ. If there is only one God who merely appears in different forms in history, one must question whether Jesus Christ was truly man, or if he only appeared to be, as in the heresy of Docetism. If Jesus Christ is not fully God and fully man, then he cannot be the one mediator between God and man.

On a final, practical note, some other religions, particularly the Jehovah's Witnesses and Mormons, see Christianity as Sabellian. Since many of the errors that these groups ascribe to mainstream Christianity are actually Sabellian in nature, it is useful to know the middle road that orthodox doctrine strikes between unity and distinction. Being able to articulate concisely what the Trinity is, how it makes the best sense of Scripture, and how it affects our salvation and the worship of God can be valuable in witnessing to others as well as developing our own relationship with God.

VI. ARIANISM

Arius argued that Jesus was a lesser god. Arius, a third century Alexandrian presbyter, the Son was the first created being. He writes: "There exists a trinity (*trias*) in unequal glories." The Father is "the Monad," so that "the Father is God [even] when the Son does not exist."[27] Semi Arians taught that the Son and the Father were of a similar essence (*homoiousios*) and denied that they were of the same essence (*homoousios*).[28]

1. *Historical Background*

Sudden chaos overtook Alexandria in 318. A riot broke out and people streamed into the street chanting, "There was a time when Christ was not!" Meanwhile, another large group of Christians stood their ground with the bishop against this movement, insisting that Christ is the eternal God along with the Father. Eventually this conflict spilled over to the rest of the empire and threatened to break apart the unity of the church. What began this crisis? It really came down to one man—Arius (ca. 256–336).

Arius was a presbyter in Alexandria, the home of the brilliant theologian Origen (184–230). He came under the influence of Lucian of Antioch, a headmaster at a Christian school, and went to school with Eusebius of Nicomedia, who eventually became an important and influential bishop. Arius eventually went

---

27   Rowan William quotes Arius's poem "Thalia" in Arius: *Heresy and Tradition*, p. 102.
28   Horton, *The Christian Faith*, 280.

on to become a presbyter in Alexandria. Like most in Antioch, all three erred on the side of emphasizing the humanity of Christ rather than his divinity. They firmly rejected Sabellius's Modalism, because that would imply that God the Father died and was crucified on the cross. And lest they put their respective church positions in jeopardy, they knew they could not publicly embrace Paul of Samosata's Adoptionism (the idea that a human person named Jesus was adopted into divinity). A new solution needed to be developed. Based partly on Origen's teachings on the Trinity, Arius developed a theory of the nature of God that firmly separated Jesus from the Father.

Since part of Arius's responsibility as presbyter was to direct a school of biblical interpretation for priests and laypersons who wished to teach, his theories quickly gained traction with the next generation of Christian leaders. Over time he began to openly criticize Alexander, bishop of Alexandria. Alexander has been described in history as a gentle and tolerant soul who did not relish conflicts. Nevertheless, the bishop took the field against Arius and insisted that the Son is just as much God as the Father. Arius then accused Alexander of being sympathetic to Sabellius's Modalism.

A time came when the Arian movement became so popular that Alexander could no longer fight Arius's criticism with mere sermons and correspondences. He called a synod of bishops to discuss whether Arius's views were orthodox. Before they made a decision, Arius rallied his followers to pour out into the streets to add pressure to the leaders. Arius's sympathizers wrote songs to fire up the working class. The mob got caught up in the passion of the slogans, songs, and Arius's personality, but they did not necessarily grasp the theological issues. In response, Alexander's supporters likewise marched in the streets against Arius. When the two groups met, a riot broke out.

But the synod went on. More than a hundred bishops from various parts of the eastern Roman Empire listened to Alexander critique Arius's teachings. He accused Arius of resurrecting Paul of Samosata's Adoptionism in a more sophisticated way. It did not matter whether the Logos was created before or after time began, Alexander argued. The difference was slight. The fact of the matter was that Arius denied the deity of Christ, which is why Paul of Samosata's teaching was rejected. Alexander insisted that salvation depends on God's uniting himself with humanity in the person of Jesus Christ so that we can be saved. After hearing this, the synod decided that Arius's view was heretical and forced him to leave the city.

2. *Heretical Teaching*

Arius was not trying to start a crisis; he thought that the relationship between God and Jesus was simple and needed to be freed from over-complication. After all, "Trinity" was not a common term at the time, and it had not yet been precisely defined. The word "Trinity" is not found in Scripture (it was first used by Tertullian), and it is best described as shorthand for all the teachings of Scripture on the nature of God. Since the age of the apostles, Jesus had always been considered divine in at least some sense, but his precise relationship to the Godhead had not yet been articulated. Yet the church still had an unspoken sense of what the Trinity isn't. This was why Sabellius was rejected for teaching that God is sometimes the Father, at other times the Son, and then at another time the Spirit, but never all at once (Modalism). Paul of Samosata, likewise, was rejected, because he taught that Jesus started out as a mere man who was "adopted" by God to become the Son of God (Adoptionism). Those early explanations were deemed incompatible with Scripture and therefore heresies.

Arius's own conceptions of the Trinity can be traced back to Origen (184–253), a brilliant and imaginative Egyptian theologian.[29] Two streams of thought flowed in Origen's teachings concerning the Son, and followers gravitated to one of the two streams. In one stream, Origen strongly affirmed that the Son is equal to the Father. In the other stream, Origen wrote that the Son is eternally subordinate to the Father. The implication of the second stream communicated to some that the Son is somehow a lesser being than the Father, though Origen did not elaborate.[30] The lack of a fuller explanation of the second stream of Origen's thought left the door wide open for further suggestions.

To understand Arius's theory, we must mention two common presumptions about God that were derived from the logic of Greek philosophy. First, God does not change (immutability). Change implies imperfection. For good or bad, if God changes, then he cannot be deemed absolutely perfect because he has either improved or regressed. God is already at the peak of perfection, so there is no room to grow, and he is fixed at that peak of perfection, so he cannot regress. Second, the other presumption is that God cannot suffer; he is "passionless"

---

29   Church historian Kenneth Latourette remarks, "Origen was so outstanding a mind, so radiant a spirit, and so stimulating a teacher and author, that for more than a century after his death he profoundly moulded the minds of Christian thinkers." Kenneth Scott Latourette, *A History of Christianity: Beginnings to 1500* (Peabody, MA: Prince Press, 2005), 151.
30   Roger E. Olson, *The Story of Christian Theology: Twenty Centuries of Tradition and Reform* (Downers Grove, IL: InterVarsity, 1999), 143.

(impassibility). Most early theologians believed in these two attributes of God.

Arius and his followers exploited these two attributes to advance their argument that the Son is not coeternal with the Father but is the supreme creation. He acknowledged that everyone believed that Jesus Christ is the incarnation of the Logos (the Word). No problem there. The problem lay with the following: "If the Logos is divine in the same sense that God the Father is divine, then God's nature would be changed by the human life of Jesus in time and God would have suffered in him."[31] The implication that God changes and suffers seemed blasphemous! So it must be then, Arius concluded, that only God the Father is without beginning. The Son came into existence through the will of the Father. To avoid charges of Adoption-ism, Arius taught that the Logos was begotten "timelessly"[32]—that is, before Genesis 1:1. "In the beginning," the Logos was created and was given all things from the Father to share.[33] With this solution it was not God the Father who grew up and eventually suffered on the cross but only the Logos experienced this on behalf of God and humanity. Thus, when the Scriptures speak of Jesus as the Son of God, this is merely a title of honor—a title given to Jesus as the one on whom the Father had lavished a special grace.

Arius believed that the Father and the Son are two separate beings and that the biblical model for their relationship is one of eternal subordination: the Father is the one who decides matters and the Son is the one who obeys. That the Son would yield to the Father's preferences was a natural conclusion, since in Arius's model the Son is simply a loyal creature serving his creator. Arius explained the sharpness of his division in reasonable terms: "For God to implant His substance to some other being, however exalted, would imply that He is divisible and subject to change, which is inconceivable. Moreover, if any other being were to participate in the divine nature in any valid sense, there would result a duality of divine beings, whereas the Godhead is by definition unique."[34] According to Arius, if the Father and the Son were of the same essence, it is difficult to see how in the incarnation the Father would not become passible.

Arius argued that the Son was created before time. He is not coeternal with the Father. As he put it, "Before he was begotten or created or appointed or

---

31 Ibid., 144.
32 Arius, "Arius' Letter to Alexander of Alexandria," in *Trinitarian Controversies, Sources of Early Christianity*, ed. and trans. William G. Rusch (Minneapolis: Fortress, 1980), 25.
33 Ibid.
34 J. N. D. Kelly, *Early Christian Doctrines*, rev. ed. (New York: Harper Collins, 1978), 227.

established, he did not exist; for he was not unbegotten."[35] Furthermore, the Son is not of one divine substance with the Father. He is rather of a similar substance with the Father (Greek *homoiousios*). On this view, the divine qualities of the Son are derivative (contingent, not essential), given to the Son by the Father. As Arius described Jesus, "He is not God truly, but by participation in grace...He too is called God in name only."[36]

3. *Orthodox Response*

The Arian division caught Emperor Constantine's attention. Although Christianity was not the official religion, Constantine hoped to use Christianity as a glue to hold the already shaky empire together. As Christianity went, so went the empire. Thus, he called the Council of Nicaea in 325 to resolve the situation.[37] After dramatic rounds of debates, the majority in the council stood with Alexander and condemned Arianism. They added to the Apostle's Creed precise wording to clearly denounce Arianism with the following: "We believe...in one Lord Jesus Christ, the Son of God, begotten from the Father [only-begotten; that is, of the essence of the Father, God of God], Light of Light, very God of very God, begotten not made, being of one substance [*homoousious*] with the Father..."[38]

They adopted the term *homoousious*, meaning, "of the same substance," to describe the Son's relation to the Father. This horrified the Arians, but the orthodox bishops, such as Alexander and his young protege Athanasius, were overjoyed. However, even this council could not quell the rising popularity of Arianism. In fact, the council served as a catalyst for it to grow even more rapidly! So much so that Constantine began to doubt the wording of the Nicene Creed and thought about rewriting it in favor of Arianism. One man stood in his way: Athanasius (ca. 296–373).

The torch passed on from Alexander to Athanasius to defend orthodoxy even when it was starting to become unpopular. Elected as the new Bishop of Alexandria in 328, Athanasius found it appalling that Arius insisted that the Son is a creature. He had no time for Arius's "smooth sophistry."[39] A creature is a creature. What other

---

35 Arius, "Letter to Eusebius," in *Documents of the Christian Church,* ed. Henry Bettenson and Chris Maunder, 3rd ed. (New York: Oxford Univ. Press, 1999), 43.
36 Kelly, *Early Christian Doctrines,* 229.
37 Justo Gonzalez, *A History of Christian Thought,* vol. 1, From the Beginnings of the Council of Chalcedon, rev. ed. (Nashville: Abingdon, 1992), 266 – 67.
38 Taken from Philip Schaff, *The Creeds of Christendom,* vol.1 (1931; Grand Rapids, MI: Baker, 1993), 29.
39 Athanasius, "Four Discourses against the Arians," in *Nicene and Post-Nicene Fathers: Second Series* (hereafter NPNF), vol. 4, trans. Cardinal Newman, ed. Philip Schaff and Henry Wace, reprint (Peabody, MA:

types of creatures are there? Athanasius argued two negative consequences make Arianism dangerous and unacceptable.[40]

First, Athanasius argued that only God can save humanity. No creature can cancel the power of sin and death, and thereby offer eternal life to other creatures. Only the Creator can do this. He argued that Arianism makes salvation impossible, because—no matter how high his status—the Son is still only a creature. Since everybody in the church recognizes that Jesus Christ saves, it stands to reason that Jesus is therefore God.

Second, looking at the common liturgy taking place in the fourth century, it was clear that the church prayed to and worshiped Jesus Christ. If the Son is only a creature, then the church is making a grave mistake in its public worship. Clearly, the first of the Ten Commandments forbids the people of God from worshiping anything else but God. If Arianism were true, Christians were committing idolatry.[41] The church should not be worshiping Christ if he is merely a creature. So, either Arians are right in their doctrine of the Son or the Church is right in its practice of worshiping the Son. Both cannot be right. Athanasius argued the church was right to worship the Son, because the Son is God.[42]

Athanasius called the heresy of Arius the "forerunner of the Anti-christ."[43] Athanasius proposed an alternative interpretation: since God created the world through Christ, and since Christ alone is said to be from the Father, it is proper to understand Christ and the Father as both being God.[44] According to Athanasius, the Son was eternally begotten from the Father such that he can be said to be of the same essence (*homo-ousios*) with the Father: "The Son is other in kind and

---

Hendrickson, 1995), 306.

40   Taken from Alister E. McGrath, *Historical Theology: An Introduction to the History of Christian Thought* (Malden, MA: Blackwell, 1998), 49 – 51.

41   Harold O. J. Brown points out, "[Adolf] Harnack observes that Arius 'is a strict monotheist only with respect to cosmology; as a theologian, he is a polytheist.'" Harold O. J. Brown, *Heresies: Heresy and Orthodoxy in the History of the Church* (Peabody, MA: Hendrickson, 2003), 115.

42   For details on Athanasius's exegetical arguments concerning the divinity of the Son, see "Four Discourses against the Arians," in NPNF, 303 – 447.

43   Athanasius, *Orations against the Arians* 1:1.

44   Athanasius, "Defense of the Nicene Creed," V. Athanasius writes, "For though all things be said to be from God, yet this is not in the sense in which the Son is from Him; for as to the creatures, 'of God' is said of them on this account, in that they exist not at random or spontaneously, nor came to be by chance, according to those philosophers who refer them to the combination of atoms, and to elements of similar structure, nor as certain heretics speak of a distinct Framer, nor as other again say that the constitution of all things is from certain Angels; but, in that whereas God is, it was by Him that all things were brought into being, not being before, through His Word; but as to the Word, since He is not a creature, He alone is both called and is 'from the Father'; and it is significant of this sense to say that the Son is 'from the essence of the Father,' for to nothing originate does this attach."

nature than the creatures, or rather belongs to the Father's substance and is of the same nature as He."[45] Although the word "begotten" (which Athanasius borrowed from John 3:16) might suggest a one-time event, Athanasius relied on the unchanging nature of God to explain that the Father is eternally begetting and the Son is eternally begotten. If that sounds confusing, remember Tertullian's early analogy of the different parts of a tree. There is the root, which carries water into the trunk, which then distributes it to the branches—a constant process as long as the tree is alive.

Moreover, Athanasius heavily emphasized the idea of salvation through theosis, a concept that had been popular with Origen and other Alexandrian intellectuals of his day. The doctrine of theosis said that the ultimate purpose of salvation is to make humans god-like—the image of God in humankind would be made pristine. It's roughly equivalent to what Protestant churches call "glorification." According to Athanasius, it is nonsensical to say that a nondivine creature could make others divine. His thoughts are worth quoting in full:

> For humanity would not have been deified if joined to a creature, or unless the Son were true God. Nor would humanity have been drawn into the Father's presence, unless the one who had put on the body was the true Word by nature. And as we would not have been delivered from sin and the curse, unless it had been by nature human flesh which the Word put on (for we would have had nothing in common with what was foreign), so also humanity would not have been deified, unless the Word who became flesh had been by nature from the Father and true and proper to him...Therefore let those who deny that the Son is from the Father by nature and proper to his essence deny also that he took true human flesh of Mary Ever-Virgin. For in neither case would it have profited us human beings, if the Word had not been true Son of God by nature, or the flesh not true which he assumed.[46]

Defending his arguments proved to be a difficult task for Athanasius. In 332, Constantine restored Arius to his position as presbyter under immense political pressure. Athanasius was asked to accept this, but he refused. So he was exiled to the

---

45   Athanasius, *Contra Arianos* III.
46   Athanasius, *Contra Arianos* II:70.

farthest outpost in Germany. Along his way to his exile, he met with several bishops in the West. They began to favor his view and Athanasius was seen as somewhat of a hero for standing up to Constantine. Disappointments, after all, still brewed in the West over the moving of the capitol from Rome to Constantinople.

So, ironically, Athanasius's exile helped bring back momentum for orthodoxy. Not only was Athanasius building up a network of support in the West but the church in Alexandria refused to replace Athanasius. So, he was still technically a bishop. Arius never did return to his position; he died a day before he was to be reinstalled (336). Constantine died a few months later (337).

Constantine's son and successor, Constantius, allowed Athanasius to return to his position in Alexandria. But their relationship was a tumultuous one. Constantius, like his father, wanted stability for the empire. To maintain this, he thought the Semi-Arian view could be a good compromise between the Arians and the orthodox doctrines. They proposed replacing the word *homoousious* (meaning "of the same substance") with the word *homoiousious* (meaning "of similar substance"). The words were differentiated in Latin by one little letter. Surely, Constantius thought, there is no harm in compromising with some slight differences. To Athanasius, this was no small matter. That little letter made all the difference in the world in understanding how the Father relates to the Son. Salvation depends on Christ's being God, not "like God." He still insisted only God can save humanity. He argued that "salvation is not...possible through an hierarchical chain, from the Father through an intermediate Son to creatures. For an intermediary separates as much as he unites creatures with the Father."[47] The essentials to the gospel remained: Jesus Christ must be truly God and truly human in order to be the perfect mediator.

Athanasius had to endure five exiles. In his forty-six years as bishop, he spent only seventeen in Alexandria. But he stubbornly stuck to the truth despite being up against what seemed like the world, and he is now recognized as perhaps the foremost defender of Nicene orthodoxy and the most prolific writer of orthodox Trinitarian doctrine in the fourth century. A few years after he died, his friends, the Cappadocian fathers—Basil the Great, Gregory of Nyssa, and Gregory of Nazianzus—carried the torch to win the fight against Arianism and Semi-Arianism at the Council of Constantinople in 381.

---

47 Quoted in Olson, *Story of Christian Theology,* 164–65. See also Alvyn Pettersen, Athanasius (Harrisburg, PA: Morehouse, 1995), 175.

4. *Relevance*

When it comes to the Trinity, a helpful caution might be in order. We can and should confess what the Trinity is, but no matter how deep we may probe into God's nature, we cannot possibly begin to understand it fully. Evangelical theologian Harold O. J. Brown elaborates:

> Without a coherent doctrine of the Trinity, the New Testament witness to the activity of God in Christ and in the work of the Holy Spirit will tend to force one either into modalism or a kind of tritheism. But if one begins with a doctrine of Trinity—as a number of orthodox Protestant theologians do—there is the danger that doctrine will take precedence over the New Testament witness and turn living, personal faith into theological metaphysics. It seems apparent that the safest course is to let theological understanding and personal faith go hand in hand. Too much enthusiastic faith without a corresponding degree of theological understanding is almost certain to lead to error, perhaps to serious heresy. Too much doctrine unaccompanied by a living and growing faith is the recipe for dead orthodoxy.[48]

Though we can apprehend the doctrine of the Trinity, we cannot fully comprehend it. Despite that fact, it is vital to maintain a Trinitarian faith. The doctrine of the Trinity impacts one's understanding of salvation. Additionally, it also affects the way we worship. James B. Torrance describes the impact of the Trinity on worship as follows:

> As we reflect on the wide varieties of forms of worship...we can discern two different views. The unitarian view. Probably the most common and widespread view is that worship is something which we, religious people, do—mainly in church on Sunday. We go to church, we sing our psalms and hymns to God, we intercede for the world, we listen to the sermon (too often simply an exhortation), we offer our money, time and talents to God. No doubt we need God's grace to help us do it. We do it because Jesus taught us to do it and left us an example of how to do it. But worship is what we do before

---

48   Brown, *Heresies,* 154.

> God...Indeed this view of worship is in practice unitarian, has no doctrine of the mediator or sole priesthood of Christ, is human-centered, has no proper doctrine of the Holy Spirit, is too often non- sacramental, and can engender weariness... The trinitarian view. The second view of worship is that it is the gift of participating through the Spirit in the incarnate Son's communion with the Father. It means participating in union with Christ, in what he has done for us once and for all, in his self-offering to the Father, in his life and death on the cross. It also means participating in what he is continuing to do for us in the presence of the Father and in his mission from the Father to the world. There is only one true Priest through whom and with whom we draw near to God our Father...It takes seriously the New Testament teaching about the sole priesthood and headship of Christ, his self-offering for us to the Father and our life in the union with Christ through the Spirit, with a vision of the Church as the body of Christ...[God] lifts us up out of ourselves to participate in the very life and communion of the Godhead, that life of communion for which we were created.[49]

Athanasius saw the deity of Christ and the Trinity as essential to the practice of the church. Not only were baptismal and Eucharistic confessions bound up in Trinitarian language but so also were prayers. The Son was adored, prayed to, and believed to be present in the Eucharist, and if he was not really God, the worshipers were depriving God of the worship which is his due. But more than this, Athanasius saw that if the Son were not divine, the salvation of humans was called into question. In the same way that Gregory of Nazianzus argued that Jesus Christ must be fully human (as opposed to the claims of Apollinarianism) if he were to be the mediator between God and men, Athanasius argued that Jesus must be fully divine:

> For it became Him, for Whom are all things, and through Whom are all things, in bringing many sons unto glory, to make the Captain of their salvation perfect through suffering;" by which words He means that it belonged to none other to bring man back from the corruption which had begun, than the Word

---

49   James B. Torrance, *Worship, Community and the Triune God of Grace* (Downers Grove, IL: InterVarsity, 1997), 20 – 22.

of God, Who had also made them from the beginning. And that it was in order to [become] the sacrifice for bodies such as His own that the Word Himself also assumed a body, to this, also, they refer in these words: "Forasmuch then as the children are the sharers in blood and flesh, He also Himself in like manner partook of the same, that through death He might bring to naught Him that had the power of death, that is, the devil; and might deliver them who, through fear of death, were all their lifetime subject to bondage.[50]

Athanasius saw an intimate connection between the salvation of humanity and the deity of Christ. Even though some sects like the Jehovah's Witnesses still repeat elements of Arian teaching, Jesus claimed to be God, and the Christian tradition has maintained Athanasius's belief in an intimate connection between salvation and the deity of Christ.

We are saved from God by God. Only a divine Savior can bear the weight of God's wrath in atonement. Only Jesus as the God-man can satisfy the enormous debt and penalty caused by human sin against God. No mere human could bridge that gap. Only a divine Savior can pay the costly price for redeeming us from our bondage to sin and death. Only the God-man can conquer all his people's enemies. Our salvation is dependent on the infinite divine capacity of our Savior, Jesus Christ.

VII. CONCLUSION

As Michael Horton writes, "Each person of the Trinity goes out to the other in mutual joy and fellowship and in that complete fullness creates a nondivine world to share analogically in this extroverted communion."[51] The beauty of this is lost with the Sabellianism and Arianism.

The doctrine of the Trinity proclaims a triune God, who turns toward humanity in the person of Jesus, the God-man who suffered, died, rose again, and ascended. The fact that Jesus and the Holy Spirit are just as much God as the Father is a nonnegotiable part of Christianity. Since questions about the relationship between Jesus, the Holy Spirit, and God the Father are inevitable, they needed to be answered well. Trinitarian orthodoxy encapsulates what Scripture says about

---

50   Athanasius, *On the Incarnation* 10.
51   Horton, *Christian Faith*, 238.

that relationship and acknowledges the mystery of it.

If Christianity had agreed with Arius that Jesus could be a lesser god—if it had failed to defend monotheism, if it had fallen into the trench of professing three unrelated deities—it may have dissolved into the religion of Rome and its pantheons of false gods. If the early Christians had lost their nerve and conceded the "lesser divinity" of Jesus, whatever that might mean, then the work of God in Christ for our salvation would have been rendered meaningless. No mere man, nor half god, could possibly intervene to save fallen and sinful humanity, let alone restore all of creation. Only the Creator can enter creation to fix its brokenness and redeem its original, latent purpose. Athanasius explored this truth in On the Incarnation, defending the claim that the Father and the Son share one common substance (*homoousios*). Only the Creator can recreate. Only the Maker can remake. Only God can save us from our sins.

Because the Father and the Son are one substance, we can also be assured that we actually know God in Jesus Christ. Without confidence that Jesus is God, united in substance with the Father, we could not be sure that Jesus can speak for God, forgive sins for God, declare righteousness for God, or do anything to make us children of the Father.

While Trinitarian orthodoxy encapsulates what Scripture says about God being one in essence and three in person, it also acknowledges the mystery of it. To speak about God, to speak about the Trinity, is different from speaking about any other thing. God is categorically separate from all other subjects. God is God. And nothing else is. So when we discuss the Trinity, we are peering into what theologians call the "aseity" of God—God as he is a se, to himself. God presents himself fully only to himself. We know about the Trinity only because God lovingly reveals aspects of his attributes and character to us.

Trinitarian orthodoxy means worshiping one God who is revealed to be Father, Son, and Holy Spirit for "their glory is equal, their majesty coeternal."[52] It guides the worshiper through key aspects of divinity, qualities or attributes of God, that are shared by all three persons of the Trinity. God is uncreated. God is unlimited. God is eternal. Each person of the Trinity is each of these things. This does not mean that there are three separate divinities. The Father is uncreated. The Son is uncreated. The Spirit is uncreated.

---

52 "Aequalis gloria, coaeterna maiestas."

In every external work of the Trinity the Father is the origin and cause, the Son is the medium and content, and the Spirit brings about the work's intended effect within creation. In every external work of the Godhead—creation, providence, redemption, and consummation—the Father speaks his Word in the Son through the perfecting power of the Spirit.[53]

Scripture records and reveals to us that God is one and it also reveals interactions between the Father, Son, and Holy Spirit. The orthodox reading of the Bible is more difficult to understand than simple monotheism or separating the three persons altogether, but it is most faithful to Scripture.

---

53   Horton, *The Christian Faith*, 131.

Contributors

DR. WOLE ADEGBILE | Nigeria/Rwanda | pg. 181
Senior Lecturer and Director of Quality Assurance,
Africa College of Theology

TSEDEY ALEMAYEHU GEBREHIWOT | Ethiopia | pg. 197
Lecturer in Biblical Studies/Old Testament
Ministry Program Manager, Samaritan's Purse

DR. GRACE AL-ZOUGHBI | Palestine | pg. 143
Assistant Professor,
Arab Baptist Theological Seminary
Accreditation Officer, M.E.N.A.T.E.

DR. SHERIF A. FAHIM | Egypt | pg. 115
Professor and New Testament Chair,
Alexandria School of Theology
General Director of El-Soora Ministries

REV. DR. JUSTIN S. HOLCOMB | USA | pg. 13 | pg. 239
Bishop of the Episcopal Diocese of Central Florida
Senior Fellow with Theo Global
Professor, Reformed Theological Seminary

DR. MICHAEL S. HORTON | USA | pg. 89 | pg. 221
Founder and Editor-in-Chief, Sola Media
Professor of Systematic Theology and Apologetics,
Westminster Seminary California

DR. WILSON JEREMIAH | Indonesia | pg. 55
Lecturer in Systematic Theology,
Southeast Asia Bible Seminary

DR. DAVID MUTHUKUMAR SIVASUBRAMANIAN | India | pg. 33
Associate Professor,
South Asia Institute of Advanced Christian Studies

DR. KENETH PERVAIZ | Pakistan | pg. 133
Assistant Professor, Forman Christian College

DR. MICHAEL PHIRI | Malawi | pg. 73
Lecturer, Quality Assurance Officer and Head of Research
Evangelical Bible College of Malawi

DR. VIJAI SINGH TAGORE | India | pg. 163
Associate Professor of New Testament,
Presbyterian Theological Seminary